1002076 MEYE ... glish
HJ ... music

D0301517

ISBN 0 85315 411 2

HERTFORDSHIRE LIBRARY SERVICE
Please return this book on or before the
last date shown or ask for it to be renewed

L 32/rev '81

Please renew or return items by the date
shown on your receipt

www.hertsdirect.org/libraries

Renewals and enquiries: 0300 123 4049

Textphone for hearing or   0300 123 4041
speech impaired users:

L32

EARLY ENGLISH CHAMBER MUSIC

Early English Chamber Music

From the Middle Ages to Purcell

Ernst H. Meyer

Second, revised, edition
edited by
the author and Diana Poulton

LAWRENCE AND WISHART
London

Lawrence and Wishart Ltd
39 Museum Street
London WC1

First published as *English Chamber Music*, 1946
Reprinted 1951
New and completely revised edition first published 1982
© Ernst H. Meyer 1982

Printed and bound in Great Britain at
The Camelot Press Ltd, Southampton

To my daughter Eva Irene

Contents

Musical Examples in Text

(*Unless stated, examples are instrumental*)

c = complete example : Q = quotation (incomplete)

Musical Examples in Appendix

Preface to the First Edition

This book has its origin in events which date back to my student days in Berlin in the late twenties when I was doing some research on the early instrumental music of various European countries. I soon became fascinated by the wealth of material slumbering on the shelves of the ancient French, Dutch and German monasteries and music schools and I remember my excitement as I found more and more scores which were often anonymous and in some cases not even listed.

It was the well-ordered catalogues of the British Museum and the Oxford Christ Church libraries which first drew my attention to early English chamber music. According to these catalogues there still survived a considerable body of 'fantasias' and other forms of music for stringed instruments composed in sixteenth- and seventeenth-century England, of whose existence continental musicians and musicologists seemed to have little knowledge. My curiosity was aroused and finally I succeeded in securing one or two of the few English publications of such music. It was chiefly these scores (I believe it was the 3-part fantasias by Orlando Gibbons) which induced me to apply for an academic scholarship to enable me to study the whole period more closely. This scholarship was granted in 1931 by the Notgemeinschaft der Deutschen Wissenschaft.

Events in Germany prevented me from writing at once a full account of all this music – the same events that were to lead me later on to settle in this country, this time for a much longer stay. However, the plan for such a book was in my mind all the time.

When I did set to work on it, I found myself faced with these very puzzling problems: What was the reason for the appearance of so extensive and significant a period of art? and why was its music unknown on the continent? Why was it not the pride and boast of at least the English people?

It was first the reading of the works of some English historians, especially those of Tawney and Trevelyan, which made the facts of the history of music appear to me in a new light, and it was my study of the works of Karl Marx and Friedrich Engels which finally led me to venture to attempt to represent a period of musical history as a natural part of a general social development.

It has not been an easy task to complete this book. The main part of the actual writing was done in London in 1940 and 1941 when libraries were closed and difficulties of other kinds existed in abundance. The book might never have been finished in the circumstances prevailing during these years, had it not been for the advice and assistance of a number of colleagues and friends. I am deeply indebted to the Incorporated Society of Authors who made a grant from their Crompton Bequest Fund towards the publication costs of this book – an act of generosity by which I feel both honoured and encouraged.

My heartfelt gratitude is also due to my friend Russell Ferguson. He not only corrected and improved the English of the book which I had to write in a language not native to me, but moreover took part in the conception of important sections of the text. My sincere thanks also go out to Gerald Hayes, Dona Torr, Professor R. H. Tawney, Arnold Goldsbrough, Diana Poulton, Professor Wormington, Storm Jameson, Benjamin Frankel, C. B. Oldman, F. D. Klingender, Dr H. S. Middleton and many other friends too numerous to thank individually, but whose help has been invaluable.

Ernst H. Meyer
London, 1946

Preface to the Second Edition

More than thirty years have passed by since this book first appeared. A new edition (note the changed title) must necessarily take into account new facts brought to light in this period on the subject of early English instrumental chamber music – and these were numerous. Much has happened in this field, and no doubt more discoveries will be made in the future, new points of view will be expressed on matters of principle and on details regarding the story told in the book.

Assessing this great age of English music is a process within which the reissue of the present book is but a link in a chain. It does not claim to be more. The first edition of this study roughly coincided with my departure from England, the country which gave me asylum from fascist persecution. During the past thirty years I have lived in Berlin, my home-town in the German Democratic Republic from where I followed the growing interest in England in the music described in this essay.

I am greatly indebted to Diana Poulton for all the help she extended to me in making possible an up-to-date reissue of my book. All the days and weeks she spent providing new facts and information, correcting errors and shortcomings which due to force of circumstance were bound to be contained in the original version of the book. . . . I am honoured by the active and devoted interest displayed by her in supervising the new edition.

Of great importance was the help given by Commander Gordon Dodd and Mr Peter Holman who not only drew up long lists of items improving numerous passages and eliminating faults, and generously allowed me to include results of their own research work in several instances, but also sacrificed much time in going through the text with me. My warmest thanks to these two learned colleagues, also to Dr Andrew Ashbee who supplied valuable material on the life and work of John Jenkins. I am very grateful to Nathalie Dolmetsch, a life-long friend, who has been sending me books and journals over many years, enabling me to remain informed on the advance of research in England.

I shall be happy if *English Chamber Music* in its second and revised edition and with its new title, will stimulate further interest in this subject on the presentation of which I spent years of my life.

Ernst H. Meyer
Berlin

Editorial Note

Through the work of Arnold Dolmetsch, until the time of his death in 1940, the wealth of English chamber music of the sixteenth and seventeenth centuries was gradually being brought to the attention of the English music-loving public, but no attempt had then been made to trace the long process of development that led to this particular flowering of the English musical genius, or to give a coherent account of the historical and social conditions which made such a flowering possible at that particular time. When Ernst Hermann Meyer's *English Chamber Music* was published in 1946 it was a pioneering study of the first importance.

Since then research into many aspects of this subject has been carried out by a number of experts, but no one has attempted to supplant this work and it remains the only book which presents an overall picture of the rise, supreme achievement and eventual decay of this great school of English musicians.

When I was asked by Lawrence and Wishart to collaborate with Ernst Meyer in bringing this book up-to-date, my immediate reaction was a feeling of inadequacy; however, the generous help of experts such as Andrew Ashbee, Gordon Dodd and Peter Holman made my part in the revision infinitely easier than I had expected.

It has been a great pleasure to renew a friendship with the author which had fallen into abeyance since his return to Berlin after the war, and to find the same enthusiasm and love for his subject that enlivened all our discussions in wartime London.

Diana Poulton

Introduction

Chamber music, the most intimate and elaborate of all musical forms, is also one of the youngest of the arts. While painting, sculpture, architecture and literature look back on a development of thousands of years, while music itself, taken as a whole, has accompanied mankind throughout the ages, chamber music in its present form is not more than four centuries old.

Not that a combination of several individual players co-operating was impossible before the sixteenth century. On the contrary, there is plenty of proof that at all times both inside and outside Europe more or less informal gatherings of small numbers of musicians took place. But the essential feature of that particular practice which we are accustomed to define as 'chamber music' (and in this book only *instrumental group music* will be discussed), that particular relationship between the few players who take part in the execution of the music, the attitude of the players and listeners towards their art, is entirely new; it is, in England, a creation of the age of Henry VIII and Elizabeth.

The essential attitude of the chamber musician is a kind of inwardness, a devotion to music for what it says to the player rather than for any effect on the audience, a devotion to the free, pure and self-sufficient creation of a seemingly abstract beauty. It is this attitude on the part of composers and players which sets chamber music in such striking contrast to all medieval music. Neither the spirit of religious devotion as in the choral masterpieces of the middle ages, nor the stirring movement of medieval dance tunes, nor the pageantry and splendour of ceremonial Court music will be found in the new domestic chamber music of Reformation and post-Reformation times. A performance of chamber music seems to originate solely in the desire of the musicians to seek diversion and enjoyment through their own playing. They use chamber music as a means of expressing what is working within them, and of satisfying and solving what seems unsatisfiable and insoluble by any other means of expression.

It is true that the 'chamber music attitude' of the sixteenth and seventeenth centuries is in many respects different from that of our own age. In particular there are varying degrees of distinction between the kind of entirely 'free' chamber music just characterised, and certain small-scale musical activities at the courts of the sixteenth and seventeenth centuries which were to some extent functional. But to a high degree this element of privacy and detachment from any visible purpose is already found in very early examples of 16th century chamber music. It is essentially music to be played without audience or, at most, to a very small one.

Among all the musical centres of Europe in the sixteenth and seventeenth centuries Britain was first and foremost in the realm of chamber music. In this field the supremacy of this country was undisputed. For decades English instrumental music influenced all kinds of instrumental art in other nations, and after 1600 many English musicians, especially string players, were engaged by foreign courts and chapels, just as, before, Netherlands composers and, later, Italian bel-cantists swept Europe.

Chamber music occupies an important place in the development of a national culture in post-Reformation England. Indeed the part it played in English cultural life was for a considerable time of a significance that was only equalled by the poetry of the same age.

Here is a passage from Fletcher:

> Orpheus with his Lute made Trees
> And the Mountaine tops that freeze
> Bow themselves when he did sing.
> To his Musike, Plants and Flowers
> Ever sprung; as Sunne and Showers,
> There had made a lasting Spring.
> Everything that heard him play,
> Even the Billowes of the Sea,
> Hung their heads, and then lay by.
> In sweet Musicke is such Art,
> Killing care, and griefe of heart,
> Fall asleape, or hearing die.

And here is an example of the very sort of music Fletcher must have had in mind – a fantasia by his great contemporary Orlando Gibbons:

Example 1: Fantasia for three viols by Orlando Gibbons.[1]

[1] From Dublin, Marsh Library, MS. Z.2, 1, 13, no. 6 of the set.

Now Fletcher's poem and the poetry of his age are loved wherever the English language is spoken. There are also individual enthusiastic admirers of early English madrigals and quite a number of choral societies which perform to a certain extent such sonnets in the musical settings of seventeenth-century musicians. But this fantasia by Gibbons, together with the rest of the instrumental music of his age, was neglected by the musical public for a long time; only during the past thirty years have the high creative qualities of early English chamber music been recognised by large numbers of music-lovers in England and in other countries. The poets of that day and age were themselves great admirers of instrumental music and have left their testimony as to the emotional power and beauty of the chamber music of their time. Gibbons's fantasia, a representative example, is a beautiful piece of work, highly wrought and deeply felt. But for some reason it was for a long time looked upon as 'music of the past'.

Bach's music was also once regarded as music of the past, until certain discerning musicians became aware of the wonderful qualities to which generations before them had been insensitive, and initiated a revival of Bach which has since become one of the most interesting musical phenomena of recent times.

Of late the popularity of John Donne and other seventeenth-century poets has borne witness to the fact that the poetry of the period is peculiarly meet for today. During my studies in the early thirties I became convinced – as did other scholars at that period – that the chamber music of that great age is also particularly suitable for the present time, for reasons which in due course will appear in this study.

But it is not quite so easy to bring to life the music of the past as it is to revive the poetry of a bygone age. The difference between poetry and music has many aspects, but that which most concerns us now is this: whereas we are accustomed to read literature and drama in the context of history, recognising that a poet or a dramatist speaks out of his time and period, our study of music is not yet conducted in the same way. Even some highly cultured musicians mistakenly assume that the old music yields up its secrets at a casual hearing.

If we take old music as it is, straight from the century-old dust of the libraries, if we listen to it as too many people listen to a Mozart Symphony, that is to say, without considering the life and spirit of the time and the circumstances in which it was produced, then we run the risk of finding all such music dull and lifeless, completely remote from our normal musical experience.

The style and meaning of the music of a period cannot be thoroughly understood if it is to be detached from its living back-ground. If we are to understand the distinctive structure, style and character of the music of any period we must first ask, what kind of people composed and performed it and for what sort of audience? Who commissioned the music and especially, why and for what purpose was it produced? Was it to furnish pleasant distraction from everyday life, or to instil religious devotion, or rouse enthusiasm?

*

This is the first discussion *in extenso* of the great age of English chamber music, but it certainly does not claim to be the first work which has drawn attention to the period. Great tribute is due to the work of a few musicologists and practitioners who in the face of utter indifference and even violent opposition or ridicule spent their lives revealing some of the uncounted treasures of early English instrumental art.

First and most important of all is Arnold Dolmetsch, who not only unearthed much of this music but also searched for and found ways of presenting it to enthusiastic if small audiences. With admirable patience and scientific exactitude he rebuilt the old instruments on which this music had once been performed, and successfully evolved a proper technique and style in the playing of them. The annual performances of his consorts of viols and recorders in London and Haslemere will always be remembered by musicians and musicologists, amateur and professional. Now, after the master's death, it is manifest that his work marked the turning point in the battle for the recognition of ancient music in England.[1]

A whole school of eager and understanding scholars and students gathered round Dolmetsch and his family. Outstanding among them is Gerald R. Hayes: he was the first to collect and produce systematically all the historical matter that had so far been neglected; this was done in his classic work, *Musical Instruments and their Music.*[2] This book is at the same time an introduction to the nature of early instruments and a general survey of the music written for them. It contains valuable material concerning the production of this music. *King's Music* by the same author[3] is most important in its scholarly exposition of the development of the Chapel Royal and in its method of research: it not only states the facts but also shows them in their historical relationship. Hayes' *Lute's Apology* is a treasury of information, especially on the

[1] A treatise by A. Dolmetsch on *The Interpretation of the Music of the 17th and 18th Centuries* appeared in 1915. Several gramophone records of old music played by the Dolmetsch family were published by the Columbia Gramophone Co.

[2] London, 1930.

[3] London, 1941.

technique of the lutes, citterns, guitars and other plucked instruments.[1]

In any account of work on the subject of early English instruments and their music, F. W. Galpin's *Old English Instruments of Music* must be particularly noted.[2] There are, further, E. H. Hunt's brief but fine studies on music for the recorders,[3] and among the works of older writers, H. St George's *The Bow, its History, Manufacture and Use*,[4] H. C. de Lafontaine's *The King's Musick: A Transcript of Records* (1460–1700),[5] and E. Van der Straeten's *The Romance of the Fiddle*[6] and *History of the Violoncello*.[7]

Grove's and Scholes' dictionaries contain welcome material upon our subject,[8] as do also J. Pulver's dictionaries of old music,[9] and editions by E. H. Fellowes, Sir R. Terry and other scholars of old music.[10]

In general works on the history of music, references to early English chamber music are mostly few and short, with the exception of Eric Blom's *Music in England*,[11] G. Reese's *Music in the Middle Ages*,[12] and P. H. Láng's *Music in Western Civilisation*,[13] though some of the instrumental works of a few individual composers such as Byrd, Gibbons and Purcell have been treated with great care and understanding by their respective biographers.[14] Soon after the end

[1] London, 1941 (the plates of this book were, alas, destroyed during the bombing of London).

[2] London, 1910.

[3] The *Recorder or English Flute*, London, 1936. Cf. also Hunt's *Recorder News-Letters*, 1940 ff. Far less scholarly, Christopher Welch on the same subject, London, 1911.

[4] London, 1895.

[5] London, 1909; reprinted 1973.

[6] London, 1911.

[7] London, 1915.

[8] Grove, fifth ed., 1954; Scholes's *Oxford Companion to Music*, 1939.

[9] Chiefly the *Biographical Dictionary of Old English Music*, 1927.

[10] Fantasia for 6 instruments by W. Byrd, 8 Elizabethan Dance Tunes, 9 Fantasias a 3 and 1 a 4 by O. Gibbons, Pavan and Galliard a 6 by Gibbons, 1 Fantasia a 6 by Tomkins, all ed. E. H. Fellowes (Stainer and Bell); 2 In Nomines by Parsons and Parsley, ed. Sir R. R. Terry (London, 1923); Sonatas by W. Young, ed. by G. Whittaker (Oxford University Press); instrumental works by Purcell, ed. P. Warlock (London, 1923); 6 Fantasias by Locke, ed. P. Warlock (1932, ibid. a suite for 3 stringed instruments); Incidental Music to *The Tempest*, by Locke, ed. G. Whittaker (London, 1936), and small publications of works by Morley and others. In Hayes' *King's Musick* there are some publications of works by Henry VIII, Ferrabosco, W. Lawes and others.

[11] Penguin Books, 1942, pp. 34–70.

[12] London, 1941.

[13] London, 1942.

[14] E. H. Fellowes, *Byrd*, 1936; F. Howes, *Byrd*, 1928; E. H. Fellowes, *Gibbons*, 1925; J. A. Westrup, *Purcell*, 1937.

of the Second World War a number of musicologists brought out
important studies on various composers and their work as well as
on musical forms, instruments and instrumental techniques and
published a considerable amount of chamber music of the
sixteenth and seventeenth centuries. R. Thurston Dart wrote essays
on *Morley's Consort Lessons of 1599*,[1] 'The Printed Fantasies of
Orlando Gibbons',[2] 'The Cibell',[3] 'The Cittern and its English
Music'[4] a 'Hand-List of English Instrumental Music',[5] as well as on
other subjects, and published, together with William Coates, a
series of fantasias, airs and dances by Coperario, Ward, Tomkins,
etc., as, for instance, in *Jacobean Consort Music*.[6] Of great importance
are G. Reese's *Music in the Renaissance,*[7] Helen Joy Sleeper's *Fancies
and Ayres: John Jenkins*,[8] Nathalie Dolmetsch's 'The Chest of Viols',[9]
William Coates's 'English Two-part Viol Music at King's College,
Cambridge'[10] and P. Evans' informative article on 'Seventeenth-
Century Chamber Music Manuscripts at Durham Cathedral'.[11]

During the past twenty years great strides forward have been
made by a considerable number of experts and research students
in popularising early English chamber music; this was made
possible to a large extent by the admirable work of the Viola da
Gamba Society (President Nathalie Dolmetsch, following the late
Sir Jack Westrup), which was founded in 1948. This Society issues a
journal *Chelys* (annually) in which much excellent and very detailed
and scholarly research work is published; it has made invaluable
contributions to rendering early chamber music a permanent part
of musical practice inside and outside England. In 1980 it issued a
thematic index of music for viols (see Bibliography). I gratefully
accept these indexes as valid and important, as a consequence of
which I have been able to make revisions of incomplete or
erroneous statements in earlier writings of mine. There are now
several other societies devoted to investigating various other

[1] *Proceedings of the Royal Musical Association*, 1947.
[2] *Music and Letters*, 1956.
[3] *Revue Belge de Musicologie*, VI, 1952, facs, 1.
[4] *Galpin, Soc. Journal*, March 1948.
[5] ibid., March 1955.
[6] Stainer & Bell, London, 1955 (Vol. IX, *Musica Britannica*).
[7] London, 1954.
[8] Wellesley College, Mass. (USA), 1950 (this publication contains works by this composer
for 3–6 instruments).
[9] *The Consort*, Vol. II, 1950.
[10] *Music and Letters*, XXXIII, 1952.
[11] *Music and Letters*, XXXVI, July 1955.

instruments of the period, as well as a number of performing groups.

Further literature as well as editions are referred to in R. de Smet's *Published Music for the Viola da Gamba and Other Viols*, Detroit Studies in Music Bibliography 18, Detroit, 1971 (which includes music with instruments other than viols), among them J. L. Jackman, *15th Century Basse Dances*, Wellesley Edition No. 6, Wellesley College (Mass.); Cecily Arnold and M. Johnson 'The English Fantasy Suite', *Proceedings of the Royal Musical Association*, LXXXII, 1958; H. Danks, 'The English Viols', *The Strad*, LXVI, 1956; Nathalie Dolmetsch, *The Viola da Gamba, Its Origin and History, Its Technique and Musical Resources* (Second Edn) London, Hinrichsen, 1968; H. Alkor, *Recorder Music Bibliography*, Heinrichshofen, 1966; *The American Viola da Gamba Society Journal*; W. W. Cobbett, *Cobbett's Cyclopedic Survey of Chamber Music* (Second Edn, revised, 3 vols), 1962–3; M. Lefkowitz, *William Lawes*, London, 1960; D. Stevens, *Thomas Tomkins*, London, 1957; F. B. Zimmerman, *Henry Purcell, 1659–1695*, London, 1963; P. Le Huray, *Music and the Reformation in England, 1549–1660*, London, 1967.

In *Chelys* there have so far appeared short studies by A. Ashbee 'John Jenkins's Fantasie-Suites for Treble, two Basses and Organ' (Vol. I, 1969 and Vol. II, 1970); A. W. Marshall 'The Viola da Gamba Music of Godfrey Finger' (Vol. I, 1969); M. Pallis on 'The Instrumentation of English Viol Consort Music' (Vol. I, 1969); G. Dodd on 'The Coperario-Lupo Five-part Books at Washington' (Vol. I, 1969) and 'The Chest of Viols reconsidered' (Vol. III, 1971); Carolyn Coxon, 'Some Notes on English Graces for the Viol' (Vol. II, 1970); A. Woodford on 'Music for Viol in Tablature' (Vol. II, 1970);R. Nicholson on 'Jenkins and "Musica Britannica" XXVI (Vol. II, 1970); F. Baines on 'Fantasias for the Great Dooble Base' (Vol. II, 1970); J. M. Jennings on 'The Fantasias of Thomas Lupo' (Vol. III, 1971); Colette Harris on 'Tobias Hume' (Vol. III, 1971) and 'The Viol Lyra Way' (Vol. IV, 1972); J. Whittaker, 'As Others Saw Us' (Vol. III, 1971); Margaret Crum on 'The Consort Music from Kirtling' (Vol. IV, 1972); D. Pinto on 'William Lawes' Consort Suites for the Viols' (Vol. IV, 1972); and C. H. Ågren on 'The Sound of Viols' (Vol. IV, 1972); as well as useful book reviews.

An enormous amount of sixteenth- and seventeenth-century music for two to seven instruments has been edited and published since this book first appeared. The reader may again be referred to

R. de Smet's catalogue and to the publications of the Viola da Gamba Society as well as to H. Alkor's and W. W. Cobbett's bibliographies.

Sixteenth- and seventeenth-century chamber music, recommended so beautifully by poets and chroniclers, must have fulfilled a significant function in a considerable stratum of the society of that age. It must have taught listeners and players alike – while enjoying playing and listening to this music – much about man, about man's greatness, his thoughts and his feelings, his daring and his suffering, his hopes and his forlorn hopes. It was composed by human beings for human beings, conveying important messages to them, thus influencing their attitude to life, helping to shape their consciousness.

The subject has led me to investigate certain aspects of the interrelationship between music and social forces which to some might appear to lie outside the scope of musicology. I have not hesitated to follow where the subject has led me, believing such inquiries to be essential to the true appraisal of a really great period of music and to its worthy celebration in present-day musical practice.

CHAPTER I

The Medieval Background

The age in which chamber music reached maturity may be characterised as a decisive stage in the fight between an old and a new principle of social structure, the fight between social, economic and cultural conservatism, represented by the feudal order of the middle ages,[1] and the rising middle classes who demanded greater individual freedom in every sphere of life.

In the sphere of religion which played so vital a part in the development of music in the middle ages, this struggle appears as the antagonism between Catholicism and all the religious movements that led up to Protestantism.

Far from being merely a religious creed, medieval Catholicism strove to be the spiritual authority that would direct and inspire the entire social life of the 'community of the faithful'. The political and social aspirations of the Church had first been formulated in St Augustine's *De Civitate Dei* – and in this 'State of God' it was the mission of the *papal hierarchy* to determine and control mankind's temporal organisation, so as to guide man through the fallacies of earthly life to his celestial salvation.

The Catholic Church of the middle ages was the strongest bulwark of the static order of society. It stood and fell with the principle of absolute authority and the divinely ordained unchangeability of things. Being itself built on the fixed system of landownership the Church struggled to keep down such tendencies as those which were being spread by the rising secular forces of the later middle ages, especially by the merchants. The world outlook of medieval Catholicism was static – as static as the social order based on self-sufficient agrarian economy and rights in land, as static as the universe of which the secular order of things is taken to be but a dim reflection. 'Credo ut intellegam', wrote Anselm – *the belief* prevails, the immutability of things is accepted. And the Church had to foster as the ideal attitude of popular religious opinion towards the external world of social institutions and economic relations, a creed which would 'stand on one side in

---

[1] In the use of the term 'feudal' we shall follow as closely as possible the definition given by H. Pirenne in his *History of Europe*, 1917; English edition (Allen & Unwin, 1939), pp. 146–160.

ascetic aloofness and regard them as in their very nature the sphere of unrighteousness – from which men *may* escape – from which, if they consider their souls, they *will* escape – but which they can conquer only by flight'.[1]

Music played an essential part in this 'creation of mentalities', The musical expression of this Catholic attitude of mind, the reiterated assertion of the unchallenged stability of Church and the worldly order of things, came to be choral polyphony.

Choral polyphony, the music of the later medieval Christian Church, is an important part of the foundation of the music of Europe, and is especially relevant to chamber music. As such we must give it some consideration.

Vocal music in general, carrying the message of the ritual, and increasing its effect and intensity both by musical and acoustic means, has been used in every kind of service almost as long as religious cults have existed. When a text is expounded by a musical choir the power of its religious message is intensified. The Christian Church has made use of this power ever since its beginnings in the catacombs of Rome and North Africa. In this practice the suggestive and emotional possibilities of music were made entirely subservient to the purpose of the biblical texts. The Gregorian Chant, that great collection of melodies used in the Catholic service, was codified, fixed and authorised in a deliberate official recognition of the power which music can be made to wield.

From the tenth century onwards the effect of the choral interpretation of the gospel was further broadened and deepened by the introduction of polyphony, i.e. the co-operation of all parts of the choir in the building of a contrapuntal whole. The crowning period of choral polyphony was the time of the so-called Netherlandish Schools which flourished during the fifteenth and sixteenth centuries. Throughout this period the polyphony of Church music was continuously elaborated, until towards the middle of the sixteenth century the holy melodies of the Gregorian choral, through the medium of which the liturgical message was announced, were finally produced by all the three, four, five or six voice-groups of the choir, each of them moving along independent contrapuntal lines, and all being of equal musical importance. The effect of this intense and highly 'organised' music was hypnotic.

This music, calm, majestic, and magnificently uniform, echoing

[1] R. H. Tawney, *Religion and the Rise of Capitalism*, 1926, p. 16.

through the twilight of the Gothic cathedrals in a neutral and unbroken flow, never failed to consolidate in the minds of the listeners a firm belief in the immutability of world, Church and established society – such indeed was its purpose. The fact that the Latin language was used in the music of the service essentially contributed to the impersonal and magic effect of the singing.

It will be easy to understand why the official art, especially of the earlier part of the middle ages, was vocal religious music, and why, indeed, no musical practice could ever hope for any official encouragement unless it were devoted to religion. St Augustine, in his *Confessiones* (about A.D. 400) says that he 'inclined . . . to allow the old usage of singing in the church; that so by the delight taken in by his ears, the weaker minds be roused up into some feeling of devotion'.

Hence the primacy of vocal music throughout the middle ages. The position of instrumental music is contrary and complementary.

As everywhere on the continent, the use of musical instruments declined in England with the eclipse of the Roman Empire. In ancient times musical instruments had occupied an all-important place in social life, in philosophy and even in politics. Non-Christian communities always believed in the magic power of instruments. But Christian culture shrank from activities so devilish and heathenish as the artificial working-up of profane emotions by aulos and cithara.

During the first centuries A.D. young Christianity proscribed musical instruments as symbols of the imperial age as Roman rule had meant slavery and unspeakable suffering to innumerable peoples. Musical instruments were employed in the temple, in the army, at state receptions, at noisy and brutally displayed pageants and especially at the debaucheries of degenerate Roman aristocracy; they even sounded when Christians were thrown to the lions. Christian communities of the 'poor and lowly', wherever and whenever they were formed, encouraged *singing* in the service. Their resistance to musical instruments can already be seen at very early times (soon after A.D. 100).

Not the singing itself belongs to the puerile stage, but the singing accompanied by instruments which have no souls, and by dancing and stamping. Therefore instrumental accompaniment in the churches has been abolished and only the pure singing has been kept.[1]

St Clement of Alexandria, one of the oldest patristic writers, says: 'Only one instrument do we use, viz., the word of peace wherewith we honor God, no longer the old psaltery, trumpet, drum and flute.' St Chrysostom (d. 407) is just as uncompromising:

> David formerly sang in psalms, also we sing today with him; he had a lyre with lifeless strings, the Church has a lyre with living strings. Our tongues are the strings of the lyre, with a different tone indeed, but with a more accordant piety.[2]

That was the attitude of the young Christian Church towards musical instruments and their music, and the suspicions surrounding instrumental music were never completely allayed throughout the middle ages. On the contrary, the hostility of the Church towards instruments and those who used them, intensified during the sixth and seventh centuries, although there were new reasons for this policy on the part of the Church.

In the early middle ages the activities of the Church were directed first and foremost against the Roman Empire and against everything that supported and represented it. Towards the end of the migration, however, especially from the time the Frankish Empire had consolidated its power, the old enemy was conquered: the victory of slaveless feudalism over the last remainders of slave society was complete (at least in Europe) – and this victory meant considerable improvements in the lot of the people and a new purpose in life for them. In the opinion of all its believers it was chiefly the Church which had led this struggle to success, resulting in both material and spiritual betterment.

It may be that in the times of Celtic Christianity before the Synod of Whitby (664) the Church in Britain exercised somewhat greater tolerance towards the ancient practice of instrumental music (as the stories of Caedmon and his harp seem to indicate), for the pre-Roman Church in England contained quite a number of relics

---

[1] *Quæstiones et Responsiones ad Orthodoxos* (A.D.370). F. W. Galpin mentions that occasionally lyras and cytharas had been used in the very earliest stages of the Christian Church, accompanying religious worship. Such cases were, however, isolated and confined to certain places. See F. W. Galpin, *Old English Instruments of Music*, London, 1910, p. 273.

[2] See E. Dickinson, *Music in the History of the Western Church*, London, 1902, pp. 54 ff.

from the times of tribal paganism. But it seems most probable that after the establishment of Roman Catholic rule the Church behaved more and more unkindly towards the 'soulless' musical instruments in this country just as it did everywhere else.

In all the cultures subsequently conquered by Christianity where instrumental music still played an important part in the official life of the community, the full power of the 'ecclesia militans' was mobilised to subdue it. In England the old instrumental art of the Bards and Celts which up to the seventh century was considered as something divine and supernaturally powerful, was pushed back during the process of cultural unification under the rule of Christianity.[1] The Church had to establish its universal sway by breaking down tribal gods, tribal separateness, and many tribal customs.

It must be stressed that during the first centuries of Christianity the stand of the Church against profane instrumental music had its progressive aspects inasmuch as it was directed against the decaying system of the Roman slave-empire and against tribal pagan influences. After all, the Church had brought a new moral standard to the masses, it had given economic security to its subjects, it had created a literate class and a new standard of art and learning which developed enormously with the further consolidation of the clerical organisation. In fact, during the early middle ages it was the great civilising force that prevented Europe from relapsing into barbarism. The austerity prescribed by all the patristic writers was part of the spiritual armour of the young movement. Yet the same Church, with the feudal order now firmly in the saddle, became an apologist for a new system of class privileges to an increasing degree; the issue was forthwith to protect and strengthen this new order by means of its entire religious and philosophical superstructure, at the same time to subdue those who were unwilling to bow to the new rulers.

Among the latter there were numerous peoples and tribes especially in north-western, northern and eastern Europe who had not yet adopted the Christian religion; those the Church had to convert to Christianity or, if necessary, to subjugate. Tribal communities in all these vast regions believed in the magic power

[1] As early as in the fourth century the art of harp playing among the Celtic Bards was recognised as an important part of their cultural activities. See Ammianus Marcellinus, L. XV, chapter IX: '. . . the Bards of the Celts celebrated the actions of illustrious men in heroic poems which they sang to the sweet sounds of the lyre.' For more details on harps in early medieval England see Galpin, Chap. I; also Burney's *History of Music*, II, pp. 352 ff.

of musical instruments. These were held in high esteem, they were sacred and surrounded with a symbolism that spelt life and prosperity to the tribe as a whole.

However, it was exactly because of their role in the magic rituals among the old gentile tribes that the Christian Church condemned musical instruments most severely, for its fight had now to be directed against magic and primitive cults which were the strongest ideological bulwark of all those communities not yet won over to Christianity.

Thus the conspicuous continuity in Church policy in questions concerning instrumental music throughout the middle ages may be explained – the Church first having to wage a fight, so to speak, against forces 'above', later on against those 'below', i.e. against the cultural independence of peoples and tribes upon which the Church had to enforce its authority.

St Augustine pleaded that it was better even to plough on the Lord's day than to desecrate it with dancing and riot.[1] In the ninth century it was decreed that bishops and abbots must not possess birds of prey, dogs or jugglers (minstrels),[2] Prohibitions of minstrels, worded in the strongest possible terms, were decreed at various councils,[3] such as Cavaillon (650), Tours (813), Glasgow (747), and in particular Mainz (847 and 852).[4] This policy stands out despite the appearance of some very ancient British instruments such as the rotta[5] in eighth and ninth century pictures in early psalters or in carvings in churches.[6] For it was even more the player of an instrument than the instrument itself which incurred the disfavour of the Church.

So the heralds of Christianity waged a holy war against those people who still continued the forbidden practice. No value was attached to any instrumental activity. To say the least, it was considered useless; just empty 'playing'. One must remember that from the early middle ages a musical instrument was 'played', 'gespielt', 'joué', etc., in nearly all the European languages, while in pre-Christian languages the respective terms were mostly

[1] *De Decem Chordis,* serm. ix, para. 3. See G. G. Coulton, *The Medieval Village,* Cambridge, 1925, p. 93.

[2] Boretius, *Capitularia Regum Francorum,* 1883, I, 64.

[3] See P. H. Láng, *Music in Western Civilization,* 1942, p. 83.

[4] See Boretius, *Capitularia,* and E. K. Chambers, *The Medieval Stage,* 1903, pp. 38 ff.

[5] Rotta is the triangular or U-shaped harp of the early middle ages, often identical with the chrotta (crwth, crowder, cruit or chorus), the rectangular harp, which was at first plucked, later often bowed.

[6] Galpin, pp. 4, 5, and *passim.*

'blown', 'plucked', 'struck' or 'sounded'.[1] Basically the English
development differed in no way from that on the Continent. When
King Alfred disguised himself as a harpist to get into the camp of
the Danes before the battle of Edington (878) he did so in order to
conceal his Christian state from his enemies. His harp showed him
to be a heathen, for it was an instrument of pagan culture which the
Christian Church did not tolerate.[2] Alcuin (Albinus Flaccus of
York, 735–804), friend and teacher of Charlemagne, warned a
friend in a letter which he wrote in 791 that he apparently did not
realise that 'by inviting jugglers and dancers to his house he
admitted a mass of unclean spirits'.[3] At the end of the 11th century
John Cotton, well-known English theoretician, in his treatise
Joannis Cottonis Musica speaks very contemptuously about wind
instruments in particular. In his opinion these instruments sound
'indiscretely' (which means dissonantly), 'like the laughter or the
groaning of men, the barking of dogs or the roaring of lions'. Only
the well-tempered movement of voices can be called music – this
Cotton felt obliged to use as an argument against those 'idiots who
are stupid enough to call *any* sound music'.[4]

It was stated as an exceptional and daring venture that St
Adhelm, Bishop of Sherborne (about 640–709), should have
deemed it necessary to attract people to the church by playing a
harp – only then, having played the pagan instrument, did he
succeed in gathering around him an audience sufficiently large to

---

[1] In Spain, however, the words 'tañer' or 'tocar', 'to touch', were used, not 'jugar', 'to
play'; and 'toccare' in Italy.
[2] E. H. Poole, in his essay on *Music in the Early Drama*, mentions a similar incident of the
year 457 which occurred in York during the wars between Saxons and Britons; there is also
the story of Baldulph, given in Chappell's *Old English Popular Music*, 1893, p. 6. Nevertheless,
the Utrecht Psalter (eighth to ninth centuries) has many pictures of harps being played
among groups of musicians surrounding the Psalmist.
[3] Quoted by A. Schering, *Handbuch der Musikgeschichte*, 1923, p. 97.
[4] See M. Gerbert, *Scriptores ecclesiastici de musica*, II, p. 234: 'Artificiale vero instrumentum
est, quod non per naturam sed per artificium ad reddendum sonitum adaptatur. Naturalis
autem sonus alius est discretus, alius indiscretus; discretus est, qui alias habet consonantias;
indiscretus est, in quo nulla discerni potest consonantia, ut in risu vel gemitu hominum, et
latratu canum, aut rugitu leonum. Simili modo discretum et indiscretum sonum in
artificiali perpendere potes. Fistula namque illa, qua decipiuntur aviculæ, vel etiam illa
pergameno superducta, unde pueri ludere solent, indiscretum reddunt sonitum. At vero in
sambuca, in fidibus, in cymbalis, atque in organis consonantiarum bene et distincte
discernitur diversitas. Illum ergo sonum, quem indiscretum esse diximus, musica
nequaquam recipit: solus autem dumtaxat discretus, qui etiam proprie phthongus vocatur,
ad musicam pertinet; est enim musica nihil aliud quam vocum congrua motio. Hæc autem
contra idiotas præcipue diximus, quo illorum compesceremus errorem, qui quemlibet
sonum esse musicum stulte autumant.'

enable him to deliver his sermon.[1] And Bishop Dunstan (tenth century) had the uncomfortable experience of being called a sorcerer for having constructed an Æolian harp which sounded when placed against a crevice in a wall.[2] Only for a short time immediately after the Norman invasion do we find some court 'jongleurs' brought over by the conquering noblemen such as Berdic, William's minstrel – while the remainder of the English-speaking minstrelsy were now driven into hiding by the Normans and forthwith rambled up and down the country as enemies of the authorities.

*

On the other hand, however, we can at least say – with all due caution – that on balance the persecution of instrumental music by the Church in England was progressively, if slightly, relaxed during the twelfth and thirteenth centuries. As we reach the twelfth century we can begin to speak of something like a reluctant (and certainly temporary) toleration of certain instruments by the Church.

The fact is that popular musical activities outside the Church were decidedly on the increase in the twelfth century.

Instrumental music was the cheerful accompaniment of the growth of the new burgher classes. The nobility, too, especially the continental knights at the time of the crusades, had contributed substantially to the consolidation of secular music in general and instrumental music in particular. Much as the Church disliked this development, it could not ignore it.

For many centuries it had kept down instrumental activity. Whilst trying to utilise painting, literature, pageantry, and many pagan festivals and customs (such as Yule) by gently diverting them into Christian channels, instrumental music it either vituperated or brutally persecuted. Not only did it appear valueless to the Church, for the simple reason that the music of the vielles, pipes and shalms seemed to contain hardly any elements worth mentioning which could be transformed and thus utilised for Church purposes – it was positively harmful to the souls of the people. Instrumental music introduced an element of secular pleasure; it disturbed the atmosphere of devotion, the unity of the service. It distracted the churchgoers from their sacred duties.

[1] Galpin, p. 17.
[2] Ibid., p. 72.

Altogether the listening to and particularly the playing of musical instruments had an activising effect on human beings as individuals – an influence small in appearance but dangerous in its possible consequences. If St Jerome preached that 'a Christian maiden ought not even to know what a lyre or a flute is, or what it is used for',[1] he must have had his reasons.[2]

But instrumental music became more and more powerful, and by 1150 it had become a deeply-rooted 'evil'. And now the Church was repeatedly compelled to come to terms with instrumental music, in an effort to absorb what it could not destroy.

The Church had to give in and try to make use of musical instruments (or at least of some of them) by taking the pagan stigma from them and incorporating them in its own inventory of recognised service furniture. This indeed the Church authorities did by having angels and saints pictured praising the Lord no longer merely by singing, but by playing harps and dulcimers; sometimes indeed they actually had them played in the monasteries and cathedrals. In such a way the Church no doubt hoped to attract the villagers back to the service and to close a dangerous gulf between itself and the people at large.

The twelfth century was a time when the Church in England could afford this temporary relaxation. For then the position of the Church was still relatively secure. From the times of the Norman invasion approximately till the thirteenth century, feudalism in England existed in its most complete form (and the Church was 'implicated to the hilt in its economic fabric, especially on the side of agriculture and land tenure'.[3] Feudal landowning and villeinage, which formed the secular basis of the power of the Church, were then most stabilised and worked well, while spiritually and intellectually the Church was certainly the dominant influence.

[1] Dickinson, p. 55.

[2] Antagonism to instrumental music in the Christian service reappears as a feature of several later movements. Here is the opinion on the matter as expressed by Dr Kippis, well-known dissenter of the end of the eighteenth century: 'The use of instrumental music in Christian worship has no foundation in the New Testament, which is the standard of our faith and practice. If once we depart from this standard there will be no end to innovations. An opening will be laid to the introduction of one superstition after another, till the simplicity and purity of the Gospel service are wholly lost. *Every thing, therefore, which tends to divert men from a rational inward devotion to external pomp and ceremony ought to be discouraged as much as possible.*' From *A Tractate against Instrumental Music in Churches*, by Dr Samuel Green, Controversial Tracts, 5.

[3] Tawney, p. 56.

So the 'ecclesia triumphans' for a time made it its policy to compromise with the allurements of popular entertainment. In fact, quite a number of strange happenings occurred in twelfth- and early thirteenth-century churches in the way of pageantry and music, especially on the Continent. In this country there are several instances of people choosing the churches or churchyards of all places for singing vulgar songs and love carols and performing quick step dances (Giraldus Cambrensis, in his *Gemma ecclesiastica*, has a whole chapter against dancing and singing in churches). Among the first instruments that played a certain part in the service we name the organ – it was the only instrument which hardly ever incurred the disfavour of the Church. This great instrument was very early adopted for use in the service. Its majestic and somewhat otherworldly (if in its young days somewhat harsh) sound made it particularly apt for this function.[1] Baudri of Bourgeuil (1046–1130) expressed his admiration for the organ at Worcester Church with great eloquence:

> The organ, whence harmonious voices run,
> Is joy that gives our lives their ordering.
> Driven on varying ways, we draw to one:
> As one we chant the praises of our King.
> The power of unity in different voices
> Is that which spreads our energies, yet controls.
> The driven air along each reed rejoices:
> So God combines with flesh our struggling souls,
> To blend our lives in mystic symphony.
> His breath of power, unifying, blows
> And many lives within one life are furled,
> The secret glory that sustains the world.
> Thus from concordant hearts the music flows.
> Great Prior, here's the song you asked of me.[2]

Under the favour of the Church organ music was able to develop freely.[3]

---

[1] As early as the eighth century an illumination in the Utrecht Psalter shows two monks playing the organ. Dunstan, in the tenth century, is said to have made an organ with brass pipes. At the same time a gigantic organ at Winchester Cathedral is mentioned. There are numerous illustrations showing organs being used in the service in the eleventh and twelfth centuries. See also H. Davey, *History of English Music*, 2nd ed. (1921), pp. 9 ff., and F. W. Galpin, *Old English Instruments of Music*, 1910, picture plates.

[2] From Jack Lindsay, *Medieval Latin Poets*, 1934, p. 112.

[3] We possess a highly important document which is generally considered as the earliest

Moreover, after 1100 some soft-toned stringed instruments make their appearance in sacred surroundings more and more frequently, chiefly the organistrum,[1] the psaltery[2] and the dulcimer.[3] Even trumpets and other brass instruments are sometimes pictured in Church MSS. where the biblical context justifies it;[4] and such examples are on the increase during the twelfth and thirteenth centuries.

Around 1300 a theoretician tells us of string, wind and keyboard instruments which reinforce the sound of the voices 'to the greater praise of the holiest divine glory'.[5] Just about the same time Bishop de Swinfield of Hereford is reported to have allowed some minstrels to play to him in one of his pastoral rounds. After listening for a while, he ordered that each of them should be given

---

specimen of organ music; it is of the fourteenth century and not immediately connected with the service itself. It consists of two parchment leaves which are annexed to a register of Robertsbridge Abbey; now Brit. Museum, MS. Add. 28550 (see also Wooldridge, *Early English Harmony*, pp. 42–45). These contain several purely instrumental movements, partly intavolaturas of vocal pieces, among others from the French Roman de Fauvel (beginning of fourteenth century; see J. Wolf's *Geschichte der Mensuralnotation*, I, pp. 357 ff.). The other keyboard music consists of three dances in *estampie* form (one incomplete), which may be either for organ or clavichord. See John Caldwell, *Keyboard Music before the 19th Century* (1973). They are 2-part pieces which expand into 3-part harmony towards the cadences. All are influenced by the continental 'ars nova' with its greater rhythmic decision, although they are, on the whole, kept in the stricter style of the earlier middle ages. The general appearance of the pieces is of such completeness and security of style as to suggest that they were results of a long tradition. There is one more indication of what early English organ music might have been like; it is contained in the Treatise from Bury St Edmunds written by an English thirteenth-century writer, generally known as 'Anonymus 4' in Coussemaker's *Scriptures*. He talks about 'bordunos organorum' which suggests an instrumental bordune tone, a sustained note kept in the bass in a similar way as in the music of our Scotch pipers, while other voices play or sing melodic counterpoint. See Charles E. H. de Coussemaker, *Scriptores de musica medii ævi*, 1864–76, I, p. 327; also Marius Schneider, *Geschichte der Mehrstimmigkeit*, II, 1935, pp. 19 ff. and pp. 43 ff.

[1] The hurdy-gurdy, also called symphony; with an internal circular bow turned round by way of an external handle.

[2] Psalterium; a flat hollow box with a stringboard; the strings are played with a plectrum or the fingers.

[3] Like the psaltery, but the strings are played with hammers.

[4] King David is sometimes shown with his musicians; there are also pictures of the trombones of Jericho, of Saul's instrumental ensemble, etc. It must be stressed, however, that the appearance of pictures of an instrument in certain sacred surroundings does not necessarily prove that it had in fact been used in the service.

[5] The treatise of this anonymous writer is called *De Sinemenis* and is affixed to that of the thirteenth-century English 'Anonymus 4' in Coussemaker's *Scriptores*. The passage in question runs: 'Quæ quidem supradicta ad sanctissimam gloriam divinam multiplicandam cum quibusdam aliis, prout in cordis, in flatu, in cimbalis bene sonantibus' (Coussemaker, I, p. 365).

the sum of 'a penny a piece'.[1] We even come across such thirteenth-century stories as that of Benedictus of Abingdon who turned out two itinerant priests in disappointment that they were not minstrels to entertain him.[2]

There is a beautiful continental example of this temporary change of policy on the part of the Church in a situation similar to the English. It is contained in a late thirteenth-century treatise by Johannes de Grocheo. Talking about Stantipes and Ductia, Grocheo describes the object of these dance-cantilenas which were either instrumental or vocal as purely moral. These tunes which originally derived from popular practice he represents as intended to distract the minds of young ladies and gentlemen from wicked thoughts and lead them, by their great degree of difficulty, away from 'that passion which is called love' to assiduous study and other praiseworthy activities.[3]

The modification of the attitude of the Church towards musical instruments after 1150 roughly coincides with the first appearance of vernacular poetry in England after the Norman Conquest. Although the old Anglo-Saxon heroic tradition and alliterative verse lived on in new transformations, the development in the Middle English period proceeds towards the greater freedom in narrative, lyrical and romantic poetry which was to culminate in the fourteenth century with Chaucer.

One is tempted to consider these two facts, the rise of lyrical poetry and the greater tolerance shown by the Church towards instruments, together, as two aspects of one and the same development: the growing consolidation and independence of cultural activities outside the Church. So the second half of the twelfth century appears as a time dividing the middle ages into two main periods, the later centuries being characterised by the growing emancipation of the secular burgher and middle classes from clerical tutelage.

But at the same time the developments in poetry show quite

---

[1] Jusserand, *English Wayfaring Life in the Middle Ages* (fourteenth century), London, 1920, p. 202. A penny at the time would equal about 17½p in present currency (1980): see G. G. Coulton, *The Meaning of Medieval Moneys*, Hist. Ass. Leaflet No. 95, 1934.

[2] Anthony à Wood, *Hist. Antiq. Oxon.,* Vol. I, p. 67.

[3] 'Stantipes . . . facit animos iuvenum et puellarum propter sui difficultatem circa hanc stare et eos a cogitatione prava devertit . . .' 'Ductia vero est cantilena levis et velox in ascensu et descensu, quæ in choris a iuvenibus et puellis decantatur. . . . Hæc enim ducit corda puellarum et iuvenum et a vanitate removet et contra passionem, quæ dicitur amor . . . valere dicitur.' See J. Wolf's article in *Sammelbände der Internationalen Musikgesellschaft*, I, pp. 93 f.

clearly that it would be wrong to see the art of the later middle ages in a straight-line oppositional development of 'Church *versus* middle classes'. The latter were always intensely religious, and in general there was a continuous and strong interplay of the cultural elements of both forces, as well as vivid interaction of the art of the court, serfs, the educated individuals at universities and monasteries, and the wandering scholars.

Just as 'the first popular songs of the modern world were the hymns of St Ambrose and the oldest fashion of popular tunes is derived from the Church',[1] so in the later middle ages many songs sung by the people were produced by musically highly skilled monks. A striking example is the famous 'Summer Canon' (about 1280):[2]

Example 2: The Summer Canon.

This piece was for a long time considered a typical 'popular' song, typical of both the simplicity of the musical thinking of the ordinary country folk and of elements of style peculiar exclusively to the English. Neither opinion can be completely refuted, but it is important to see that there are in pieces like the 'Summer Canon' elements of the style of the music of the highly educated classes (as well as of foreign countries, which in this case is not the point to be discussed). It has been called 'a learned composer's adaptation of a reverie or chant of welcome to the spring',[3] and those who look more closely will find how true this is, for there are many evidences of a truly ingenious mind contained in the score. Its musical form is closely related to the contemporary French isorhythmic secular 'minstrels' motet, which is certainly based on a highly difficult and

[1] W. P. Ker, *Medieval English Literature*, 1912, p. 76.

[2] Dr M. Bukofzer (*Sumer is icumen in, a revision*; University of California Publications in Music, 1944) believes that this famous *rota* cannot possibly have been written before 1280. See also E. J. Dent in *The Music Review*, vol. VI, No. 2 (May 1945), pp. 107–109.

[3] E. K. Chambers and F. Sidgwick, *Early English Lyrics*, 1907.

even refined pattern.[1] Moreover the original copy of the song has a Latin text as well as an English one (Latin had long ceased to be the language of the common people in England). At the same time there certainly are popular influences and sources clearly discernible in this piece; one of them is the popular French rondeau as exemplified in the following melody:[2]

Example 3: thirteenth-century 3-part round (Northern French).

Hé Dieu qu' eile m'a_ tra - hi_ qui m'a tol - lu mon_ a - mi

The trend of French influences in thirteenth-century English poetry and music thus shows just this interaction of social forces. These influences came from popular *as well* as 'polite' circles and they affected the fashionable and courtly efforts of good society over here *as well* as popular activities in country and town (for instance such festivals as celebrate the coming of May with dances and games).

Such considerations are important if we want to see the development of spiritual life outside the Church in its proper perspective. However, it will not be denied that behind this changing interplay of social forces and influences there *are* these two antagonistic factors, Church and burgherdom, as guiding spirits of the development. One of the manifestations of this hostility was the suspicious attitude of the Church towards many expressions of secular gaiety – it will presently be shown that this struggle was to become violently obvious in our own field of instrumental music, and even during the era of compromise between 1150 and 1300 we cannot say that the Church was exactly kindly disposed towards it.

In the words of B. L. Manning, it 'sanctioned what it was obliged – after many protests – to tolerate'.[3] And even during this period the critics of instrumental music were active enough: e.g. Nigellus, præcentor in the Church of Canterbury and favourite of Bishop William de Longchamps.[4] In *Aldhelmi Ænigmata* there is a very rude

---

[1] See H. Besseler, *Musik des Mittelalters und der Renaissance,* Potsdam, 1934, pp. 170 ff.

[2] From Joh. Wolf, *Geschichte der Musik,* I, 1930, p. 62, the second and third voices come in in the second and third bars.

[3] *The People's Faith in the Time of Wyclif,* 1919, p. 124.

[4] In his 'Speculum Stultorum' (The Mirror of Fools), *Rerum Britannicarum medii ævi scriptores, Satirical Poets and Epigrammatists* (twelfth century), Vol. I, 1872 (ed. Thomas Wright).

poem directed against various instruments,[1] also a sharp satire on a trumpet.[2] A picture of about 1200 shows a recorder blown by a bear,[3] and on a capital of the crypt at Canterbury Cathedral we see a shalm[4] played by a really abhorrent goat (a donkey next to it holds a cornet).[5]

The popular notion of Satanas with his fiddle or pipe, viewed in this historical context, appears in a new light: it was the Church that gave him the fiddle or pipe, not to dignify him, we may be sure, but to degrade the instrument.

> A Winnock Bunker in the East –
> There sat Auld Nick in Shape o' Beast;
> A Towzy Tyke, Black, Grim, and Large –
> To gie them Music was his Charge.
> He screwed the Pipes, and gart them skirl
> Till Roof and Rafters a' did dirl.[6]

It would be interesting to find out to what degree musical instruments in the middle ages played their part in witchcraft. It has been said that many ordinary men who felt that Church and state were leagued against them turned for consolation to the old enemy of Christian mythology, the Devil. The French historian Michelet declares that 'the medieval peasant would have burst but for his hope in Beelzebub'. Witchcraft must have been widespread and dangerous in its uncontrollable fierceness, and musical instruments have been connected with magic beliefs as long as music has existed, from the fertility charms of the ancient bullroarer to the 'hautboys' for the witches' cave in Shakespeare's *Macbeth*.[7] Even such a distinguished writer as Alanus Anglicus (twelfth century)[8] emphasises the *magic* powers of music. There is

[1] Ibid., Vol. II, 1872, p. 540. Here is the poem and a rough translation:

De barbito sive organo	*On the lute, or perhaps the organ*

Quamvis ære cavo salpinctis classica clangant
Et citharæ crepitant, strepituque tubæ
  modulentor:
Centenos tamen eructant mea viscera cantus,
Meque strepente stupent mox musica corda fibrarum.
	Though the battle signals of the trumpet bellow out
	  through the hollow brass.
	And the harps clatter, and the trombones move noisily
	  up and down;
	Yet my bowels belch up chants by the hundred,
	And when I start all those soulful musical gut-strings are
	  dumbed as I blurt on.

[2] *De Salpinge*, ibid., II, 556.

[3] Galpin, p. 137.

[4] Early predecessor of the oboe family.

[5] For pictures see Galpin, pp. 80, 140, 159, 170, and 190.

[6] *Tam o' Shanter*, by Robert Burns.

[7] See also Chaucer, *House of Fame*, I, 169, on jugglers and witchcraft.

[8] Alani Anglici Anticlaudianus; see *Rerum Britannicarum medii ævi scriptores*, Satirical Poets and Epigrammatists, Vol. 2, 1872, pp. 323 ff.

the story of the Sacrilegious Carollers (1303): thirteen persons of both sexes (the chief being the priest's daughter) danced in a churchyard and instrumental musicians accompanying the ceremony are shown in a picture illustrating the incident.[1] We know from the end of the middle ages that instrumental music was an integral part of witchcraft ceremonies. In the fifteenth and sixteenth centuries 'trumps' or 'Jew's harps' (jaw's harps) were played at such celebrations.[2] Jonet Lucas at Aberdeen was accused that 'thou and they was under the conduct of thy master the Devil, dancing in a ring, and playing melodiously upon one instrument'.[3] Occasionally one person held the position of 'piper to the Devil', and indeed pipes (as accompaniment of the dances) or sometimes citterns seem to have been the most frequent instruments on such occasions.

In view of the often anticlerical use of many instruments of music some churchmen extended their hatred of such instruments to every kind of instrumental practice. A vivid example of this radical attitude is contained in a sermon by Ethelred Abbot of Rivaulx, Yorkshire (end of the twelfth century), who did not even approve of the use of organs: 'To what purpose, I pray you, is that terrible blowing of Belloes, expressing rather the crakes of Thunder, than the sweetness of a voyce?' But when the attempt was made to introduce instruments apart from the organ into the churches Ethelred boiled over with rage: 'The common people standing by, trembling and astonished, admire the sounds of the Organ, the noyse of the Cymballs and Musicall Instruments, the Harmony of the Pipes and Cornets.'[4] When it actually happened that honours were granted to minstrels or other secular musicians there were protests from some high Church officials such as John of Salisbury who, in the twelfth century, thundered against the 'fools of this age who pour out rewards to minstrels and monsters of that sort'.[5]

*

After the brief interlude of the twelfth and part of the thirteenth century the attitude of the Church towards instruments underwent a new change. It is perhaps too early to pass a final opinion on the

[1] Margaret A. Murray, *The God of the Witches*, p. 113 and plate XIV.
[2] M. A. Murray, *Witchcraft in Western Europe*, 1921, p. 55.
[3] *God of the Witches*, p. 67.
[4] Translated by Prynne; see Davey, p. 16.
[5] Chappell, *Old English Popular Music*, 1893, I, p. 5.

exact nature of this change, since the evidence at our disposal is
scanty and somewhat contradictory. But as far as can be
ascertained, it seems that the Church authorities had more or less
generally accepted the organ in the service. There are also a
number of examples of certain stringed instruments and some
privileged musicians having been tolerated. But in general the
Church authorities resumed their denunciation of instrumental
playing. In the struggle for and against these 'devil's tools' their
antagonists had won the day and their hatred became most violent
when it was directed against the *itinerant* musicians (who formed
the vast majority of minstrels in later medieval England).

The reason for this stiffening of the opposition to musical
instruments is not far to seek.

In its early days the *ecclesia militans* had to proscribe as unholy
anything that recalled the sins of its Roman and pagan opponents.
From the middle of the thirteenth century onwards the Church
once more (and even more passionately) attacked instrumental
music, but now it was on the defence against the new and
progressive middle classes which began to challenge the very basis
of its existence. About 1300 the old medieval order was definitely
on the decline. The old domainal and manorial system which
formed the economic foundation of Church and nobility, had
given stability, but now it 'checked progress and denied freedom'.[1]
With the increasing demand of the popular masses for greater
social, national and economic independence the Church progressively lost its moral and intellectual leadership – especially
when from the fourteenth century onwards the prophets of new
spiritual and social freedom appeared within its own ranks.[2] The

---

[1] G. M. Trevelyan, *History of England*, 1934, p. 237.

[2] Here is one of the stories that illustrate the somewhat changed attitude of many ordinary
people to Church music which was becoming a more and more isolated and intellectual
affair: 'Jacobus de Vetriato tellis how that ther was a preste that trowid he was a passand
gude synger, not-with-standyng he was not so. So on a day there was a gentyl-womman that
satt behynd hym and hard hym syng, and sho began to wepe; and he, trowyng that sho
wepid for swettnes of his voyse, began to syng lowder than he did tofor; and ay the hyer sho
hard hym sung, the faster wepud sho. Than this preste askid hur whi sho wepud so as sho
did, and sho answerd hym agayn and sayd: "Sur, I am a pure gentill-womman, and the
laste day I had no calfe bud one, and the wulfe come and had it away fro me and evur when
that I here you syng, onone I remember me how that my calfe and ye cried (a)like." And
when the preste hard this, onone he thoght shame, and remembred hym that the thing (th)at
he thought was grete lovyng unto God, was unto Him grete shame and velany; and fro thens
furth he sang nevur so lowde.' (From Coulton, *Social Life in Britain*, 1919, p. 266).

Church, however, 'refused every concession, effected no reform and called in brute force to repress heresy'.[1]

The development of its attitude towards music reflects the change which was going on in the wider field of Church policy. The minstrel's art of instrumental playing, grudgingly tolerated for a transitory period, had become too powerful. The unorthodox element in the long run must not be allowed to invade the medieval church in the form of recorders, shalms and fiddles. And many minstrels really must have become quite a menace if we are to believe such witnesses as the Abbot of Rivaulx.

The fight against the minstrels and their instruments was not, on the whole, as violent in England as on the Continent. There these 'joculatores', 'mimi', 'ministeriales' or 'histriones' were often outlawed 'while alive' or at least prevented by law from entering towns. Minstrels were often excluded from the mass. To mention only one of many examples, the 'Sachsenspiegel', a German juridical code of the thirteenth century, contains a law according to which a minstrel was only allowed to hit the *shadow* of anyone who might have done him wrong.[2] The famous Bull of Pope John XXII, decreed from Avignon (1322) against the 'secularisation' of service music, is an illustration of the same policy,[3] yet to quite a high degree the later medieval English Church too did its best to discourage the minstrelsy and, as a matter of fact, all kinds of secular activities. There were repeated attempts to stop dancing[4] and from 1337 onwards to prohibit even games as apparently harmless as play-ball,[5] wrestling, the stone-throwing sport, etc., where many fellows 'vainly glory in their bodily strength and exercise themselves in such like things'.[6]

The Council of Oxford, following the rule of the Lateran Council, decided that members of the clergy 'must not listen to actors, jigglers and minstrels'.[7]

---

[1] G. M. Trevelyan, *History of England*, 1934, p. 245. Nevertheless, musical instruments still made their appearance in church artefacts. E.g. the angel on horseback playing a lute on the Steeple Aston Cope (fourteenth century).

[2] Johannes Wolf, *Geschichte der Musik*, Berlin, 1930, I, p. 35. H. Riemann, *Geschichte der Musiktheorie*, Leipzig, 1898, p. 210, says that instruments were generally out of the church by the advent of the thirteenth century. But on the basis of our evidence the date should be put slightly later, as far as England is concerned.

[3] See E. Dickinson, *Music in the History of the Western Church*, 1902, p. 146.

[4] G. G. Coulton, *The Medieval Village*, Cambridge, 1925, pp. 559–600.

[5] Ibid., p. 93 (Law of 1382).

[6] Ibid., p. 561 (Decree of 1401).

[7] E. K. Chambers, *The Mediæval Stage*, 1903, p. 39.

The Statutes of St Paul's of the year 1450 direct the beadles 'to keep off and throw out the minstrels who make their noises, void of devotion, openly before the altar of the Virgin and the Cross'.[1] Scottish minstrels were handled even more roughly. In 1449 the King, obviously on the instigation of the very discredited Scottish Church, asked the minstrels to live decently or to leave the country; any minstrels found forthwith should have their ears cut off and, if caught again, be hanged.[2]

Musical theorists often followed the lead of the authorities. Simon Tunstede, writer about 1350, refers contemptuously to minstrels whose music had nothing to do with art.[3] In a treatise called *De Origine et Effectu Musicæ*, written by an English monk about 1400, it is asserted that 'Roundellas, Ballads, Carollas and Springas' (that is to say, the secular songs and dances which were often played by instruments) are 'fantastic and frivolous', and that 'no good musical writer has ever thought it worth to explain their texture'.[4]

Many musical instruments disappeared from the churches

[1] '. . . quod menestrallos coram altaribus Virginis et Crucis indevote strepitantes arceant et ejiciant', Statutes, i. 5, 4, cf. W. S. Simpson, *Register of St Paul's*, 1873, p. 72.

[2] 'Gif there be onie that makis them fuiles (jesters), and ar bairdes or uthers sik like runnaris about, and gif onie sik be fundin, that they be put in the king's waird, or in his irons (stocks) for their trespasses, als lang as they haue any gudes of their awin to liue upon – that their eares be nailed to the trone (pillory) or till ane uther tree, and their eare cutted off, and banished the cuntrie – and gift thereafter they be funden againe, that they be hanged.' See W. Dauney, *Ancient Scottish Melodies*, Edinburgh, 1838, p. 72. More decrees against histriones (especially during the second half of the thirteenth to the end of the fourteenth century) are quoted by Helen Waddell, *The Wandering Scholars*, 1932, pp. 261 and 265 ff. Orders dealing with Welsh minstrels are contained in Brit. Mus. MS. Add. 15003 and MS. Add. 15038; they contain a statute attributed to Griffith ap Cynan (1055–1137) relating to minstrelsy, and the ancient order of Deheubarth, 'Llyma Drefn ar wyr wrth Gerdd Dafawd' (before Griffith).

[3] Coussemaker, *Scriptores, IV*, pp. 295 f.

[4] See Hawkins, *General History of the Science and Practice of Music*, I, 246. A fifteenth-century monk complains that most singers sing 'naughty' songs for 'empty renown'; he warns his colleagues 'for God's sake' not to do so, so that they may be led 'to the everlasting fatherland':

> Cantatores sunt plerique
> Quorum artes sunt inique.
> Vanam querunt gloriam.
> Libens cane non inane
> Propter deum ut in evum
> Ducaris in patriam.

This verse occurs in a poem composed in motet style contained in the 'Old Hall' MS. which is assumed to have been completed between 1438 and 1444. The Old Hall MS. (large collection of motets mostly liturgic) was transcribed and edited by A. Hughes and M. Bent (Rome, 1969) Corpus mensurabilis musicae 46.

during the fourteenth century, especially the small ones that could be carried about and thus smelt of 'wayfaring'.

Robert Manning, in 1303, still mentions some of them in a poem about the life of Bishop Groteste (1253):

> Yn Harpe and Taborn and Symphan gle
> Worschippe God yn Trumpes and Sautre;
> In Cordes, yn Orgones and Bellis ringyng,
> Yn all these worschippe the hevenes Kinge.[1]

But in 1397 Bartholomæus de Glanville triumphantly announces: 'And nowe holy chyrche useth only this instrument of musyk (the organ), in proses, sequences, and ympnes: and forsakyth for men's use of minstralsye all other instruments of musyk.'[2] Here we have proof that the whole question of instrumental music was not a side-issue, but that the Church considered it of great importance, and that it had a well-considered policy towards it. And if the Church in the fourteenth and fifteenth centuries was no longer strong enough to suppress such instrumental music as was produced outside its immediate jurisdiction, at least it kept it out of its service as far as possible.

There were exceptions to the rule. But they only confirm the vigour of the rising forces of secular music that defied the strictures of the Church; the minstrels were not ecclesiastical but *secular* musicians.

These exceptions, one of which has already been mentioned,[3] are found chiefly in the popular mystery plays. These, however, were not organised by the Church but by craft guilds through private theatre companies and they are but another indication that in some measure an interaction of the cultural activities of the various social forces was taking place all the time. These plays formed a connecting link between the Church and the secular world. There is often great freedom and popular originality in the mystery plays. They were sometimes enormous in scope, size, duration and expense. The people developed them further and further away from the Church pattern of religious practice. They express ideas of a religion with which the people were at home and which they freely developed in their own comic imagination. There were comic episodes in the middle of these performances, there

---

[1] Galpin, p. 56.
[2] *De proprietatibus rerum*, 1397. See Hawkins, p. 268.
[3] See above, p. 24.

were shepherds' dances and other secular scenes. It is quite true that there were many condemnations of clergy who took part in them.[1] Such condemnations expressed the anxiety of the Church to prevent these plays (and with them clerical control of the people's religious belief) from getting out of hand. But just as often these plays enjoyed a certain amount of patronage or at least the connivance of the Church. It must be remembered that the craft guilds of the towns which organised these plays in many cases helped both to build and to endow the churches outside which they were conducting the plays.

Minstrels were often asked to perform in such plays. In the account books of the companies there are mentioned minstrels as pipers, harpists, lutists, drummers, and flutists. Much of this music must have been purely instrumental; altogether instruments appear to have been used in these plays because of the great appeal they had for the popular masses, for whom the mystery plays were intended as propaganda so-to-speak 'in their own language.' In the 'Assumption of the Virgin,' shown in Coventry about and after 1400, a remark is found: 'Here the angel descends while citherns play.' In 'Origo Mundi,' of Cornwall, of the same period, the minstrels are asked 'in the name of the Father to pipe immediately.[2]

There is further the question of the slow 'tenores' (cantus firmi) in the motets in the already mentioned Old Hall Manuscript.[3] This collection contains pieces mostly liturgic which were used in the Royal Chapel, presumably during Henry VI's reign. Some of these complicated vocal scores contain biblical cantus firmi with extremely long notes which seem to be unfit for vocal performance; these may, indeed, have been intended for organs, but it is just possible (though perhaps unlikely) that they were played by some soft wind or string instruments of long sustaining power.[4]

As far as can be seen there are few definite instances of instrumental music (harps and dulcimers only) having been used within fourteenth- and fifteenth-century churches.[5] In the account

[1] See Coulton, *The Medieval Village*, Vol. II (Appendices).

[2] H. E. Poole gives more examples from 'Creation and Fall and Death of Abel' (Chester, fourteenth and fifteenth centuries).

[3] See above, p. 32, footnote 4.

[4] As a typical example we mention Th. Damett's Salvatoris mater pia, No. 107, pp. 89b, 90a.

[5] Early in the fifteenth century a train of pilgrims were allowed to have bagpipes with

books of certain priories, such as Thetford, Maxstoke, and Durham, we find occasional evidence of the use of instruments in churches. Few though the instances of monks practising gitterns or listening to minstrels' vielles in the fourteenth and fifteenth centuries may be, we may, I think, be sure that they represent a spiritual revolt within the Church. The anomalous fact that, though the Church did not want instruments, in some churches they were heard all the same, illustrates a breach within the clerical organisation itself. In fact, the Church was seething with controversy, with an uneasy, sinister expectancy of approaching climax.

Although there were these belated compromises on the part of the Church the general trend of its policy towards instrumental music stands out – a policy which was the musical counterpart of the ecclesiastical obscurantism of the opponents of the Lollards and the jailers of Bishop Pecock. And this policy was fraught with danger.

Rejected and despised, the outlawed musicians turned against their persecutors and criticised the established order. During the fourteenth century, especially during its latter half, instrumental minstrels and other itinerant musicians sometimes became a real menace to the authority of Church and State.[1] Now the true nature of medieval instrumental music as part of the struggle of the lower classes for individual freedom and secular gaiety begins to be obvious. While the authorities 'showed indulgence to the armed retainers of the great, they feared the rounds made by those glee men with no other arms than their vielle or tabor, but sowing sometimes strange, disquieting doctrines under colour of songs. These were more than liberal, and went at times so far as to recommend social or political revolt.'[2] They sang of the heavy taxes imposed on the peasantry by monasteries and manors alike;

---

them to cheer them up on their journey; see Galpin, p. 176. A number of instruments once again appear as ornaments in churches (again almost exclusively lutes, crowds and psalteries). Burney mentions that in the annual account-roll of the Augustine priory of Bicester (Oxfordshire) for the year 1431, an entry is made of a fee expended for a harpist; see *History of Music*, II, 428. In the Maxstoke Priory account books there are two items of rewards given to minstrels ('cuidam citharistæ, 6d.') and a sum to 'Duobus citharistis de Coventry.' Further examples given in E. K. Chambers, *The Mediæval Stage*, 1903, pp. 243–245.

[1] See the treatise of Thomas de Cobham (Bishop of Salisbury) (1303) against the minstrelsy; cf. E. K. Chambers, *The Mediæval Stage*, I, pp. 60 f. and II, pp. 262–263.

[2] Jusserand, pp. 211–212.

they sang of the vice of the monks and the infamy of many distinguished rogues.

A minstrel (reign of Edward II) sings about the lot of husbandmen of his time:

> Ich herde men upo mold make much mon,
> Hon he beth – tened of here tilyynge,
> Gode yeres and corn bothe beth a-gon,
> Ne kepeth here no sawe ne song syng.
> Now we mote worche, nis there non other won,
> Mai ich no lengore lyve with my lesinge;
> Yet ther is a bitterore bid to the bon,
> For ever the furthe peni mot to the kynge.[1]

In 1402 the House of Commons accused by name the Welsh minstrels as fomentors of trouble and causers of rebellion:

> Item: That no westours and rimers, minstrels or vagabonds, be maintained in Wales, to make kymorthas or quyllages on the common people, who by their divinations, lies, and exhortations are partly cause of the insurrection and rebellion now in Wales. Reply: Le roy le veut.[2]

The songs of the Peasant Wars are known examples of such 'exhortations'.[3] Outstanding among them is 'The Cutty Wren' which, it is interesting to note, is composed in an ancient Church

---

[1] *The Political Songs of England*, ed. Th. Wright, Edinburgh (Bibliotheca curiosa), 1884 Vol. II p. 78 ff. Ibid. songs against the clergy, the King's taxes, etc. (Vol. III, pp. 30, 60, and others). – Here is a rough translation of the above song:

> I heard men on the land making much moan,
> Mournful they are, anxious over their tilling,
> Good years and corn are both gone,
> and here there is no talking, nor no song sung.
> Now we must (seek) work, there is nothing else for it,
> I can no longer live with my loss (my gleaning?)
> Yet there is still a bitterer burden to their complaint,
> For every fourth penny must (go) to the King.

[2] *Rolls of Parliament III*, 508 (quoted by Jusserand, p. 212). A German musician (piper), the shepherd Hans Boeheim of Niklashausen, usually called Pfeifferhans, actually started the movement of the Peasants' Revolts in Central and Southern Germany (1491). In this country the great ecclesiastical and historical writer Giraldus Cambrensis (Gerald de Barri; see below, p. 40) was once accused of inciting the Welshmen to rebellion (see *Encycl. Brit.* under Giraldus Cambrensis).

[3] Full text of John Ball's sermon in G. G. Coulton's *Social Life in Britain*, 1919, p. 359.

mode (Mixolydian).[1] Robin Hood, the friend of the poor and ordinary folk, was a favoured champion of minstrels' songs and ballads:[2]

> I can rymes of Roben Hood and Randal of Chester,
> But of our Lord and Lady I lerne nothyng at all.
>
> (*Piers Plowman*)

The 'Scholares vagantes' were considered to be particularly dangerous and anti-clerical. One of them (late thirteenth century, presumably English or Northern French) lets fly thus:

> ... Rome that is the head of the world, but this head is unclean, and unclean is whatever it touches. ... It is but a great market where they sell and buy prebends. ... If you come before the Pope, always remember: the poor has no position before him, his favour only goes to him who brings gold and silver with him.[3]

From the middle of the fourteenth century onwards, it was particularly the Jig which was connected or associated with oppositional and even seditious anti-Catholic plays. In the fifteenth century, the Jig (later Gigue) was a dance in fast and stirring rhythms, well suited for the purpose of inciting people to disaffection.

One might gain the impression from the number of references quoted that instrumental music was, after all, just as much in the foreground of official medieval life as poetry or singing in the churches. But this is not the case. Let us state then once again quite unequivocally that instrumental music as a whole was of small importance in *official* medieval life compared with vocal music, especially vocal religious music.

True, in later medieval England the instrumental music of the popular classes was never quite so repressed as for instance in Germany and Spain. But even in England instrumental music, hampered and pursued by continual ecclesiastical attacks, could advance only slowly and painfully.

---

[1] See also A. L. Lloyd on 'The Hunt of the Wren' (Manx) and other songs from the Peasant Wars (*The Singing Englishman*, London, 1944.) The 'Cutty Wren' has been published and recorded by the Workers' Music Association, London, 1939.

[2] See also J. Ritson, *Robin Hood Ballads*, London, 1865.

[3] From a poem 'Utar contra vitia carmine rebelli', contained in Brit. Mus. MS., Harley 978. See also O. Hubatsch, *Die lateinischen Vagantenlieder des Mittelalters*. Goerlitz, 1870, pp. 52 f., and J. A. Schmeller, *Carmina Burana*, 1883.

Yet the ordinary folk in old England succeeded in keeping instrumental music alive and active all the time. Popular instrumental music, which was kept down through all the centuries of the middle ages, thus appears as a matter of great importance as an *unofficial* and often underground musical activity.

A fourteenth-century village poet[1] confesses bashfully that sometimes when idleness overcomes him – and only then! – he takes to playing musical instruments. Thus speaks Idleness:

> I teche hem daunce,
> And also, ffor ther lady sake,
> Endyte lettyrs, and songys make
> Up-on the glade somerys dayes,
> Balladys, Roundelays, vyrelayes.
> I teche hem ek, (lyk ther ententys,)
> To pleye on sondry Instrumentys,
> On harpe, lut, and on gyterne,
> And to revelle at taverne,
> Wyth al merthe and mellodye,
> On rebube and on symphonye.

This passage shows that instrumental performance was popularly regarded as an accomplishment even while it was discouraged by the Church. Instrumental music grew up original and healthy in the atmosphere of natural naivety which only popular practice could provide. In Germany the minstrels of the central middle ages were expected to be able (apart from throwing little apples and catching them with knives, imitating animals' voices, etc.) to play not less than nine string and wind instruments.[2] Pictures from this country suggest a parallel development over here. The minstrel accompanied his singing by playing the vielle[3] and other instruments, or he played purely instrumental music.

Chaucer was fond of playing harp and dulcimer and of listening to purely instrumental music of which he talks as of something well-established:

> Many thousand tymes twelve
> That maden loude menstralcyes
> In cornemuse, and shalmyes

---

[1] Quoted by H. S. Bennett, *England from Chaucer to Caxton*, London, 1928, p. 91.

[2] J. Wolf, *Geschichte der Musik*, I, 1930, pp. 34 f.

[3] 'Emisit cantum viellando', as it says in a Latin story of the fourteenth century; see *Latin Stories*, ed. Th. Wright (Percy Society), 1842, p. 83.

And many other maner pype,
That craftely pype
Both in dulcet and in rede,
That ben at festes with the brede;
And many floute and lilting-horne,
And pypes made of grene corne.[1]

A considerable variety of instruments appeared and disappeared in the course of the middle ages. We find almost all the
names that are familiar to us now, together with names of
instruments like 'nabulum', 'tintinnabulum' (presumably a small
set of bells), 'pennola', 'bombylium'[2] the exact identity of which is
difficult to define. There are the predecessors of the violin and viol,
such as gigue, rebec, rubebe or rybyb, rota (or rotys of Alemayne,
probably imported from Germany), vielle and fiddle. The
metamorphosis of the crwth can be followed up in the long series
of lyras, clarsechs or telyns and other harp instruments, while there
are innumerable forms of lutes and cythers like the cytele or cythol,
with a variety of hurdy-gurdy instruments. The forerunners of the
pianoforte as well as of the harpsichord, such as dulcimer, dulsate,
psaltery or tympan, are found to have been played in England just
as much as on the continent; and there are many wind
instruments: bagpipes such as the cornamuse (also called
tympanum, symphony, or sambuca), reed instruments such as the
shepherd's pipe, oboe, wait, shalm, pommer and others,
instruments of the flute and recorder family, such as pipes or fyfes
(tibiæ), sordines, rackets; furthermore horns, cornets, trumpets,
trombones, and percussion instruments like bells, drums, tabors,
nakers, and triangles.[3] The rich variety of the instruments invented
in the middle ages shows clearly the vigour of the popular musical
interest that produced them. Several of these instruments were
introduced from Moslem and other non-European and pagan
sources (though certainly not by the Church authorities).

During the earlier centuries of the middle ages large wind
instruments with majestic and far-reaching sounds were every-

---

[1] From *House of Fame*, book III, 1199 ff. For more quotations from Chaucer, see Sister M.
E. Whitmore, *Mediæval English Domestic Life and Amusements in the Works of Chaucer*, The
Catholic University of America, Washington, 1937.

[2] Mentioned in Cotton MS., Tiberius C 6 (beginning of eleventh century). Explanation of
some of the names is given in 'De proprietatibus rerum', see Hawkins, pp. 268 ff.

[3] For details, see G. Hayes, *Musical Instruments and their Music*, London, 1930; Canon F. W.
Galpin, *Old English Instruments of Music*, London, 1910; also K. Schlesinger, *Modern Orchestral
Instruments and Early Records of the Precursors of the Violin Family*, London, 1910.

where more highly esteemed than stringed instruments. This was obviously because horns and trumpets were more in use at the courts, especially at hunts, and in the army. The change in the respective valuation of instruments seems to have occurred during the eleventh, twelfth and thirteenth centuries. Johannes de Grocheo found that stringed instruments 'occupy first place among all instruments'. It was the vielle which was most popular among stringed instruments, and a stringed instrument was considered to be able 'to move the souls of those listening much more than trumpets or drums could have affected them'.[1]

And what of the nature of the music itself?

There is little to be said of the instrumental practice of the earlier middle ages. No traces of any music have so far been found in our libraries, with the exception of a seventeenth-century MS.[2] containing notations of harp music which the writer of the MS. claims to be ancient Welsh (unfortunately he does not state how he obtained this music).

Only about 1250 does more reliable information appear, and it seems that from the fourteenth century onwards instrumental music developed along its own lines. We hear more and more often of instruments played not only in accompaniment of singing but also without singing.

Giraldus Cambrensis, famous writer (1146–1220), praises popular music in Ireland, Wales and Scotland in the most enthusiastic terms. He has a low opinion of the Irish of his time, but thinks that their instrumental music is superb and that 'their musical skill is better than that of any other people'.[3] Reading his essay one must assume that instrumental music was very much alive. In England it is said to have been of a less vivid character at this time,[4] although towards the end of the thirteenth century we learn from another source that popular instrumental playing in England was developing as elaborately as anywhere: Anonymus 4 (Coussemaker, *Scriptores*) talks about the division of longer notes

---

[1] *Sammelbände der Internationalen Musikgesellschaft*, 1899–1900, pp. 96 ff.

[2] British Museum, MS. Add. 14905.

[3] *Giraldi Opera*, vol. V, p. 135 (Descriptio Hiberniæ): 'In musicis solum instrumentis commendabilem invenio gentis istius diligentiam. In quibus, præ omni natione quam vidimus, incomparabiliter instructa est.' Giraldus also says that the Scots knew citharas, bagpipes and crowds, the Welsh citharas, tibias and crowds, and the Irish citharas and the tympanum.

[4] Ibid. '. . . in Britannicis quibus assueti sumus instrumentis, tarda et morosa est modulatio . . .'

into many small ones in instrumental music as opposed to vocal music, obviously meaning fast passages, scales and figuration.[1] The same writer even speaks of the chromatic possibilities of instruments ('falsa musica'), as does John de Garlandia, another English writer on music, at the beginning of the thirteenth century.[2] A later theoretician discusses consonances (he only admits thirds, fifths, sixths and octaves) and continues: 'Such treatment is obvious whether voices are used or instruments, either stringed instruments or the organ.'[3]

The general observations of such theorists are particularly valuable in view of the almost complete absence of written examples of the music of the times; on the whole the transmission of folk music through the tradition of mere practice is part of its essence. Least of all was any kind of instrumental music of the earlier and central middle ages preserved by writing, in view of the small value attached to it and the low social status of its bearers. But towards the end of the thirteenth century Anonymus 4[4] describes among other things that 'simple dots' were used in notation of music for every sort of instrument. This means that at that time there was not only a firm tradition of instrumental playing but possibly also a system of notation. Then, towards 1300, there is evidence that instrumental music *was* written out, a fact that indicates that it was holding its ground, and that even theorists were beginning to take an interest in this popular art which proved so obstinately immune to the antagonism of the Church.

There is a tune from the same period still preserved in the Bodleian Library at Oxford[5] which gives at least some notion of

[1] Coussemaker, *Scriptores*, I, p. 328: 'Iterato sunt et alii modi prout modi supradicti frangunt brevem vel breves in duas, tres vel quatuor, etc., prout in instrumentis. . . . Sonus sub uno tempore dici sonus acceptus sub tempore non minimo non maximo sed medio legitimo breviter sumpto, quod possit frangi veloci motu in duobus, tribus vel quatuor plus in voce humana, quamvis in instrumentis possit aliter fieri.' Ibid.: 'Et ulterius per consuetudinem raro frangimus, videlicet non monimus quator pro brevi in voce humana, sed in instrumentis sepius bene fit.'

[2] Coussemaker, *Scriptores*, I, p. 166: 'Videndum est de falsa musica (i.e. chromatic alterations) quæ instrumentis musicalibus multum est necessaria, specialiter in organis.'

[3] Fauxbourdon Anonymous 9 (from Brit. Mus. MS. Add. 21455), quoted by M. Bukofzer, *Geschichte des englischen Diskants und des Fauxbourdons nach englischen Quellen*, Strassburg, 1936, p. 138. The treatise was presumably written about 1400.

[4] Coussemaker, *Scriptores*, I, p. 339 (the treatise is shortly after 1272): 'Simplicia puncta quedam accipiuntur, prout . . . utuntur in quolibet genere omnium instrumentorum.' See also J. Wolf, *Notationskunde*, II, pp. 5 f.

[5] MS. Douce 139 (about 1270); facsimile in Stainer's *Early Bodleian Music*, London, 1902. See also L. Schrade, *Die handschriftliche Überlieferung der ältesten Instrumentalmusik*, Lahr (Baden), 1931.

what popular instrumental tunes must have been like towards the later middle ages. It is a dance-like piece in unison which spreads into three parts shortly before the end (the upper part might be for drum or tabor); here are a few extracts:

Example 4: thirteenth-century dance tune.

How unlike the music of the Church!

Most conspicuous is the rhythmical simplicity of the piece. Its structure has nothing in common with the intricacies of contemporary vocal (i.e. ecclesiastical) compositions. At the same time this music requires quite a high degree of dexterity on the part of the performer, and the musical language is outspokenly instrumental in several respects if we consider the unvocal leaps of fifths up and down, the tone repetitions, and the rows of sequences throughout the piece. Such instrumentalisms are completely missing in all medieval music apart from instrumental composition.

The rhythmic qualities of the tune raise important problems of the relationship between medieval music and poetry. In the earlier centuries of the middle ages the boundaries between music and poetry must have been vague, as vague as those between vocal and instrumental music. The instrumental accompaniment of the singing of the Anglo-Saxon scop was presumably based on the same non-metrical, rhetoric-rhythmic style as the verses themselves, and the continental production shows that secular vocal music until 1000 was on the whole most closely related in style to religious music.

An important change occurred in certain eleventh- and twelfth-century forms of Latin poetry, chiefly the 'sequentia' of these centuries which consisted of Latin rhymed verses with words set to the freely improvised melodies of the 'Allelujah' in the Mass. These words were rhythmically and metrically regular, imitating the poetic style and form of the older Christian hymni. The music was accordingly rhythmically regular and based on equally long repeat periods:

Example 5: Sequence 'Prosa de Sancto Dionysio', by Adam of St Victor.[1]

The influence of Latin hymns, tropes, and sequences on the development of rhythm and metre in France as well as in England was most marked. The songs of the troubadours and trouvères used the metres of the ancient Greeks: trochæics, iambics, dactyls, etc., thus bringing rhythmically measured music with 'bars' in the modern sense a stage nearer.

These changes are not peculiar to English or even to French history, but since England was part of the Christian world of that time they have to be mentioned here. The change from the non-metrical to the 'measured' rhythmic structures of the 'modi' clearly corresponds with the change from Anglo-Saxon alliterative and declamatory poetry to Middle-English accent, rhyme and metre, with Latin quantitative and accented measures representing a transitional period; and again popular music, as closely linked up

[1] From Joh. Wolf, *Geschichte der Musik*, I, p. 22.

with popular poetry, was bound to be most strongly affected by this change.

With metre and rhyme comes a greater degree of clarity within the secular melodies themselves. We observe the appearance of parallel lines and periods in many songs and tunes. The 'melodic energy' is more and more concentrated into the *end* of each melodic period. The melodic development of each melodic line is to be rounded off satisfactorily, in conformance with the rhymes in poetry.

The final stage in this vital process of shaping rhythm and metre is the so-called 'mensural' music (from the thirteenth century) which provides definite time values for each single note (maxima = 2 longæ; longa = 2 breves; brevis = 2 semibreves; semi-brevis = 2 minimæ; etc.) as well as definite bar measures (triple rhythm, common time, etc.). Mensural notation is, of course, quite indispensable as part-singing and part-playing (especially polyphonic part-singing) develop and the parts have to be rhythmically co-ordinated.

Popular instrumental music, wherever it was least affected by the more artistic treatment of musically more educated individuals, seems to have been far ahead of both Church and secular vocal music in the evolution of rhythmic clarity and metrical decision. It is as though the theorists who laid down the new systems of practice, performance and notation, were in fact guided by the rules and customs of the wandering minstrel. There are clear parallel periods and distinct phrases. Similar vocal forms such as the Northern French 'lai' and 'rondeau', seem here reduced to the utmost metrical simplicity.

A further change is that our little dance tune is in common time (two-in-a-measure) which in the thirteenth century is still little used in Church music. The Church prescribed 'triple rhythm' (three-in-a-measure) as a symbol of the Holy Trinity.[1] Two-in-a-measure at that time is almost invariably non-Church and often enough anti-Church.

Yet at least as important as the rhythmic and other instrumental peculiarities of this tune is its harmonic and tonal structure. The whole popular approach to music, as opposed to the ecclesiastical use of the art, is here illustrated in one simple example. For the frequently observed phenomenon that early English popular

[1] See below, p. 73. This theory has recently been contested. (Dart, Waite).

music uses full-grown major and minor 'modes'[1] is clearly confirmed in this little tune, and the question of these melodic modes is of the utmost importance.

The Church did not employ major and minor, although towards the end of the middle ages they were theoretically admitted in the modal system as 'Ionian' and 'Æolian'.[2] The Dorian, Lydian, and other modes of the Gregorian choral suited the purpose of the Christian liturgy best, for the following reasons. First, these basic modes of the medieval chant, are based not on a complete scale ranging from prime to octave but rather on hexachords.[3] They have no 'leading note' which like b to c, leads back to the 'finalis', the tonic note of a piece, by a half-tone, the shortest possible interval of the scale. That means that the close functional relationship between dominant and tonic (in the sense of modern harmony) is foreign to the Church modes; which again signifies that the most important means of building up emotional developments is denied to the Church modes.[4] Secondly, the Church modes are not organised (and cannot be organised) upon the harmonic base of consonant triads, consisting of prime, third, and fifth, upon which all recent music (except some of the most recent) is built. The Church modes are usually based on two melodic 'axis' tones: the 'finalis' on which the song starts and ends, and the 'repercussio', the tone round which the melodic line mainly circles during the song. The 'repercussio' is in the main modes either a fifth (Dorian, Lydian and Mixolydian) or a sixth (Phrygian) above the 'finalis':

---

[1] The term 'mode' (modus) has a variety of meanings in medieval music. In this case 'mode' means 'type of scale' and should not be confused with the use of the word as characterising 'rhythmic patterns' as it did in the previous paragraphs.

[2] Notker Balbulus names the tones of the scale 'A' to 'G' which suggests minor; but it is interesting to note that in doing so he refers to *instruments* (psalterium and lyra). See Gerbert, *Scriptores*, I, p. 96.

[3] Scales that consist of only six tones, e.g. the Dorian hexachord consists of d, e, f, g, a and b.

[4] As late as the fifteenth century the seventh (i.e. the leading note) is considered an evil by some theorists; e.g. the author of *De Origine et Effectu Musicæ* (cf. Burney, II, p. 416). Many players and singers, however, sharpened the sevenths in the old modes as they played and sang, even though church composers continued to write strictly 'modally'. See E. Blom, *Music in England*, 1942, p. 14.

The Lydian mode on F (modus quintus) which also contained the E as a possible leading note to F, was by far the least frequent among the *permitted* modes of medieval Church music.

Example 6: Antiphon 'Statuit'.[1]

The melody is in the Dorian mode. 'D' is finalis, 'a' is repercussio. It must be emphasised that although the repercussio is mostly the fifth tone of the hexachord scale, its relationship to the finalis is *not* harmonic in the sense of our modern dominant. The ancient repercussio is a kind of second 'home' note for the melody. It 'dominates' the *melody* of the Gregorian chant, but it is not the *harmonically* functional dominant.

How absolutely foreign the harmonic triad was to all early Catholic Church music will become clear if one considers the fact that the 'third' – major as well as minor – was considered and treated as a dissonance or, at best, an 'imperfect consonance' up to the thirteenth century.[2]

It is these two qualities of the Church modes, the *absence of the 'leading note'* (which denied the dramatic dominant-tonic progression to the music of the Church) and the *non-chordal structure* (which did not allow for the forming of those colourful major and minor triads), which make all medieval Church music appear so neutral, ethereal and mystical. Only the major and minor modes could express secular joy or distress, and for such elements there was no room in Church music. At the same time, the major and minor modes contain the 'leading note' which held out the possibility of providing the dramatic tension of the dominant and the satisfactory solution of the tonic. Therefore the major and the minor, the step-children of the system of Church modes, became the modes of the secular, the popular forces of society.

---

[1] From Cod. 339, St Gallen, p. 27; published in Adler, *Handbuch der Musikgeschichte*, II, ed. 1930, vol. II, p. 112.

[2] Two English theorists of the second half of the thirteenth century, Walter Odington and Anonymus 4 (Coussemaker), advocated for the first time the recognition of the thirds as consonances. See Coussemaker, *Scriptores*, I, pp. 200 and 358. The great influence of the popular modes (major and minor) and harmonies on 'official' music in England during the fourteenth and fifteenth centuries is shown in Guilelmi Monachi *De preceptis artis musice* (fifteenth century; see Coussemaker, *Scriptores*, III, pp. 289 f.). See also below, p. 52.

The secular musicians . . . had a special predilection for the tonality on C. . . . For this very reason it was looked at askance by the ecclesiastical teachers and designated as 'tonus lascivus.' The itinerant musicians were more progressive than the theorists.[1]

One of the new features which developed together with and within the major scale is the *melodic cadence*. The feeling of finality at the end of a melody in the major scale is strengthened by certain melodic formulæ which appear with increasing frequency in the secular music of the late Middle Ages. They laid the foundations of the later *harmonic cadences* which were to play such an important part in all post-Reformation music.

Is the major key found more frequently in medieval English than in continental music? The answer is in the affirmative. Indeed we may justly speak of it (together with the harmonic-melodic technique of the 'fauxbourdon' which will be discussed later on) as one of the first signs of a national character in the music of this country, as Gerald Hayes suggests in his analysis of the problem.[2] There was, moreover, a growth of nationalism among the people of England during the fourteenth and fifteenth centuries, due chiefly to the gradual permeation of feudal life with new social elements, more individualistic and less cosmopolitan in character, largely derived from new developments in trade and manufacture at home, particularly in relation to wool and cloth. In fact this new nationalism was expressed in the field of music towards the end of the fifteenth century by such men as John Major (born 1469 in N. Berwick), when writing of Cambridge where he was in 1493:

The bells of St Osenay are the best in England, and *as in music the English excel all other nations*, so they excel in the sweet and artistic modulation of their bells.[3]

[1] Carl Nef, *An Outline of the History of Music*, New York, 1935. Tonus lascivus: 'the wanton mode'.

Already Glareanus remarked in his *Dodekachordon* (1547) on the *popular* nature of the major key; it was, according to him, the key of folk-songs and folk-dances. It would be interesting to find out whether the development of major and minor was directly assisted by the playing of certain wind instruments. The ancient horns, trumpets, etc. produced the *natural scale* (harmonic series) in which the first five harmonics constitute the major triad. In a MS., dated 1567, the lutenist, Jacomo Gorzanis of Trieste, wrote out a set of 24 passamezzo-saltarello suites on all the major and minor keys in ascending chromatic progression.

[2] *King's Music*, London, 1937, p. 39. Hayes mentions Welsh influences in connection with the spreading of the 'modus lascivus'.

[3] *A Miscellany Presented to J. M. Mackay*, 1914, p. 249.

National characteristics in the cultural life of a country are and always have been chiefly determined by the characteristics of its *popular* art, and it has invariably been the transition from feudal to modern society that brought these characteristics to the surface. The secular gaiety chiefly of the major key remained one of the typical features of English music for centuries.

John Cotton (about 1100) was the first to consider beautiful a melody based on major and minor triads.[1]

Among the numerous instances of major and minor in early English music we refer once again to the Summer Canon (Example 2). After 1400 major and minor tonality as well as melodies based on triads, are found more and more often in the works of Church composers, for instance, in those of John Dunstable.[2]

To the major scale we have to add the pentatonic scale which has been the other mainspring of English and Scottish folksong;

the scale on which 'Auld Lang Syne' and so many other songs are based. It is difficult to say, at the present stage of research, what part the pentatonic scale played in medieval instrumental music, but it is a fact that the pentatonic scale is a very ancient feature of English and Scottish music in general. This is not the place to discuss the possibility of prehistoric connections between this scale and the Chinese and other Far-Eastern scale systems which are also pentatonic.

Recent analysis has also stressed that there exists a certain pentatonicism in the Gregorian melodies and that it is connected with the pentatonic elements in ancient Greek music. It seems to be a fact, however, that the pentatonicism of medieval English folk music has other roots and developed quite independently of the Church.[3]

Out of the popular practice of instrumental playing there also grew the tendency to group several instruments together, as is shown in the three-part episode towards the end of our thirteenth-century dance tune.

[1] See Gerbert, *Scriptores*, II, p. 254.

[2] In Stainer's list of Dunstable's works, thirty-three among forty-six pieces are in the major, the others mostly in the minor. See *Sammelbände der Internationalen Musikgesellschaft*, II, pp. 1–16.

[3] It is mentioned by John Cotton; see M. Gerbert, *Scriptores*, II, p. 234, also Lederer, *Über Heimat und Ursprung der mehrstimmigen Tonkunst*, Leipzig, 1906, I, pp. 287 and 348, and J. Yasser, *Mediæval Quartal Harmony*, New York, 1938.

We know from Giraldus Cambrensis that part-*singing* was known in popular vocal music as early as the twelfth century. He states that 'in Wales they made descants to their tunes, in the same way that singers did to the plainsong of the Church', also that 'singing in two parts was common in the North of England, and children tried to imitate it'. The latter statement, which suggests singing in simple parallels, has been confirmed by the discovery of a Northern hymn to St Magnus:[1]

Example 7: Hymn to St Magnus.

No - bi - lis   hu - mi - lis   ma - gne mar - tir   sta - bi - lis

Furthermore Giraldus says in his frequently quoted *Descriptio Cambriæ* that the Welsh not only sang in two but often in many parts.

Instrumental group music – chamber music – is first foreshadowed in such purely popular activities as the already mentioned 'bordune' practice,[2] i.e. the holding out of one sustained note while all kinds of melodic figuration took place in other instrumental or vocal parts. Originally these activities represented quite a casual co-operation of several instrumental players. As far as can be seen these tendencies were at first confined to the peasantry and the independent popular minstrelsy.

Again, the Abbot of Rivaulx's sermon[3] seems to have been directed against a still further advanced stage of combination of several instrumental parts when he denounced the 'harmony of the pipes and cornets'. Further, several pictures of very early times show in a primitive way ensembles of such instrumentalists; for instance, there is a picture of a procession of musicians (eleventh century) where we can see rote, rebecs, and psalteries together, and a particularly beautiful scene from the twelfth century where not less than nine musicians are active: chime-bells, harp, rebec, viol, recorder, pan-pipes, organistrum, psaltery and hand-bells. In a picture of an acrobatic performance from the fourteenth century

[1] From Wolf, *Geschichte der Musik,* I, p. 62.

[2] See above, p. 24, footnote about Anonymus 4. Giraldus Cambrensis gives this description of such instrumental 'ostinati' (pedals): '. . . sub obtuso grossioris chordæ sonitu, gracilium tinnitus licentius ludent, latentius delectant, lasciviusque demulcent' (*Descriptio Cambriæ,* VI, 189).

[3] See above, p. 29.

there are two musicians, obviously 'ioculatores' (jugglers), playing pipe and tabor, while a third person performs a dangerous acrobatic trick.[1]

Now we need not necessarily conclude from these instances that instruments appearing together in a picture were actually played together, although the possibility that that might have been so has to be admitted.[2] But certain it is that wandering minstrels meeting casually or travelling together *did* increase the fun (and the art value, for that matter) of their activity by playing on different instruments in consort (at first presumably they played in unison). There is some contemporary evidence to that effect.

In a parable translated by Wycliffe there is this sentence: '. . . when he cam neere, he herde a symphonie and a crowde.'[3] Ensemble music extended to brass instruments. In the *Confessio Amantis* Gower speaks of the 'sounds of bumbarde and of clarionne with cornemuse and shalmele' (1393). In the *Sqyr of Low Degree* (about 1400) we are told that:

> Ther was myrth and melody,
> With harpe, getron, and sawtry,
> With rote, ribible and clokarde,
> With pypes, organ and bumbarde,
> With other mynstrelles them amonge,
> With sytolphe and with sawtry songe,
> With fydle, recorde, and dowcemere,
> With trumpette and with claryon clere,
> With dulcet pipes of many cordes.[4]

It seems that groups mostly (and more or less naturally) formed within similar categories of instruments: trumpets do not often occur in the company of dulcimers; string instruments are usually mentioned together – soft with soft and loud with loud.

But for the evidence of the continuous growth of instrumental group music in the middle ages we are not dependent only upon pictorial and literary references.

---

[1] F. W. Galpin, plates 21, 20 and 28. Similar scenes are on reliefs of the eleventh century; see Duncan and Crowest, *The Story of the Minstrelsy*, 1907, pp. 22–23.

[2] Ibid., p. 274. Canon Galpin himself has doubts whether the instruments shown together in some pictures have really been used together. Quotations from literary sources to this end are, of course, more convincing.

[3] F. W. Galpin, p. 106.

[4] Ibid., p. 64.

There are three more dance tunes still in existence, from which we can get an impression of the character of thirteenth-century instrumental group music, in particular of the polyphonic technique of the early forerunners of chamber music. These dances,[1] which are all in triple rhythm, are to be considered as music of the rising middle classes; such and similar types are described by Johannes de Grocheo[2] as Stantipes, Ductia and other dance forms.[3] They are all in two-part harmony; there is always a consonance (either a perfect consonance such as a fifth, octave or unison, or a so-called 'imperfect' consonance, which means a third or sixth) on the *main* beat of the bar, while all sorts of dissonances, consecutive fifths, consecutive octaves, etc., may occur during the latter part of the bar. The movement of the two parts is very largely opposite. Everywhere there are dance-like periods of 8 or 16 bars. One part has the real dance tune; in the following example the tune is to be found in the bass, while the counterpoint in the superior part was obviously composed *after* the bass melody:

Example 8: thirteenth-century dance tune (for two instruments).

continued overleaf

---

[1] Brit. Mus. MS. Harley 978; MS. after 1225. Full transcription of the dances by J. Wolf, *Die Tænze des Mittelalters,* Archiv. f. Musikwissenschaft I, 1918–19, pp. 10 ff.

[2] See J. Wolf, *Die Musiklehre des Johannes de Grocheo, Sammelbände der Internat. Musikgesellschaft,* I, 1899, pp. 93 ff. See also above, p. 22.

[3] These forms were used in Italy about 1300; see above, p. 22.

There follows a repetition of the whole of the three sections in the bass while a different counterpoint appears in the top part. There are simple periods; there is always a 'question' (*a*) and an 'answer' (*b*), without much artificial complication or embarrassment. The speed is moderate. Again here is the radiant major key, as familiar in early English folk music as it is rare in Church music of the same time.

Church or no Church, in all its simplicity popular instrumental music appears as an art which had its own logic and its own laws of æsthetics. Yet the example just shown is only the first indication of the style which instrumental music was finding for itself. About the middle of the fourteenth century it became evident that the struggle of instrumental music for legitimate acknowledgement had entered a new phase.

Indeed, much was being altered in the public estimation of instrumental music as well as in the organisation and development of the minstrelsy itself. Approximately up to the first part of the fourteenth century instrumental music was 'unofficial' in every respect: always kept down though sometimes tolerated and never successfully suppressed. After this time it became more and more respectable.

The close fabric of medieval society was gradually loosened.

Not that the secular power of the Church had gone; its loss of moral prestige did not prevent it from retaining, for the time being, its privileges, its wealth and its mighty organisation.

But freedom of the individual, freedom of the mind – these basic demands of later English life and culture began to be announced in earnest. With the increasing influence of secular circles, as opposed to the overwhelming power of the Church, instrumental music gained, first of all, more recognition among the middle classes. In this development the influence of the peasant movement was of great importance: the cultural life of the peasantry, so vital for the development of instrumental music in the middle ages, was made known to the inhabitants of the towns. True, throughout the middle ages there had been a continuous trickle of villeins escaping to the towns. Invariably they had taken with them on their flight the tunes of the wandering minstrels, the dances and rounds of the village green.

But the art of the peasantry and the art of the townsfolk mingled to a far larger extent when both classes achieved a greater degree of emancipation from feudal rule. The cultural life of the towns in particular became more intensive and independent as they became powerful factors in the country's social life, especially in the fifteenth century when the textile industry was spreading into the rural districts and the great manufacturing colonies of Yorkshire, Gloucestershire, Wiltshire, and East Anglia.

The 'franklins' or free yeomen were of particular importance for the development of music. Much of the balladry came from them, and certainly many of the early folksongs. They remained a vital cultural force for centuries and laid the foundation of much of the musical greatness of the sixteenth century.

These independent peasants were closely akin to craftsmen in the towns. The towns, on the other hand, had developed their own forms of instrumental playing. In some of them (e.g. London, Coventry, Bristol, Norwich, Chester, York, Beverley, Lynn, and Leicester) the consolidation of a musical profession is expressed in the formation of guilds of 'waytes' or 'waits'. These watchmen of the fourteenth, fifteenth, and sixteenth centuries were employed by the town councils. They had oboe-like reed instruments which were also called waits.[1] About 1500 they also used sagbuts, horns and even strings. It was their duty as municipal bands to perform musical functions on great occasions, such as public plays, pageants, and other festivities (among them the mystery plays mentioned earlier), but they also had to do actual watchmen's service.

> This day it is agreed . . . that the waytes of this Citie . . . shall bewixte the hours of 6 and 8 of the clok at night, blow and playe upon their instruments the space of half an houre, to the rejoicing and comfort of the hearers thereof.

This order of Norwich city council[2] indicates an important part of the regular duties of the waits.[3] In view of the nature of this kind of performance as well as of the number and variety of instruments ('blow and playe') it must be assumed that not only unison music was produced but also some kind of harmonies, preparing the ground for chamber music in yet another aspect.

Yet not only the rising merchant class but also feudal noblemen of various kinds began to take to the enjoyment instrumental music could provide. It found its way into the houses of more and more counts, dukes and princes, as a kind of secondary pleasure. In fact, in the thirteenth century minstrels had become quite welcome guests at many castles of the aristocracy, for they could entertain the knights as well as glorify in song their deeds and those of their ancestors.[4] Feudal lords, in particular of the fourteenth century, borrowed the popular music of the peasantry and towns, and only too often misused it. At that time instrumental music served, in such houses, as the seasoning of meals. During these dinners of the rich the music was frequently interrupted by the loud conversation and roaring laughter of the diners, but also by the 'crunching of the bones gnawed by the dogs under the tables, by the quarrels of the same, or by the sharp cry of some ill-bred falcon; for many noblemen kept during dinner these favourite

---

[1] Medieval instrumentalists were often named after their instruments: pipe, drum, etc. In the case of the waits the instruments were named after the function of the players.

[2] See J. C. Bridge, *Town Waits and their Tunes,* Musical Association Proceedings, 1927–8.

[3] Rewards for the work of the waits increased during the fifteenth century. The town council of Lynn decreed in 1431 'that the three players shall serve the community this year for 21 sh. and their clothing to be had of every house'. A few years later they received 20s. each, and clothing; in return they had to 'go through the town with their instruments from the festival of All Saints to the Feast of the Purification'. See Mrs A. Green, *Town Life in the Fifteenth Century,* 1894, p. 65.

[4] For details, cf. Jusserand, p. 199.

birds on a perch behind them'.[1] Some distinguished people took a more active part. A highly-placed traveller of the second half of the fourteenth century was reported to have had great pleasure in listening to musicians at an inn. 'Then come forward into the lord's presence the trumpeters and horn-blowers with their frestles (pipes) and clarions, and begin to play and blow very loud, and then the lord with his squires begin to move, to sway, to dance, to utter and sing fine carols till midnight, without ceasing.'[2]

On the whole the medieval courts showed more tolerance towards the minstrelsy, vocal and instrumental, than the Church did. There are certainly numerous instances of early medieval courts having followed the Church in its denunciation of minstrels. To mention only one of them, Louis the Pious (d. 840) decreed that minstrels (histriones) should not be admitted to the palace, and in his edict minstrels are called 'vile and infamous people' and ranked with thieves and prostitutes.[3] Yet from the time of the ancient scop to the wandering minstrel of the thirteenth century, stories tell of many musicians visiting courts and castles, and of kings offering the minstrels generous rewards.

'Sir Orfeo' in the famous thirteenth-century romance is the symbol of the wandering minstrel. He is admitted to the 'fair high castle of gold and silver and precious stones' and brought before the King and Queen. 'How do you come here?' said the King; 'I never sent for you, and never before have I known a man so hardy as to come unbidden.' 'It is our manner,' Sir Orfeo said, 'to come to every man's house unbidden,

> And though we nought welcome be
> Yet we must proffer our game or glee.'

Then he played on his harp, and the King offered him whatever he should ask:

> 'Minstrel, me liketh thy glee.'

Orfeo asked for the lady bright. 'Nay,' said the King, 'that were a foul match, for in her there is no blemish but thou art rough and black.' 'Fouler still,' said Orfeo, 'to hear a leasing from a king's mouth'; but the King let him go with good wishes.[4]

[1] Ibid., p. 203.
[2] *La Manière de Langage*, composed by an Englishman in French in the fourteenth century; ed. P. Meyer, *Revue Critique*, Vol. X (1870), p. 273. See also Jusserand, p. 202.
[3] Boretius, *Capitularia*, I, p. 334.
[4] Retold by W. P. Ker, *Medieval English Literature*, p. 125.

The story of instrumental music in the service of medieval kings has been described so exhaustively by Gerald Hayes that we may confine ourselves to a few summarising remarks.

In the earlier middle ages Court music was supplied chiefly by trumpets and trombones apparently in mere fanfares which cannot really be called composed music.

But from the times of Henry III and Edward I (both thirteenth century) more and more is heard of musicians of all instruments gathering at the court. True, trumpeters, shalmists, and pipers alone appear to have at first belonged to the permanent staff of the royal music. But slowly viellists, harpists and others are engaged for certain occasions. In 1252 there is for the first time a mention of 'the harpist of the King'.[1]

And after instrumental music had staged its spectacular return to public life in the thirteenth century, it never vanished again from the royal households, but found indeed one of its main strongholds at the Court. Some kings even took an active interest in the art as composers or players, notably Richard II and Henry VI.

In the absence of any musical examples little can be said about the instrumental music itself which they loved and played. Certainly Court representation, display of pomp and might, always played a vital part:

> The princes, that war riche on raw
> Gert nakers strike and trumpets blaw
> And made mirth at thaire might.[2]

However, the vigorous dances of the peasantry, too, the homely tunes of the town waits, and the dainty rounds and virelais of French troubadours – they all were practised at the English courts by English, French and Spanish artists. The chronicles report occasional musical events on a considerable scale, such as the Westminster Feast of 1306 where 25 harpers, 22 trumpeters, 9 violists, 8 crowders, 6 taborers, 3 gigours, 2 organists, 2 psaltry players, 2 bagpipes, and one lutenist, gitarist, citoler, nakers and chimes player were employed.[3]

Another famous instance is Richard of Maidstone's description

---

[1] Hayes, *King's Music*, p. 30.

[2] From a Song on King Edward's Wars, by Laurence Minot; about 1352. See *Political Poems and Songs*, ed. Th. Wright, London, 1859, I, p. 69.

[3] Hayes, p. 31.

of a great musical show given in 1393 on the reconciliation of
Richard II with the City of London. On this occasion these
instruments are said to have co-operated:

> Fistula, cistula, tibia, timpana, cum monacordo,
> Organa, psalteria, cimbala, cumque lyra,
> Zambuca, citharæ, situlæque, tubæque, viellæ,
> Buccina cum nablis, simphonicisque choris.[1]

In 1377, at an entertainment for young Prince Richard,

> in the night, one hundred and thirty citizens, disguised and well
> horsed, in a mummery, with sound of Trumpets, Sackbuts,
> Cornets, Shalmes and other minstrels . . . rode from Newgate
> . . . to . . . Kennington.[2]

And in 1502, to mention only one more event among many, a
ladies' orchestra, consisting of 12 musicians (playing on 'Clary-
cordis, dusymers, clarysymballs and such other') entertained a
distinguished audience at a pageant in Westminster Hall.[3]

The English Kings between 1250 and 1500 patronised
instrumental music:

> . . . and he called for his pipe,
> And he called for his bowl,
> And he called for his fiddlers three.

But did an original, independent art of its own derive from the
English courts before Henry VII, comparable to the art of the
Church on the one side and that of the peasantry on the other, or to
the achievements of later absolutism? Hayes believes that 'if
outwardly the Court led and the people followed, subconsciously
the Court was influenced by the cultural tendencies of the people'.

Throughout the centuries of the middle ages it certainly does not

---

[1] Davey, *History of English Music*, p. 42. The exact meaning of some of these names is
doubtful. Fistula is the recorder; cistula the citola (pear-shaped guitar with flat back); tibia is
a pipe; timpanum (timpan) is not yet the kettle-drum but either a bagpipe or (more often) an
Irish psaltery, just as psalterium and cimbalum, lyra (lyre) is a form of rebeb (rubebe, bowed
instrument); zambuca (sambuca) is either a psaltry or a bagpipe (symphony) or even a
trombone (saquebout = sagbut); cithara may be any harp, lyre, cither; situla probably again
the citola; tuba a non-specified trumpet, probably straight; viella is the vielle (bowed
minstrel's viol); buccina is the old Latin trumpet which was usually curved, (but in the
middle ages the buccina is straight and has a short tube); nablum may be either a string or a
percussion instrument (nakers?); symphonicus chorus is presumably a hurdy-gurdy.

[2] Burney, II, 368.

[3] Galpin, p. 64.

appear that the Court ever led in the field of *instrumental music*, or did more than make use of the art of the secular forces. And it never completely renounced its musical dependence on France – not even (or perhaps least of all) during the 100 years' war.

It was indeed fortunate for English music that the all-too-precious beauty of the Machaut or Landino type did not spread from the Court to popular music to such a degree as to drown it completely. Popular music never lost its originality and independence. It was always healthy, strong, and sensuous in the tonal-harmonic simplicity of its triads, in contrast to so many of the abstract, orderly constructions of the contemporary de Vitry and Bartolomeus de Padua. *It was the music of the popular forces in England which contained the elements that were to be decisive for the musical development of the whole nation.*

To recall the 'Summer Canon', we recognised French influences as well as traces of 'polite' art and of a highly technically and musically skilled mind in this amazing and prophetic little piece.[1] Here, too, we want to state again that it is the *popular* qualities of the tune which make it appear so vigorous and, after all these centuries, so delightful to sing and listen to. It is the gay beauty based on triads, thirds, and sixths which is the most conspicuous feature of this canon – this extraordinary synthesis of the simple and the complex, of the 'popular' and the 'precious'.

However, materially the instrumental minstrelsy gained much by the increasing favour of the kings. The formation of chapels especially (particularly during the fourteenth and fifteenth centuries) assisted the consolidation of the instrumentalist's profession. In the towns the minstrels had long ago formed their brotherhoods, but in 1469 permission was granted also to the minstrels at the Court to 'maintain, continue and augment a fraternity or guild'.[2]

But with the increasing patronage of the courts, coinciding with the increasing demands that were being made on the minstrelsy in the towns, a very profound change came over the social structure of the minstrelsy itself.

By 1400 those minstrels who had been able to find permanent positions in either Court or municipal service, had become well-behaved and respectable citizens with regular (and sometimes very substantial) incomes, with servants, and valuable privileges, and

[1] See above, p. 26.
[2] Jusserand, p. 436.

with the outlook of well-established guildsmen – the 'higher minstrelsy' who often accompanied the newly-elected Lord Mayor at his show through the town, and the navigator on his journey on the seas. At the same time the great mass of independent wayfaring minstrels began to degenerate. The fifteenth century saw on the one hand the evolution of the musical profession, on the other hand the rapid decline of the minstrelsy in the old sense.

It is certain that the development of the 'liveries' considerably assisted this process. The great houses especially of the fifteenth century kept huge bands of liveried retainers (private armies) – the feature of the century and of the Wars of the Roses. With these retainers a great number of minstrels were gathered and maintained by the great houses – another step towards the settlement of part of the minstrelsy and the degradation of another part.

The guilds of the town waits and of the established royal musicians watched jealously over the activities of the 'lower' or independent, non-established, and unlicensed minstrels, whom they kept away from their own places of work by rigorous means. In the efficiency of their measures against the independent minstrelsy these guilds sometimes surpassed the Church.

The wayfaring minstrels of the original medieval type kept themselves alive during the fifteenth and sixteenth centuries. But they were driven lower and lower, as they were wandering up and down the island as 'common fyddelers', 'trompoteres' or 'systolyrs', amidst a world of firmly organised guilds and professions. Their existence became increasingly difficult, and also narrowed in scope and function, with the rise of the 'higher' minstrelsy to settlement, recognition and wealth, brought about chiefly by the growing strength of the development of the burgherdom. A new class distinction made itself felt in the practice of the minstrelsy and of instrumental music itself. It expressed the rapid advance and consolidation of the towns as against the very unsettled conditions on the land; it reflected the gradual dissolution of the villeins' medieval pattern of living. The independent minstrel was lowered to the stage of a vagabond and beggar.

This process had already begun at the time of Edward II who, in 1315, decreed:

. . . to the houses of meaner men that none (no minstrel) come unlesse he be desired, and that such as shall come so, holde themselves contented with meat and drynke, and wyth such courtesie as the maister of the house wyl shewe unto them of his own good wyll, without their askying of any thyng.[1]

This already struck hard at the independent minstrels. In 1467 the town of Coventry issued an order:

. . . also yt ye wayts of yis Cite yt now be and hereaft to be shall not passe yis Cite but to Abbot's and Priors within 10 myles of yis Cite.[2]

Finally, by Edward IV's order the guild of the minstrels was authorised to 'examine the pretensions of all such as affected to exercise the minstrel profession; and to regulate, govern, and punish them throughout the realm'.[3] Nevertheless, the itinerant minstrel persisted into the eighteenth century, welcomed wherever crowds were gathered as bringer of the latest news from all over the world.

Both classes of minstrels, however, the higher as well as the lower, derived from the same source, the old picturesque juggler, the man of the common people. These itinerant musicians of the earlier middle ages up to the end of the thirteenth century – law-breaking, rebellious, scandal-mongering, dirty, scraggy and utterly useless in the opinion of many rulers – were the real forefathers of our occidental instrumental art. They accompanied and assisted the rise of a new class of citizens to power; they entertained and cheered them, and they contributed a good deal to their enlightenment. We have to express our admiration for their independence, their uncompromising courage, and their partisanship for the people and their ways and doctrines: an attitude which, in the end, led to higher and higher organisms of literary and musical forms, styles and practices.

During the fourteenth and fifteenth centuries with the rise of instrumental music from the depths of anonymity to a more honourable position, more complicated forms developed. Certain fifteenth-century literary references to instrumental music suggest already a remarkable advance of instrumental composition on the path towards respectability. In many English chansons and motets that were practised at the Court and in other high society circles

[1] Poole, *Music in Early Drama*, p. 25.
[2] Bridge, *Town Waits*.
[3] Poole, p. 25.

about and after 1400 the performers must have played single parts of the vocal score on instruments – at least *ad libitum*.

The beginning of this practice of playing some of the voice parts on instruments can already be seen in certain fourteenth-century compositions.

There are many motets, secular and religious, which contain contrapuntal parts without words. In the following piece[1] it appears not at all unlikely that the two lower parts were played by instruments:

Example 9: Motet with two presumably instrumental parts; time about 1375.

---

[1] From J. Stainer, *Early Bodleian Music*, reprint from MS. Bodl. 264. It would be useless to transpose this music into a piano score with two systems; if played on the piano it would not appear to make any sense at all. To those who would like to get an impression of the music a performance with two voices (alto and baritone) and two stringed bass instruments, preferably bass viols, is recommended. Speed of the piece is moderately slow.

Example 9—*continued*

The two parts without words keep to the style of the vocal parts in similar motets. The piece is again closely related to French motets of the time, and it is of the kind that could only have been practised by musically educated persons.

In the fifteenth century the evidence of instrumental playing in highly evolved compositions increases considerably. The famous MS. Pepys 1236 (first half of fifteenth century) contains among its many vocal motets a four-part piece without words and without religious or literary references (ff. 73b–74a). It might have been played by instruments, although it differs in no way from the usual style of vocal motets. The piece is in common time (four minims to a bar) which once again suggests secular use.

But there are also examples of parts in polyphonic music of which there can be no doubt that they were performed by instruments. In several fifteenth-century chansons there are so-called ritornells which bear, it is true, still a few traces of instrumental peculiarities but are, nevertheless, certainly intended for instrumental execution. Incidentally, they prove that most instruments were used in very aristocratic surroundings:[1]

Example 10: Ritornello to 'Now wolde y fayne sum merthis mak'.

Example 11: Ritornello to 'O kendly creature of beaute perles'.

We find in these Ritornells all the complications of the vocal music of the time: imitations, difficult counterpoint, rhythmicised

[1] Examples 10 and 11 from Stainer, *Early Bodleian Music*, II, pp. 51 and 68. Stainer remarks: 'Is it possible that the passages without words were intended for instruments alone? I think so, and if this is the case, these songs present us with very early examples of symphonies' (p. 51). Example 10 is about 1425, Example 11 about 1445.

fauxbourdon[1] and other features. They are obviously influenced
by French and Italian models – again: the music of the aristocracy
was more liable to be influenced by foreign elements than popular
dance tunes.

From the point of view of instrumental interest the most
important form of the century was, however, the non-aristocratic
(or at least only partly aristocratic) carol or carolle. Its history in
this country actually begins in the twelfth century. It was originally
a dance either accompanied by singing or by instrumental playing
(instruments were used, for instance, by the 'Sacrilegious
Carollers' at the beginning of the fourteenth century).[2] If sung it is
divided between a leader and the rest of the chorus; where
instruments were available they came in with the chorus, but at
least some of the lines and verses were also accompanied by
instruments. The form was extremely popular. Not only did it
provide the formal material for the *ballad* but it also must have
become an important field for the further development of
instrumental playing.

Here is an old Christmas Carol (time about 1460):[3]

Example 12: Fifteenth-century Christmas carol.

---

[1] A fifteenth-century technique of counterpoint in which the parts are largely conducted
in parallel thirds and sixths.

See Manfred Bukofzer, *Geschichte des englischen Diskants und des Fauxbourdon nach englischen
Quellen,* Strassburg, 1936.

[2] See above, p. 29.

[3] From Chappell, *Popular Music of the Olden Times,* p. 42.

And here is the first part of a dance in the same style and rhythm as the carol. In the copy that has come down to us it has words with it; but originally it was quite obviously instrumental, for the words are awkwardly adapted and the phrasing in the text is irregular and unsymmetrical.[1]

Example 13: English dance tune (time about 1425).

So there are indications that instrumental music was developing parallel with vocal motets and chansons, with the ballads and romances. We recognise the vigorous advance of instrumental music during the fourteenth and fifteenth centuries and its importance for the future of the art. And yet it cannot be repeated too often that even during that period, Church music was still *the* official art which absorbed most of the energies and talents of the community, even though instrumental music was, historically seen, on the increase.

In the course of the fifteenth century, the material and social basis of English musical life was slowly transformed. The years between Henry IV and Henry VII were a time of preparation, of transition, a complicated and contradictory though germinating period. At a superficial glance this last stage of pre-Tudor England offers a picture of anarchy, of piracy, of noble lords imposing their will on the bewildered Commons by parading armed bands of retainers, of murderous battles fought between rival factions of the nobility, and of churchmen hunting down heretics from cloisters, castles and colleges. But in the fifteenth century there also

---

[1] It must be said that several writers, Morley among them, criticise the bad placing of words in music originally written for voices.

appeared more numerous and more impressive signs of the coming of the new age.

Indeed the Church, after Langland and Gower, had become intellectually unproductive. Yet there were several schools of choral writing flourishing in fifteenth-century England. This, to be sure, was not due to any spiritual strength in the Church. It has already been mentioned that there was a cleavage within the Church organisation itself.[1] These schools resulted from the apparently paradoxical fact that the ancient polyphonic tradition of the Church was temporarily rejuvenated by the intrusion of just those reformatory elements which the Church endeavoured so hard to keep down. Such elements are easily recognised in the music itself: the stiff motet style (as exemplified on p. 61) gave way to greater freedom of writing, as seen chiefly in Dunstable's[2] work. The popular, tonal-harmonic fauxbourdon (faburden),[3] which was closely related to all the gay dances and rounds of the previous centuries, gained enormously in importance. Here, then, we have a parallel development to the one which was going on in instrumental music itself. The elements of secular emotion gained ground – there must have existed a strong 'human element' especially among the lower clergy. The progressive, emancipationist forces of the time certainly affected the activities of the rank and file of Church musicians.

The great feudal lords who were busy cutting each other's throats had become an anachronism, and their basis of justifiable existence was crumbling. This condition they attempted to hide by ostentation and pretended refinement in their homes.

But on the other hand commerce and the cloth trade developed at an incredible pace. In spite of its still essentially corporate character the advance of the bourgeoisie increased the demands for individual freedom; a process which is felt in all the cultural spheres of the fifteenth century. Besides, the new mercantile classes were far more educated and literate than their ancestors. They could study things for themselves and think them over by themselves.

The cultural forms of the old age decayed with the Church and crisis-stricken feudal institutions, while on the other hand the conditions for the great spiritual renaissance that was to rise in the

[1] See above, p. 35.
[2] See above, p. 48.
[3] See above, p. 64.

towns were being created (though by no means yet fulfilled). This applies to literature and art as much as to music.

For instrumental music, too, the fifteenth century was a time of preparation. Unfortunately, it must be said again, we have few musical examples (beyond the instances quoted)[1] which could give us more clues as to the nature of the music of the waits in the towns and of the minstrelsy at Court. This makes it very difficult, for the time being, to assess the actual state of instrumental art especially in the second half of the fifteenth century.

Only one thing can be stated as certain. Instrumental music could not develop freely until the road was opened to its chief promoters: the progressive popular and mercantile classes, the new forces.

---

[1] There is a piece without words (apparently a ground tenor) with the name of Dunstable added to it in the British Museum Add. MS 31922 (fol. 36b). If the piece is really by Dunstable it might be his only known instrumental composition.

CHAPTER II

On the Threshold of Modern Times

It was the time of Henry VII and Henry VIII that brought the great change.

The virtual completion of the process of liberating the serfs and the subsequent fluidity of labour; the 'triumph of the sheep' (the transformation of the land from growing corn to producing wool); the upward surge of trade and industry; the discovery of distant fair lands offering unlimited possibilities for trade; and last but not least the invention of gunpowder to blast the ancient castles of the feudal nobility – these factors had spelt death to the middle ages.

The universal adoption of the reformed English language, the reappearance of Lollardry, the revived study of Greek and Roman ideas, the growth of English nationalism and finally the invention of the printing press to enlighten new masses of citizens – such were the spiritual expressions of the great revolution that was going on.

During Henry VIII's reign a stage in the development of England had been reached where a national emancipation had to take place. In 1536–40, in what is called the English Reformation, the secular power of the Catholic Church was challenged. The monasteries had been dissolved and their property, together with that of some of the older feudal noblesse, confiscated by the King in what might be called a 'revolution from above' and distributed among merchants and certain representatives of the aristocracy. This was part of the struggle by which the national independence of England was established against the power and exploitation of the Catholic Church, and so was enthusiastically supported by the bourgeoisie and Parliament.[1]

[1] See Christopher Hill, *The English Revolution*, London, 1940, p. 21. Mrs A. Green gives a lively picture of the social developments towards the end of the fifteenth century: 'As soon as the village weaver began to make cloth for the Prussian burgher or the trader of the Black Sea instead of for his next door neighbour, the old conditions of his trade became absolutely impossible. The whole industry was before long altogether reorganised both from the commercial and the manufacturing side. The exporting merchants drew together in a new and powerful association known as the Merchant Adventurers. Meanwhile the army of workmen at home was broken up into specialised groups of spinners, weavers, larders, fullers, shearers and dyers. The seller was more and more sharply separated from the maker of goods. Managers and middlemen organised the manufacture and made provision for its distribution and sale' (*Town Life in the Fifteenth Century*, London and New York, 1894, Vol. I, p. 67).

The merchants quickly gained decisive influence. Vital rights for the merchants were established, a kind of merchant nobility settled on the land and strongly consolidated itself in the towns. With them the whole mass of middle-class citizens in the towns achieved increasing importance. The growth of the Reformation during the first half of the sixteenth century was the main spiritual indication of this change in society. But the cultural outlook of this new society was entirely different from that of the older feudal classes.[1] The attitude of the new individual towards life was no longer to stabilise the world in its status quo but, on the contrary, to change it, to create possibilities of personal freedom, of individual development, economic, political and cultural.

This atmosphere of vitality and progress could certainly leave no sphere of life and culture untouched. Quickly the outer appearance of all cultural life changed. While during the middle ages the main cultural centres in England were the churches and, to a lesser degree, the aristocratic courts, the sixteenth century, especially after the dissolution of the monasteries, brought the establishment of many new centres, the town and country seats of the new gentry.

In the middle ages town and country were as far apart in their cultural outlook as in their geographical distance, which appeared enormous in face of the primitive travelling facilities of the time. Yet when, through the settlement of the new nobility of the towns in the country, and the intermarriage of merchants and aristocracy, the two spheres were brought together, a new cultural vitality developed throughout the country with amazing rapidity.

The insularity of the medieval manor house was broken down. Before the sixteenth century 'a great house provisioned itself with little help from the outer world; the inhabitants brewed and baked, churned and ground their meal; they bred, fed and slew their beeves and sheep and brought up their pigeons and poultry at their own doors. Their horses were shod at home, their planks were sawn, their rough iron work was forged and mended.'[2]

Not that self-sufficient economy in England had ended by the middle of the sixteenth century. But a great change in the way of housekeeping was beginning to make itself felt after 1500 and continued to do so to an ever increasing degree as the sixteenth

[1] See also L. C. Knights, *Drama and Society in the Age of Jonson*, London, 1937, pp. 103–108 and p. 115.

[2] Frances P. Verney, *Memoirs of the Verney Family during the Seventeenth Century*, London, 1925, I, 5.

century and the revolution on the land progressed (particularly around London). Of Anne, second wife of Thomas, Lord Berkeley (d. 1534), we are told: 'Country huswifry seemed to be an essential part of this lady's constitution', while already the 'huswifry' of her daughter-in-law began to decline, and she 'seemed to betake herself to the delights of youth and greatness . . .'.[1] The influence of the elegance and luxury of the great towns on the country seats became very noticeable. Many gentlemen even began 'to take another course, and falling from the use of their ancestors, do now either altogether (or very much) leave to dwell in their country houses, inhabiting cities, and great towns . . .'.[2] London itself during Henry VIII's reign is described thus:

From the Tower to Westminster along, every street is full of luxuries, and their shops glister and shine of glasses, painted cruses, gay daggers, etc., that is able to make any temperate man to gaze on them and to buy somewhat, though it serve to no purpose necessary.[3]

So the spirit and tempo of life in the new cities invaded the former centres of patriarchal agrarianism. Leisure, luxury, and at the same time, a keen sense of art, science and philosophy developed in the country seats, as the gap between town and country diminished. The new 'gentlemen of importance' patronised painting (especially did they commission the best continental artists to paint their portraits) as much as architecture; numberless precious manors and castles were modernised and completely rebuilt during the sixteenth century. The country manors became comfortable living-places; they were no longer merely centres of agricultural production. Witness the wonderful beauty of many small Tudor country houses that are still in existence today. In 1577, towards the end of the century, William Harrison[4] could write:

The furniture of our houses . . . is growne in maner even to passing delicacies and herein I doo not speake of the nobilitie and gentrie only, but likewise of the lowest sort in most places of our south countrie, that have anything at all to tak to. Certes, in

[1] Berkeley MSS. II, p. 254. Quotations by Knights, p. 112.
[2] Cyvile and Uncivyle Life, 1579, Sig. B. i., V.–B. iii. Quoted by Knights, p. 115.
[3] Traill and Mann, Social England, III, p. 226, quoted by Knights, p. 118.
[4] Elizabethan England, p. 11; quoted by H. S. Bennet, The Pastons and their England, Cambridge, 1932, pp. 87 ff.

noble mens houses it is not rare to see abundance of Arras, rich hangings of tapestrie, silver vessell, and so much other plate, as may furnish sundrie cupboards, to the summe often-times of a thousand or two thousand pounds at the least. Likewise in the houses of knights, gentlemen, merchantmen, and some other wealthie citizens. . . . But as herein all these doo far exceed their elders and predecessors, and in neatness and curiositie, the merchant all other; so in time past, the costlye furniture staied there, whereas now it is descended yet lower, even unto the inferiour artificers and manie farmers, the most part learned also to garnish their cupboards with plate, their joined beds with tapestrie and silke hangings, and their tables with carpets and fine naperie.

The homes of the new half-town half-country middle classes in England henceforth became centres of art and culture. Here the vitality of the young and ascendant mercantile class was translated into cultural reality.

With the new standards of comfort and taste there arose a vivid musical culture. The production of instrumental music in particular increased with great speed.

Of great importance in this connection were the Royal Chapels. While the Church gradually lost its position as the centre of the country's musical activities, the absolutist Court of the early Tudor kings took over this function. The great innovator Henry VII contributed essentially to the revolutionary increase of instrumental music in particular. Once again we can refer to Hayes' representation of the music of the Courts of the early Tudor kings. Simultaneously with the increasing amount of music composed for instruments the percentage of instrumental players, compared with singers, increased rapidly at the Courts of Henry VIII and Edward VI (who, incidentally, added two 'makers of instruments' to his chapel).

After 1500 many private families, too, even the less wealthy, already had their private establishments of harpists and violists.[1] A favourite instrument in many country houses was the portable organ or regal, the very existence of which constituted a challenge to the Church – not to mention the music played on it, which ranged from secular arrangements of religions songs to popular tunes.

A study of the social past of the young merchant nobility reveals

[1] See Chappell, *Popular Music of the Olden Times*, pp. 55 ff.

that many of them came from the lower middle classes, or at least had very close associations with them; that is to say with artisans, craftsmen, small merchants and yeomen. The rise of these people meant at the same time the rise of music of a popular character, for the representatives of the new merchant nobility took their tunes and harmonies with them, introducing the melodies from the village green into the private gardens and drawing-rooms of the higher society.

*

The chief feature of instrumental music in England around and after 1500 is rhythmical definition, and this is the quality which most clearly shows its secular origin and purpose and sets it most obviously aside and apart from contemporary choral music, the music of the Church. Now it has been pointed out that fifteenth and early sixteenth century English Church music was generally less obscure and abstract than many continental Masses and motets of that time, especially those of the Dutch and Flemish schools. But compared with popular instrumental music, even English Church music – though very beautiful and highly evolved – appears over-complex and rhythmically blurred, like many works of music by composers living in over-developed and declining societies. Syncopes and rich ornaments in all voices make it all but impossible for the listener to discriminate between arsis and thesis in a bar:[1]

Example 14: from 'Adoramus' by Hugh Aston (d. 1521).

[1] *Tudor Church Music*, Vol. X, No. 1.

The new instrumental art, with its simplicity, shows on the other hand the qualities we found in the little folk tune in Chapter I. It has very clearly marked 2/4, 3/4 and 4/4 rhythms, and exhibits distinct accents at the beginning of bars and periods.[1] The structure, too, is outspokenly homophonic:

Example 15: Dance tune a 3 by Henry VIII.[2]

In this instrumental music, it is interesting to note, the common-time rhythm had now risen to an importance unknown in Church music. As we have seen in the first chapter, these rhythms 2/4 and 4/4 had always been outstanding rhythms of folk music, even at times when common-time was kept out of all Church music. Then triple rhythm, the three beats of which were for a long time considered symbolic of the Holy Trinity, was sacred, all other rhythms profane.[1] About 1500, at a time when rhythmical complications of all kinds dominated the 'mensural vocal' music of all countries alike as never before, in instrumental notation each note almost without any exception subdivided into *two* of the next smaller units; a breve into two semibreves, a semibreve into two minims, etc. The whole apparatus of 'ligatures', 'perfection', 'alteration', etc., in mensural music was foreign to instrumental art.[2]

The music of Henry VIII's court is typical of the art of the new bourgeois aristocracy; and music written for or at the Court was widely used outside it.[3] In and around the Court, dance tunes and dance forms constituted the main bulk of instrumental music, at least up to 1550, and indeed, of all the rapid developments of musical forms in this fast-moving century, the triumph of dance music is certainly one of the most striking.

Most of the new dance pieces of the Court and of the new aristocracy and merchant bourgeoisie were melodically fresh, simple and rhythmically clear. The easy-going melodies of the lower middle classes and peasantry of the later middle ages, worked into a slightly stylised form, were the musical material of early Tudor Court and society:

Example 16: 'Blow thy horn, hunter. . . .'[4]

Tunes of this and similar kind, known as country dances from Chaucer's time onwards, were taken from the huge reservoir of true 'music of the people'.[5] The young bourgeoisie whose interests were so largely represented by Henry VIII wanted this kind of

[1] See also P. F. H. Radcliffe in Mus. Ass. Proceedings, 1930–31, and above, p. 41, where doubts are expressed concerning this theory.

[2] See also H. Riemann, *Geschichte der Musiktheorie*, pp. 213 ff.

[3] There are numerous references to the use of court music in the houses of wealthy citizens in Galpin's book.

[4] See Chappell, *Old English Popular Music*, I, 41–53. Tune from p. 40.

[5] Mrs Walter Carr, in *Grove's Dictionary*, Vol. I (article on country dances) rightly emphasises that the country dances were English folk tunes from the very beginning, as against the notion that the country dances were in reality 'contre-danses'.

simple and jolly music and took it over, having no use for the highly architectonic contrapuntal combinations of the learned scholars in the cloisters.

Among the new Court dances there appears a species which attracts our special attention: the domps, dumpes or dompes.[1] They were of particular significance for the development of independent chamber music. For it was the domps which, as a form of instrumental music, appear chiefly to have been performed by an ensemble of instruments rather than on a keyboard. These pieces, like the rest of Henry VIII's Court dances, were rhythmically square and melodically simple. But they lacked the gaiety of the other forms. The name was always applied to slow dances of a sombre and somewhat sinister nature. Some of them must have been used at funerals; an atmosphere of mourning or solemn reflection had to be created in these pieces; it could best be brought about by a group of instruments.

Domps are built on this rhythm:

and on a repeated harmonic ground, as shown in Example 17: 'My Lady Carey's Dompe.'[2]

They consist of three, four or five strains of a varying number of bars. In the later strains the movement becomes livelier, and sometimes certain variations modify the original melodies of the dances. In these variations, we may fancy, instrumental expression is struggling to be born. On the whole the domps are stately, important and expressive in a musical sense.[3] There are pieces, for

[1] See J. M. Ward, 'The Dolfull Domps', *Journal of the American Musicological Society*, IV, 1951, pp. 111–121.

[2] Brit. Mus. MS. Roy. App. 58; time about 1520. The sharps are added editorially.

[3] Literature of the time makes frequent references to the domps. Naylor (*Shakespeare Music*, 1912, pp. 5 ff.) reminds us of the 'doleful dumps' in the first verse of Richard Edward's poem which Peter sings in *Romeo and Juliet*, IV, 5, 125. Peter's request to the musicians to

instance, like 'the Duke of Somerset's Dumpe'[1] whose particularly solemn character suggests that they were used on prominent occasions.

Later in the sixteenth century the domps lost much of their mournfulness, and some of them took on the playful character of Elizabethan tunes; witness 'Queen Marie's Dumpe' for two viols,[2] an arrangement for virginal of 'Lady Carey's Dump' towards the end of the century,[3] and an 'Irish Dump' from the Fitzwilliam Virginal Book.[4] The latter even changes the slowly striding rhythm into a 'merry' 6/8, quite in accordance with the change towards greater gaiety that so many dance forms underwent about 1600.

Although the domps are of purely English origin and, as far as can be said, confined to the musical repertoire of this country, they have a certain similarity to the more widely known 'basse danses' of the Continent which, in their very earliest stages in Spain, were called 'danzas de la muerte' (dances of death).[5] Both domps and basse danses were slow dances which included a great variety of movements and steps, and both died out towards the end of the sixteenth century. Yet it is essential to recognise the importance of the domps, which, as purely English pieces, not only give proof of the productivity of the regenerated society of this country but also prepare the ground – in their demand for *sostenuto* – for a new instrumental technique.

'play a merry dump to comfort me' (earlier in the same scene) is in reality an allusion to the sad character of the dump. It is not a 'merry' dance – he calls it 'merry' mockingly – but it is tragic and depressing.

> 'Where gripping grief the heart would wound
> And doleful dumps the mind oppress . . .'

In *Lucrece*, line 1127, we find:

> 'Distress likes dumps, when time is kept with tears.'

In Humphrey Gifford's *Gilloflowers* there is another poem called 'A Dolefull Dumpe' and two more, 'A Dumpe' and 'A Dumpe by his Friend C. C.' (See J. Pulver, *Dictionary of Old English Music*, 1927.) A piece named 'Ye Quenes dumpe' is mentioned in a list of dances of Henry VIII's time (Brit. Mus. MS. Sloane 3501, fol. 2b). A 'doleful dump' is mentioned in *Chevy Chase*, the famous ballad of the fifteenth century, re-told by a seventeenth-century writer, see *Ballads and Poems*, ed. Frank Sidgwick, Cambridge, 1913, p. 38, line 194. In Shakespeare's 'Sigh no more ladies' a 'dull and heavy dump' is mentioned. See also John Ward, 'Dolfull Domps', *Journal of the American Musicological Society*, IV, 1951, pp. 111–121.

[1] MS. Roy. App. 58, fol. 51b.
[2] Brit. Mus. MS. Add. 15118 (Bass part only).
[3] Naylor, p. 5.
[4] Ibid., p. 7.
[5] See C. Sachs, *A World History of the Dance*, New York, 1933.

Another dance form, the hornpipe (Hornpeype) played a similar, though less important part in the development of instrumental technique in chamber music. It was of greater importance to organ and virginal music, as is shown in the well-known 'Hornpype' by Hugh Aston (d. 1521), composed for a keyboard instrument, an exceedingly lively and richly figured piece of considerable technical difficulty.[1] Only a few hornpipes for chamber music combinations are known to have been written during the 16th century; several are included in a list of compositions of Henry VIII's court.[2] The hornpipe was a dance in vivid 3/2 or 3/4 rhythm; in the sixteenth century it consisted of many small symmetrical periods of two, four or eight bars. The small melodic units were as simple as those in Aston's piece.[3]

Apart from these two purely English dances, domp and hornpipe (to which the already mentioned jig and some odd forms would have to be added), we can count a great variety of dance forms of continental origin among the compositions played at Henry VIII's court. Most of them are lively, replacing the old and stiff court dances of the fifteenth century, and many are not named but are easily recognisable as early saltarellos, bransles, pivas, etc., on models familiar in contemporary French, Italian and Dutch collections such as Attaignant's editions of dances in 1529 and 1530. French influence is particularly conspicuous in the formal structure of many of these dances, but the melodies are almost invariably of the popular English type which was shown to be prevalent in the music played at Henry VIII's court.[4]

It is difficult to form an opinion as to the approximate number of dances composed at Henry VII's and Henry VIII's courts. Among the composers of such music we meet most frequently the names of Richard Pyttins, Thomas Fardying, W. Cornysshe, John Floyd (Flude), Robert Fayrfax and Thomas Churcheyarde; there

---

[1] Complete reprint in J. Wolf's *Sing- und Spielmusik*, 1925–6. See also Grove's *Dictionary*, II (3rd edn), p. 670, on the origin of the hornpipe, and Davey's *History of English Music*, 1921, p. 98, on domps and hornpipes.

[2] Brit. Mus. MS. Sloane 3501.

[3] On the whole, chamber music and music for keyboard instruments developed fairly independently of each other during the first half of the sixteenth century, as they belonged to entirely different spheres of life. The interplay of styles between keyboard and ensemble music became, however, livelier after 1550 when the brilliant technique of the virginal pieces helped to prepare the way for a more typically instrumental technique on instruments used in chamber music.

[4] There are several other dance pieces without titles or names in Add. 31922, Roy. App. 58, 74, h 76, etc.

are also instrumental pieces by Bramston, Banastir, Heywood, Ludford, R. Cooper, Dygon and Johnston.[1]

During Henry VIII's reign some pieces are found which are actually called pavanas (pavins) and galliardas (galliards).[2] They appear either as single dances or in pairs, pavana and galliards being coupled as one and the same item in a performance of dances at the Court. The pavana then provided a majestic introduction in common time while the galliarda followed suit in a faster triple rhythm. It is difficult to say at what part of this period the English musician adopted the continental habit of basing both dances on one and the same tune (the galliard appearing as a variation of the pavana at greater speed, with still stricter and stronger accents on the arsis of each bar, and usually in triple rhythm). But we can guess the reason for this economy of thematic material. As the general demand for entertainment for the common people increased and dances and similar diversions received more or less official recognition, the composers of dance music were often unable to cope with the enormous calls that were made on them. So variety and enrichment of the repertoire of dance music was achieved by simply repeating a dance tune in a different rhythm. Thomas Morley alludes to this 'Variation Suite' (the couple of pavan and galliard):

> After every pavan we usually set a galliard (that is, a kind of musicke made out of the other). . . . This is a lighter and more stirring kinde of dauncing.

Morley then gives as basic rhythm of the galliard the 'foot Trochæus': ⚬ ♩ | ⚬ ♩ | ⚬ ♩   etc.[3]

How much of the continental practice itself was known in this country is hard to say.[4] But in the connecting-up of different

---

[1] Many compositions of these masters are in Brit. Mus. Add. MS. 31922; others in the already mentioned MSS. of the time. There are two pieces a 3 and 23 a 3–5 in Roy. App. 58; among the numerous instrumental pieces contained in Brit. Mus. Add. MS. 31922, there are 30 a 3–4 by Fayrfax (d. 1521), Fardyng (d. between 1514 and 1524), Cornysshe (d. 1523) and unnamed composers.

[2] Pavanas and galliards in Brit. Mus. Stowe 389, Roy. App. 58, 74–6, etc. Some have names: 'The emperorse pavyn', 'King Harry 8th' Galliard' and others. Thomas Churcheyarde (1520–1604) appears among composers of the dance tunes of Roy. App. 75.

[3] *Plaine and Easie Introduction to Practicall Musicke*, 1597, p. 181.

[4] There seem to be some examples of this principle in Roy. App. 74–76, 'Ronda' with 'la represa' and similar pieces which include two versions of the same piece in form of variations on each other.

dances in this way, the principle of the later dance suite is recognised in these early arrangements.

Some pieces called pavanas (about 1550) are technically rounds or canons.[1] This suggests that there are certain tendencies in the pavana to 'stylise' the dance piece; probably under the influence of the polyphonic technique of contemporary church compositions.[2] But up to 1550 this feature is still of minor importance.

Towards the end of Henry VIII's reign another continental dance appears in English collections, the allemande (almand),[3] which even on arrival bears the main features of its standard seventeenth-century form; a certain gravity modified by the possibility of changing the character of the music as the dance changed. Like most other dances, the almand consists of three or more parts which are separated by complete cadences with pauses. From the beginning it is slightly more polyphonic than the domp or galliard, although in Henry's time it was still simple, hardly stylised and quite obviously essentially a 'dancing dance' and not a 'dance to be listened to' (as indeed are all but a very few of the dance forms of the period 1500–1558). Morley defines the almand: '. . . a more heavie daunce than this' (the galliard), '(fitlie representing the nature of the people, whose name it carrieth), so that no extraordinarie motions are used in the dauncing of it'.[4]

Finally there is the courante (coranto), the 3/4 dance in moderately quick time and in simple binary form. It made its appearance in England about the beginning of the reign of Elizabeth, and Shakespeare mentions it frequently. The courante became a vital factor in seventeenth-century dance music, especially in the suites.[5]

As for non-dance instrumental music, in B.M. Add. MS. 31922 (known as Henry VIII's MS.)[6] we find examples by English composers of works such as the long and intricate 'Fa la sol' for 3 instruments by William Cornyshe (c. 1465–c. 1523); puzzle canons

---

[1] Pavan 'in subdiatessarum', 'Per aliam viam reversi sunt in regiam suam' in MS. Roy. App. 74–76.

[2] See below, Chapter III.

[3] Allemande d'amor for 4 and 5 viols in MS. Roy. App. 74–76. A piece called 'ruger' in this MS. is by R. Pyttins.

[4] A Plaine and Easie Introduction, p. 181. Morley also mentions bransles, voltes and other dances.

[5] Ibid., p. 181.

[6] Music at the Court of Henry VIII. Transcribed and edited by John Stevens, Musica Britannica, Vol. 18 (1962).

for 3 and 4 instruments by John Dunstable (d. 1453) and Robert Fayrfax (d. 1521); and other consort music by Henry VIII himself and pieces by anonymous composers. The presence of works by Isaac, Agricola, Fevin after Ockeghem and a number of French *Chansons* shows that England was by no means isolated from continental developments.

In c. 1480 Johannes Tinctoris[1] remarked that lute players had become so skilful that they could play four parts on the lute. By the time the first printed lute music began to appear in the early years of the sixteenth century the ricercar and fantasia were already in a vigorous state of development, while intabulations of vocal music, both sacred and secular, called for all the skill of which Tinctoris had written. This type of non-functional music reached a high state of perfection in the compositions of masters such as Vincenzo Capirola (1474–c. 1548), Francesco da Milano (1497–1543) in Italy and Luis Milan (fl. 1536) in Spain. During the first half of the century it accounted for the greater part of all music for the lute. The same pattern presents itself in early secular keyboard music.

The presence at Henry's court of Italian and Flemish musicians such as the organist Dionisio Memo and the lute players Philip and Peter van Wilder would have strengthened tendencies towards non-dance composition which may already have been brought to England by visiting foreign musicians, and English travellers abroad.

✻

It was not, however, until about 1558 that chamber music – as an independent art – began its conquest of England. What was behind this triumphant rise? For a triumph it was if ever there was one.

The sudden development of the art was due to rapid and important changes in the spirit and 'tempo' of the times.

From about 1558 onwards a life of increasing activity developed: the spirit of enterprise, adventure, progress and intensified labour affected all parts of the population engaged in the various spheres of the new commercial life. A greater freedom of competition prepared the ground for a musical activity which was not tied by a thousand bonds to a non-musical function, but was based on the initiative of the individual composer. During the middle ages all professions, including the musical, were organised into guilds, so that the isolated individual could never have

---

[1] *De Inventione et Usu Musicae.*

achieved full consciousness of his power, nor have protected himself and advanced. The individual was only a link in a chain which was composed of equal parts, a member of a corporation or fraternity which stood for his rights, but at the same time held him captive. Now, after 1558, music moved away from the medieval way of functioning at court and church, or on municipal occasions, towards the much more independent ideal of pure chamber music.

And what part this music played in the awakening of the new age! How alive and varied it became! It had to respond to the immense and ever new, ever increasing demands of that fast-growing public of educated musical amateurs – the first stage of the 'general public' as we know it today. It has to be repeated that the chief centres of chamber music were at first the country manors of the new merchant-nobility. But more and more chamber music was called upon to counterbalance the increasingly strenuous life in the towns that developed so quickly (particularly in London). For although the growing freedom of life in the new cities offered more and more possibilities for the advance of the individual, it brought also increased strain; men became more and more entangled in its allurements and enchained by its promises, which only meant new and ever new endeavour, haste and exhaustion.

In this situation music became a means of providing recreation and pleasure. Towards the end of the sixteenth century English music shows an increasing tendency to develop quite new features pointing in that direction: in music there now is 'sweetness', 'charm', 'loveliness', 'magic' – and the minds of the listeners are carried away into an unknown sphere of harmony and immaterial beauty.

We in the twentieth century are so used to listening to music in this way that we often do not realise that it is of a comparatively recent growth, and that in the middle ages the attitude of the listener was entirely different. The predominance of the element of pleasure and diversion did not become apparent in musical life until the end of the sixteenth century. William Byrd, the greatest of Elizabethan composers, was the first to express the wish that his music 'might happely yeeld some sweetness, repose and recreation'.[1]

Chamber music offered an almost ideal medium for providing just this mental and spiritual recreation, by virtue of the privacy of the practice, its apparent remoteness from any perceptible

[1] Introduction to *Psalms, Songs and Sonnets*, 1587–8.

purpose, and the opportunity it gave for the expression of a more subjective emotionalism.

Another important point to remember in this context is that during the sixteenth century, music was regarded as fulfilling an important role in society. Within the conception of the universe it was thought that terrestrial music should reflect the divine proportions of the Music of the Spheres, which maintained the planets in their courses. Thus, according to the theoreticians, well-composed music could act as a corrective influence on the nature of man, and in this way contribute to a well-ordered society.

Let us consider for a moment instrumental music in general. It is the realm of 'absolute' sound, in which are no limits or boundaries. It addresses man's emotional life most immediately and directly; and in so doing does not rely on 'roundabout routes' as do other arts; it does not represent concrete objects from real life as painting does; nor deal with symbols of reality as literature and poetry do. In instrumental music man's emotional life is most purely reflected. Therefore man found here a practically unlimited field for developing his imagination.

With the new conception of life the artist's imagination was freed from its medieval fetters. It was instrumental music which offered itself to Elizabethans as a perfect field for the realisation in ideal terms of all those demands which the Reformation and Renaissance put forward, and in particular we shall see how in the following century instrumental music, this kaleidoscope of changing visions and emotions, became an important vehicle for the expression of the new life – modern life with its wrongs and hopes.

It must not be overlooked that this new development in the field of music, the evolution of instrumental music, contained a potential element of danger. In instrumental music the imagination of the artist could develop in two directions: he could indeed draw up plans for the battle of life which would stimulate and inspire his fellows with new energy and optimism; but he could also (and here lay the element of danger) dream himself away from life to a world of passive wish-fulfilment. It must be made clear from the start, however, that during the days of the childhood of instrumental chamber music there was hardly any question of escapism. Elizabethan composers chose the first way, for society (as will be shown in a later chapter) was more active, and more united and balanced than in most other periods of English history; and there was no need to escape from reality. There was much optimism and vitality in Elizabethan art which was in itself a healthy reaction to the religious escapism of medieval Church art.

So it was historical necessity that brought about the evolution of chamber music and of chamber music instruments. It was not (as some still suppose) through the means of 'invention' that chamber music came into being; the preparation of this art was a painful process that dragged on for centuries. Nor did some individual genius conjure this art out of nothing – some Aladdin who had only to rub his magic lamp – a whole people participated in the creation of its chamber music. Talent is indeed a necessary prerequisite of creative art, but the artist's talent is directed and developed by the fact that he is not an isolated but a social being. The individual 'creative genius' is only creative because he recognises most clearly and deeply and magnificently (though not necessarily consciously) the spiritual necessities of the society to which he belongs. His work is a factor in the development of the human community as a whole, but it is itself a product of this development,[1] and only as a result of the influences of events upon him can a creative genius himself influence them. Least of all is it blind chance or the caprice of some dark, cold destiny that is responsible for the appearance and disappearance of great periods of art. *It is the creative power of human society itself that makes the history of art.* All the finest qualities of the human race, all its warmth and beauty will be recognised in the great age of music that now begins.

[1] How far the whole conception of a 'genius' is dependent on historical necessity is most clearly shown in our own art, for the cult of the great, all-conquering 'genius' of music is a creation chiefly of the eighteenth and nineteenth centuries – the time of great careers and great personalities who struggled to rise far above their fellow human-beings, in accordance with the general trend of society which was based on industrial conquest and individualism.

CHAPTER III

The Emancipation from the Church

In the new type of instrumental music that was developing under Henry VIII, we have seen that its connection with Court functions and dancing was still essential; pleasure in instrumental sound and playing, so essential to chamber music, was not yet the chief purpose.

After all that has been said it may seem surprising that the decisive step to accomplish this was made in music that originated in the Church. The earliest real chamber music had, indeed, the form of religious works and was written by Church composers. There were important reasons for this peculiar situation.

Humanism and the Renaissance in England, propagating personal, social and cultural freedom, advanced in the cultural sphere essentially on religious grounds. It was no contradiction if instrumental music, another expression of a progressive social outlook, was connected with the Reformation. But further, Anglican Reform pursued a peculiar policy regarding music in the church. The sixteenth century was a time of fierce religious and social struggle. In all such times the emphasis in vocal music laid upon the *words* (and the text in general) becomes stronger. In all countries the movements of the Reformation and Counter-Reformation alike endeavoured to convey their messages through the medium of vocal music; this endeavour established the temporary triumph of the words and their meaning in the Musica Reservata on the Continent, in the Florentine Camerata, in the opera, and in the choral Laudes of the Jesuits – all this after the long predominance of the hyper-complex old motet-style, in which the music was all-important, drowning the text. We think further of the clarity of the declamation in the operas and songs of the French Revolution, reacting against the primacy of the purely musical element in other eighteenth-century French music which was crammed with ornaments and coloratures. We can also find similar tendencies aiming at greater distinctiveness and more effective interpretation of the text in the music of modern political movements – as against the intricate and twisted counterpoint of contemporary *l'art pour l'art* composers.

The words must be clearly understood by the listener who is

to be converted or convinced of the rightness of a new theory, philosophy, gospel or policy. So we find in sixteenth-century England, too, a stronger elaboration and clearer interpretation of the biblical words of a vocal work. In 1559 the Anglican Church decreed the simplification of the vocal score. The 49th Injunction in Cranmer's Reform asks for a 'modest and distinct song so used in all parts of the prayer that the same might be understood as if it were read without singing'. There should be but one note to one syllable, and the whole choral arrangement should be homophonic. Simultaneously the organ was temporarily silenced (organists hitherto provided excessively florid accompaniments).

It is evident that such a style offered little scope for the composers to continue in the Church their tradition of artistic and polyphonic motets. True, they wrote vocal Church music according to the new regulations, and they tried to give of their best in it. But they also had to find an outlet, another field where they could employ their technical skill and pacify their 'polyphonic consciences'. Some of the composers went on composing Catholic music in the old sense, occasionally with the disapproval of the Anglican authorities. They were, however, in the minority. But to what field did the main body of composers direct themselves? To instrumental music which, as shown, contained so many elements of attraction for the musical world of the middle of the sixteenth century. So it was the Church composers themselves who developed instrumental music from out of the environment of the Church.

This tendency has already been seen in the 'Canon Pavanas' of the first half of the sixteenth century. But these were minor examples; much more important were the instrumental works which grew directly out of the choral Church art. The old choral polyphony determined the form as well as the style of the early chamber music. Immediately before and during the early stages of the Reformation by far the most important form of Catholic church music, apart from the mass, was the *motet*, an authorised though not liturgical vocal species. This was in essence a polyphonic setting of a biblical text, having as a rule one voice reserved for the enunciation of the Gregorian chant proper to the words, the other parts moving freely in counterpoint to it. English composers of chamber music took hold of the motet, and by a kind of act of collective creation metamorphosed it into chamber music. Let us study the form and the process.

The standard type of motet of the English school during the first half of the sixteenth century was influenced by the works of the contemporary Dutch polyphonists Josquin des Près, Pierre de la Rue, Gombert, Mouton and others. This influence, it must be emphasised, was certainly very moderate compared with the subjection of the whole Continent to the Netherlandish cathedral style. But it was noticeable over here, too; just as Dutch spiritual movements, both orthodox and reformatory, moral and intellectual, made a deep impression on the English in the general sphere of religious thought.

At that time the standard type of motet still appeared mainly as 'Cantus firmus' motet or 'Tenor'[1] motet, characterised by the maintenance of a cantus firmus in one of the parts of the score throughout the piece. Every one of these cantus firmi was solely based on one of the flourishing melodies of the Gregorian Chant which from the seventh century onwards were the choral material of the Catholic service. The Gregorian melodies were considered as sacrosanct in the Church. The succession of the notes was therefore strictly kept whenever they were used as the thematic backbone of the polyphonic motets. The rhythm was altered, though; usually the plainsong in the motet of the sixteenth century moves along calmly in one of the parts in long, equal notes, regardless of all the polyphonic happenings in the other parts:

Example 18:

(*a*) Plainsong:

Et ex-ul-ta-vit

(*b*) Motet Cantus firmus:

Et ex - ul-ta - vit——

---

[1] Tenor originally meant 'ea vox quae tenet' the voice that 'holds' the main part in the motet; the term must not be confused with 'Tenor' meaning the upper part of the male voice chorus which only up to the thirteenth century really was 'ea vox quæ tenet'.

(c) 4-part Motet by John Taverner[1] (cantus firmus in the first bass):

Otherwise the form of the motet depends on the formal arrangement of the sentences of the text. While the cantus firmus is smoothly running along

Taverner (1495–1545), Tedeum:[2]

a close polyphonic net is being woven by the other parts.

The scheme of the polyphonic structure of these contrapuntal parts is usually as follows. One clause of the Latin text, 'Te eternum patrem omnis terra veneratur', is sung by one voice which introduces a melodic phrase:

A second voice enters, mostly *imitating* the melody of the first, although often pursuing a more independent course after a few notes in the beginning, while the first voice carries on a counterpoint of its own. A third voice comes in, then a fourth, until the full

[1] *Tudor Church Music*, III, p. 3.
[2] Ibid., pp. 26 ff.

polyphonic stream of the whole choir is reached. A final cadence concludes the first 'section' of the motet.[1]

Now a new sentence starts: 'Tibi cherubin et seraphin incessabili voce proclamant.' A new phrase starts in the musical composition accordingly:

Ti - bi che - ru - bin et se - ra - - phin

Fugal imitation and the whole polyphonic construction take place again, and again a cadence concludes the development. A third section begins:

Do - mi - nus De - us Sa - ba - oth _____

and so on, until the text finishes.[2]

It is true that this scheme is not always strictly followed, the fugal imitation especially, is rarely regular in all voices during the first half of the sixteenth century; there are also homophonic parts, and sections in which there is no imitation but every voice has an entirely independent contrapuntal line of its own. The sections, moreover, mostly overlap: the melody of a subsequent section comes in before the cadence of the previous section has finished.

It may be said that it was a common practice long before the middle of the sixteenth century to reinforce or even to replace one or several of the voice-parts by the organ (or perhaps by some soft stringed instruments as shown in Chapter I). But only about 1550 do we find it a general practice for all parts of a vocal score to be performed by instruments. The special attraction of the instrumental performance of a vocal piece must have been very great, for there are hundreds of instrumental arrangements of vocal works of the time – secular as well as religious – still in existence.[3] The reader may try for himself, by having any motet of

---

[1] In this particular case each of the first sections consists of two sub-sections: Te Eternum Patrem – omnis terra veneratur, and: Tibi cherubin et seraphin – incessabili voce proclamant.

[2] See also the author's 'Form in the Instrumental Music of the Seventeenth Century', *Proceedings of the Musical Association, 1938–39,* pp. 45–61.

[3] There are many titles with indications that music may be used either for voices or instruments. E. g., Thomas Whythorne's *Duos or Songs for two voyces* bear the sub-title: 'playne and easie to be sung or played on Musicall Instruments' (1590).

the time first sung by a choir and then played by instruments.[1] He
will be surprised at the discrepancy in the two performances.[2]
There are hundreds of arrangements of this kind in one large
collection alone.[3]

The instrumental arrangements of cantus firmus motets follow
the vocal line strictly. Some types of vocal motets seem to have
attracted instrumental performers more than others. For instance
there are many instrumental motets based on the Gregorian
'Miserere',[4] most of which one could identify as literal
transcriptions of vocal pieces. Yet among the numerous genres of
instrumental pieces appearing in sixteenth-century manuscripts
there is one which cannot be considered as a mere 'arrangement'!
It is the so-called 'In Nomine'.

The instrumental 'In Nomine' is composed on a cantus firmus
which in every case is identical.

Example 19: 'In Nomine' (Cantus firmus).

[1] Parts of William Byrd's *Psalms, Songs and Sonnets* of 1588 were originally composed for
one voice with instrumental accompaniment.

[2] In the old MSS. the texts of vocal and instrumental versions are identical, apart from
minor variants that occasionally appear. In a piece by Taverner, Brit. Mus. MS. Add. 31390,
107, the music is identical with the vocal motet 'Dum transisset', cf. *Tudor Church Music*, III,
37–45, except for the fact that in the instrumental version several parts have double
stoppings in the final chord!

[3] Brit. Mus. Add. 31390. Many are also in Add. 30480, such as 'Levavi oculos' by Wyllyam
More, 'harpour to Ed. VI'. A reference to the work is found in G. Hayes' *Kings's Musick;* the
whole piece is published there on pp. 26–7.

[4] There is one instrumental 'Miserere' for 4 parts, anonymous, in Brit. Mus. Add. MS.
36484, one a 5 by Bramley in Royal Coll. of Music, MS. 2049, one a 2 by Nathaniel Giles in
the King's Library RM. 24 d.2, one a 5 by Mallorie in Oxford, Bodleian D. 212–16, one a 5
by Lupo in Oxford, Christ Church MS. 2 and several other libraries, one a 5 by Stoninges in
Brit. Mus. Add. 31390, one a 5 by Chr. Tye in Oxford, Bodl. MS. Mus. School e 1–5. Morley
speaks about the 'Miserere' in the *Plaine and Easie Introduction*, p. 115 (1597).

This cantus firmus is not only common to all In Nomines; it is peculiar to them. The In Nomine is the first definite form of composed instrumental music, the forefather of all English chamber music up to the present day.[1]

The origin of this form was first traced simultaneously by R. Thurston Dart jointly with Robert Donington[2] and by Gustave Reese.[3] The melody of the In Nomine is originally an antiphon[4] in the Gregorian Choral contained in the Festival of the Holy Trinity with the words 'Gloria tibi Trinitas'. It occurs in Taverner's Mass 'Gloria tibi Trinitas', in the 'Benedictus' of which it appears with the text 'In Nomine Domini' in calm and equal long notes. Taverner's composition must have impressed composers so much that forthwith they vied with one another to write polyphonic pieces with the 'Gloria tibi Trinitas' melody serving as a cantus firmus. So this form was given the name 'In Nomine'. All these compositions were intended for instrumental performance from the time of Taverner's vocal masterpiece onwards.

It is certain that the In Nomine did not make its appearance until the middle of the sixteenth century when the Church went through its deepest crisis and when instrumental chamber music began to be the fashion. Most probably the instrumental In Nomine never had a place in the service. But why was a sacred melody used? Why was it performed instrumentally? And why was it used by so many composers up to as late as the second half of the seventeenth century? Is the right explanation that given by the Hon. Roger North, who considered the In Nomine to be a kind of test piece among composers to prove their accomplishment and skill in contrapuntal writing?[5] This seems most likely, for almost every English composer of importance from Taverner to Purcell wrote In Nomines.[6] There are about 150 In Nomines still in

---

[1] It is interesting to find two 'In Nomines' in the major mode (B flat): Lawes a 6 (Oxford Bodleian Mus. School, B.2, p. 10) and an (imitation?) by J(ohn) B(rowne), Oxford Christ Church MSS. 473–8 No. 21.

[2] 'The Origin of the "In Nomine"', *Music and Letters*, 1949 (vol. 30, No. II, pp. 101–106).

[3] 'The Origin of the English In Nomine', *Journal of the American Musicological Society*, Vol. II, No. 1 (Spring 1949).

[4] Geraert, *La Mélopée antique*, Gand, 1895, Thème 6.

[5] If the study, contrivance, and ingenuity of these compositions, to fill the harmony, carry on fuges, and intersperse discords, may pass in the account of skill, no other sort whatsoever may pretend so more'. *Memoirs of Musick*, 1728 (see *Roger North on Music*, ed. Wilson, p. 340).

[6] See list in the author's article on 'The In Nomine and the birth of Instrumental Style', *Music and Letters*, January, 1936. The riddle of the *In Nomine* and its origin has been largely solved by recent research; cf. R. Thurston Dart and R. Donington in *Music and Letters*, Vol. XXX, No. 2 (April, 1949) (authors' note:1951).

existence in our libraries; of these about 100 are of the sixteenth century. The composers of the sixteenth century turned to the In Nomine with an exalted intensity which can really only be understood if we imagine what panic the Anglican Reform must have caused among the composers of polyphonic Church music.

The In Nomines are not only historically the first harvest of the new art of chamber music, but they also exhibit items of striking musical value from the very beginning.

From the purely historical point of view the importance of the In Nomines goes far beyond the academic interest which it shares with other 'first-borns' of the history of music such as the dry experiment, Peri's 'Euridice', which was the first real opera, or the primitive attempt on the harpsichord by the obscure Dutch composer Sybrandus van Noordt which he called 'Sonata for Cimbalo Solo' – the first piano sonata in history.[1] These are single compositions, but the In Nomine was a cult, a fashion. It became the field in which an instrumental style was first developed. Freed from the vocal past, the independence of instrumental playing was established here, and the vast possibilities of a chamber-music style were first recognised in the In Nomines written by the composers of the sixteenth century.

Certainly in the oldest In Nomines the original vocal character of sixteenth-century polyphony is still very obvious. In the In Nomines by Taverner (1495–1545) and Tallis (1505–1585) we find hardly any difference from other instrumental cantus firmus motets of the time. The cantus firmus is always strictly kept; its individual notes are all of the same duration: long notes, ranging from longæ ($\wp$) to semibreves ($\mathbf{O}$).[2] The In Nomine cantus firmus is usually in one of the middle parts: only towards the end of the sixteenth century do all parts of the score become possible candidates for the honour of playing the most outstanding – yet most slow-moving – part. The sectional development of successive themes is the same as in the vocal motets, although without relation to any verbal sentences. The single parts are vocal in

[1] Printed in 1690 in Amsterdam; copies in the British Museum and the Bibliothèque Nationale, Paris. See also my essay on 'Die Vorherrschaft der Instrumentalmusik im niederländischen Barock', *Tijdskrift van de Vereeniging voor Nederlandsche Muziekgeschiedenes*, The Hague, 1938–9.

[2] This is a feature common to all In Nomines up to the end of the seventeenth century. With a few exceptions composers resist the temptation to drag the In Nomine cantus firmus into the magic polyphonic movement of the other parts; then the medieval rigidity of the equal note values melts into softer ornamental counterpoint.

character: any choir could have sung these pieces had they had texts. The melodies of the contrapuntal parts flow softly in a neutral and continuous stream:

Taverner, In Nomine[1]

But after Taverner and Tallis the In Nomines give a different impression. In the hands of the composers during the third quarter of the 16th century, Robert Parsons (d. 1569), Christopher Tye[2] (d. 1572), Robert White (1530–1574), Osbert Parsley (1511–1585), Nicholas Strogers (d. about 1585) and Alfonso Ferrabosco, sen. (1543–1588),[3] the In Nomine underwent a decisive change. The *style* had begun to take on a more instrumental character.

Nevertheless, that much of this textless ensemble music was commonly performed by groups of voices and instruments or by voices alone as well as by instruments only, until towards the end of the century and even after, is demonstrated by Warwick A. Edwards in 'The Performance of Ensemble Music in Elizabethan England'[4] where he brings forward a quantity of evidence to prove his point. Among many examples he quotes the title-page of Brit. Mus. MS. Add. 31390 which, though dated 1578, may have been written out as early as 1567 or 1568: 'A booke of In nomines & other solfainge songes of v: vj: vij: and viij: parts for voyces or Instruments.' Except for some later additions at the end of the MS. all are without texts. He adds: 'It is difficult to imagine how one can sol-fa on an instrument.' Textless 'sol-faing' songs' are also found in Brit. Mus. MSS. Add. 22597 and Add. 32377, both written in the 1580s: The practice of using the voice without words is confirmed by Thomas Morley in *A Plaine and Easie Introduction to Practicall Musicke*, printed in 1597, where on p. 179 the following passage appears: '. . . I say that all musicke for voices

[1] Add. 31390.
[2] 21 In Nomines in 4 to 6 parts are printed in Christopher Tye, *The Instrumental Music*, edited by Robert Weidner, in *Recent Researches in the Music of the Renaissance*, Vol. II (Newhaven, Con., 1967), and 3 In Nomines for lute and 4 for viols in Robert White, *The Instrumental Music*, edited by Irwin Spector, *Recent Researches in Renaissance Music*, Vol. XII (Madison, 1971).
[3] Fantasy for five viols on the 'In Nomine' theme, scored by Arnold Dolmetsch, and edited by Nathalie Dolmetsch (London, 1951).
[4] 'The Performance of Ensemble Music in Elizabethan England', published in *The Proceedings of the Royal Musical Association*, vol. 97 (1970–71), pp. 113–23.

(for onlie of that kinde have we hitherto spoken) is made either for a dittie or without a dittie.' Even as late as 1607, in *Captain Humes Poeticall Musicke* a piece called 'Sir Christopher Hattons Choice' or 'The fashion of Musicke' has a treble part in staff notation without words and carrying the instruction, 'This part is for the treble viole or the voice'.

The evidence collected by Warwick Edwards, seems to point clearly to the fact that, during most of the last quarter of the sixteenth century, music that could be performed vocally or by mixed groups of voices and instruments was in greater demand than that which could be performed by instruments only. An interesting point to which he calls attention in support of this conclusion, is the fact that the In Nomines by Tye which are most instrumental in character and contain features which, in spite of the direction 'for voyces or instruments', would make vocal performance impossible, are unique to Brit. Mus. Add. 31390, while only those which could be managed vocally were copied into later Elizabethan manuscripts.

The numerous examples that show that voices were commonly used in the performance of textless domestic music at this time may be due to the fact that, in contrast to the court, the theatre and the companies of waits, there is little evidence to confirm that complete sets of viols were in common use among amateurs. Certainly there were exceptional cases such as the group of five viol players shown in the memorial portrait of Sir Henry Unton, who died in 1596.[1] Yet no other painting of the period shows a similar domestic group, and no mention of the viol is made in any of the books which list the required subjects of study for a gentleman's education. The ability to play the virginal, the lute and other members of the plucked-stringed family seems to have been more common.

The new flexibility and more instrumental character which began to show itself may, however, have been due to composers directing their music towards professional players, together with the few amateur groups which possessed the necessary instruments. At the end of the century the situation changed and the art of viol playing began to assume far greater importance in domestic circles. From 1600 onwards music specifically for the viols assumed an immensely important part in the English musical scene.

[1] This portrait is in the National Portrait Gallery, London.

The viols are a family of instruments with 6 strings, pitched a fourth apart, except for the two middle strings which are separated by a third:[1]

Bass Viol   Tenor Viol   Treble Viol

They were played with a bow much softer and more curved than that of the violin family which was altogether different in style and appearance. In the viol family frets indicate the pitch of the notes on the finger-board. Still more important, the viols have a quality of sound which is fundamentally different from that of the modern violins and 'cellos. The sound is slightly nasal and rather soft but much more distinctive. While modern instruments respond to the utmost subjective expression (accentuation, vibrato and cantabile), the viols speak by themselves. Quite naturally so, since the music which is to be played needs an objective and somewhat neutral interpretation, compared with a violin concerto, say, by Tchaikovsky, which is nothing without the interpretation of the performer and his violin, with its extremes of emotion. In the art of the sixteenth century, the influence of the middle ages, when art was functioning in accordance with the much more static general outlook of things, is still very close. These viols offered, however, innumerable new possibilities for the introduction of extensive scales, quick figures, tone repetitions, jumps and slurs.

Several facts indicate that the In Nomine had finally left the Church in the second half of the sixteenth century. The main MS. which contains In Nomines[2] has a peculiar form of arrangement of the different parts which points to chamber music, not to Church music. The parts are written on each side of the open book so that a whole company of from 4 to 7 people sitting round the table on which the book was lying could play the piece simultaneously from one single volume. This may have been done in private houses as recreation, but surely not in a church:[3]

---

[1] For details about the viols see Gerald R. Hayes, *Musical Instruments and their Music* (1500–1750), London, 1930.

[2] Brit. Mus. MS. Add. 31390; date given as 1578, but could be as early as 1568.

[3] A similar arrangement of the parts is also found in the original printed edition of Dowland's 'Lachrimæ', London, 1605. See Edward Lowinsky, 'The Use of Scores by Sixteenth-Century Musicians', *Journal of the American Musicological Society*, Vol. 1 (1948), pp. 17–22.

ALTUS.   MEDIUS.

BASSUS.   CANTUS.

TENOR.   CONTRATENOR.

Some instrumental pieces are called 'In Nomine Pavin' and 'In Nomine Galliard', which again shows the process of secularisation to which the In Nomine was subjected. The In Nomine melody is also used as the thematic-harmonic backbone of Orlando Gibbons's merry Quodlibet, called 'The Cries of London'.

The music itself, especially some works by the most outstanding composer of In Nomines, Christopher Tye, shows most clearly this process of secularisation.

Tye may be called the first great English composer of chamber music. There are 19 In Nomines for 5, one for 4 and one for 6 parts known to be by him. Most of them have characteristic titles, such as 'Rachell weepinge', 'Weepe no more Rachell'.

The chief importance of these pieces lies in the change of the polyphonic structure which they all underwent. The melodic lines of the instruments – apart from the In Nomine cantus firmus which never altered – are no longer so extended. The phrases are no longer so indefinite. The motifs[1] are shortened and, at the same time, more characteristically shaped. We find here the first attempts at 'thematic work':[2]

[1] I am applying this term for the basic figures of a piece or a section of a piece, as far as they represent the thematic material on which the contrapuntal work is based – as against the Wagnerian meaning of the term 'Leitmotiv' which always associates musical themes with non-musical subjects, ideas or situations.

[2] From 'Weepe no more Rachell', In Nomine a 5 by Tye (Add. 31390).

We note, too, that the cadences are becoming more definite. The technique of 'overlapping' which veils the structure of the pieces and creates the impression of an 'eternal' melody still exists, but it is no longer so absolutely dominating as before. It happens occasionally in Tye's In Nomines that the sections are kept apart – the motif of a new section begins only *after* the cadence of the previous section has been heard distinctly. We further find the first signs of a tendency to unite the pieces in a-b-a formula by returning to the initial motifs towards the end of the piece; the motifs

reappear slightly modified (in normal position as well as reversed) in the last section of this piece. The full importance of this phenomenon will be discussed in a later chapter.

Instrumentalisation is developed to quite an astonishing degree in another of Tye's In Nomines, called 'Crye'.[1] This piece is based on a purely instrumental theme:

It must be said that themes like this are extremely rare at this time (c. 1560) anywhere in Europe. Tone repetitions as such are part of the technique in Jannequin's, the contemporary Frenchman's chansons; but the combination of such very fast tone repetitions with octave and fifth jumps is unique at that time. Yet even more astonishing, the whole piece consists of only two sections, each of which is a complete *fugato* development of considerable length such as was done 100 years later! Moreover the second section is a variation of the first in different rhythm:

The derivation of the second part from the first is quite in line with the habit of connecting up a pavana in common time and a galliarda in triple rhythm. We have already discussed this practice in sixteenth-century dance music. But it is difficult to account for

[1] Add. 31390.

the thematic and structural novelties in the piece. Themes like the one mentioned are surely much more likely to be encountered in a Scherzo by Bruckner than in a sixteenth-century In Nomine! Yet at a time when progress was so to speak in the air, when innumerable musicians were trying to find new ways and styles and possibilities, results were occasionally anticipated by some daring individuals which were generally arrived at only centuries later. The principle of independent instrumental music being once established, sometimes possibilities of instrumental technique were touched which, although they were the logical consequence of the instrumentalisation of music, could be generally acknowledged only a long time after the more elementary novelties had been absorbed. In France and Germany men like Jannequin or Regnart were free to break a good many rules of the 'good old times'. Approximately at the same time colleagues in Italy reached an even more advanced stage of the revolutionary spirit of conquest when anything within the reach of the composers was tried out; even the 'modulating passion' of the post-Wagner era was anticipated, as for instance in works by Gesualdo da Venosa. And did not Bacon in this country even speculate about quarter-tones and other experimental schemes?[1]

Some other composers of In Nomines are hardly less daring than Tye. Robert Parsons appears as an innovator (as well as a charming personality whose works have much more of the 'human touch' than those of his contemporaries). One In Nomine of his is of a particular warmth of sentiment which was rare at that time: the famous 'Parsons' In Nomine' (it is only one out of a whole series, but it was very famous in its time and was played all over the country for many years)[2] (Example 20, overleaf).

It has an especially fine conclusion, with its touching little descant figures above the compact harmony of the other instruments.

Parsons wrote six In Nomines, among them two for seven instruments.

All these In Nomines are harmonically in the old idiom. The

---

[1] 'We have Sound Houses where we practice and demonstrate all sounds, and their generation. We have Harmonies, which you have not, of Quarter sounds, and lesser slides of Sounds. Diverse Instruments of Musick, likewise to you unknown, some Sweeter than any you have, together with Bells and Rings that are Dainty and Sweet . . .' (*New Atlantis*, 1627, ed. Harold Osborne, London, 1937, pp. 39 ff.).

[2] Add. 31390; also in many other MSS. in the British Museum, and Oxford libraries. It also appears as 'A Dial-song' for 4 parts, composed by W. Syddael in imitation of Parsons' original, in Charles Butler's *Principles of Music*, London, 1636, p. 42.

Example 20: In Nomine a 5 by Robert Parsons.

Church modes are still dominant, especially Dorian and Mixolydian.

The In Nomines of the sixteenth century are generally on a very high average level of skill, contrapuntal ingenuity and variety of themes. There are many composers of In Nomines in the sixteenth century, of whom we know little more than their names. Here are some of them: Alcock, Allison, Baldwine, Bevin, Brewster, Buck, Cobold, Cocke, Eglestone, Edward Gibbons, Gibbs, Goldar, Hake, Johnson, Mericocke, Mudd, W. Munday, Nayler, Picforth, Poynt, Preston, Randall, Sadler, Stanner, Stoninge, Strogers, Thorne, Whitbrooke, White, Woodcocke, Woodson and Th. Work.

An In Nomine a 5 by Picforth deserves special mention. Here contrapuntal mannerism – a remnant of fifteenth- and sixteenth-century Netherlandish church music – goes far beyond the Pavin canons of Henry VIII and his fellow-composers. In this curious piece one part (the In Nomine cantus firmus) has only breves (breve symbol) throughout the piece: the second part has only equal dotted semibreves, the third simple semibreves, the fourth dotted minims, the fifth simple minims. These values are strictly kept in every one of the parts to the bitter end: an acrobatic polyphony is the outcome.

So in the In Nomine a genuine chamber-music style was established which derived straight from the Church service. Although the sixteenth-century In Nomine still shows many traces of the pre-Reformation cantus firmus motet its importance for the subsequent blossoming of chamber music simply cannot be overrated. With the exception of the structure of the tenor motet, there is nothing like the In Nomine in other countries or schools in Europe. It is a purely English form.

In the meantime a parallel process of instrumentalisation was going on within another kind of Church motet. Apart from the cantus firmus motet with its 'tenor', another polyphonic vocal form had come into being which may be called the 'free' motet. This species had the sectional arrangement of all motet compositions, but the Gregorian melodies which formed the melodic material of this kind of motet were dissolved into little segments and distributed among all the voices taking part in the performance.[1] Thus towards the middle of the sixteenth century all voices of this 'free' motet had their thematic material taken from one or other of the Gregorian melodies. The practice of imitation was practically the only method of achieving a polyphonic result. In this form the greatest triumphs of English polyphony were celebrated.

It is true that the free motet represents, on the one hand, a more rigid control of the composers, for the thematic material is now finally confined to the Gregorian melodies, while before all kinds of secular tunes could be used to make up the polyphonic texture. But on the other hand there is a strong new element of individualism and independence in the free motet. The cantus firmus in equal long notes had become a burden on the composition. The fifteenth- and sixteenth-century composer had to carry this heavy weight along as Sindbad carried the Old Man of the Sea. Now at last greater freedom in the polyphonic texture was made possible.

The musical profession itself had become more independent; it had developed in accordance with the increasing freedom of competition in the social and economic field. The more the musical profession was emancipated from the Church, the more freely could the composer treat the thematic material, even though he was not yet in a position to *invent* his motet melodies freely.

In a motet by Robert White (1530–1574), for instance, the melodic material is taken from a Gregorian melody in the Æolian mode.[2] This melody forms the fugal subject of the motet,[3] without a cantus firmus running through the whole piece.

[1] Certain signs that this process was going on can be noticed as far back as in the fifteenth century. Some motets by Dunstable show a greater degree of freedom in the treatment of the cantus firmus. See H. Davey, *History of English Music*, p. 36, and M. Bukofzer, *Geschichte des englischen Diskants*, Strassburg, 1936. The Old Hall and the Pepys MSS. (see above, p. 33, footnote 4) also contain some motets in which the cantus firmus has the same speed and is of the same strongly ornamental character as the other voices.

[2] Gevaert, *La Mélopée antique*, p. 235; characterised as belonging to the 'third type of Gregorian melodies' (thème 3):

[3] *Tudor Church Music*, V, pp. 48 ff.

Fugal imitation of this theme takes place in all parts of the score, and a conclusion in form of a cadence rounds off the first section as in the cantus firmus motet:

Example 21: from *Ad te levavi*, 6-part motet by R. White.

A new section is built up in a similar way; altogether there are eight sections in this motet.[1]

---

[1] Eight in part I; an independent second part with more sections begins with the text 'Miserere nostri'.

The distribution of the cantus firmus among the various parts and sections had begun to show a much rougher handling of the sacrosanct material of the Gregorian choral. The emancipation of an instrumental style advanced far more radically in this kind of motet than in the still rather ancient and scholastic cantus firmus motet. To watch the birth of another vital form of instrumental music out of this free motet is a fascinating study.

When, through the purely instrumental performance of a motet of this kind,[1] the motet was deprived of its immediate religious significance, the next step was to dispense with the holy melody as thematic material altogether. As all that instrumental playing sounded so new and independent and as no reminder of the sacred origin was retained in the playing, there was no more need to stick to the old melodies of the service.

The year 1570 saw a move away from plainsong cantus firmi towards secular substitutes, such as the celebrated 'Browning' (see p. 122) and 'synthetic' ones, such as the hexachord (*ut re me fa sol la*), the first six degrees of the major scale in ascending and descending order.

Many great composers such as Byrd,[2] Baldwine,[3] Ferrabosco, sen.,[4] Th. Woodson,[5] Robert Parsons,[6] later also Ferrabosco, junr.[7] Tomkins,[8] and others[9] wrote 'Ut-re-mi's'. This fashion is an important indication of the growing popularity of the major key which began gradually to replace the Church modes towards the end of the century in the work of the instrumental composers.

The next and last phase of the development is easily established. Real themes are invented, independently of any vocal origin – with the free *fantasia*. The final stage of the metamorphosis has been reached.

Fantasia, or fancy – this was the name given to many pieces which were to play such a vital part in the history of English music. Thomas Morley, one of the leading Elizabethan composers,

[1] There are many instances of this kind in Add. 31390, e.g., 'Dum transisset Sabatum', 'O Luna', 'Aspice, Domine', etc., by several composers.
[2] Add. 32377 (partly lost); by Parsons?
[3] One a 2 and one a 3 in King's Library RM. 24, d. 2.
[4] Ibid.
[5] Ibid.
[6] Add. 32377 (one part only).
[7] Oxford Christ Church; one Ut-re-mi and one La-sol-fa; by A. Ferrabosco sen.?
[8] Called 'In Nomine Ut-re-mi', Dublin, Marsh's Library, Z. 3. 4. 1–6.
[9] There is an anonymous piece called 'Re-la-re' in Add. 31390; more are in Royal College of Music, 2036 and in Add. 36484.

recognised its importance even at the time. In the instrumental fantasia he says 'may more art be showne than in any other musicke'.[1] Fantasia as a musical form has a history of its own – from one period to another, from country to country and even from instrument to instrument. The English fantasia for strings and/or other instruments has a specific quality of its own from the late sixteenth century to the time of Henry Purcell.

The name and the principle of the fantasia are certainly not of English origin. There are fantasias in continental publications such as those which are contained in Milan's *El Maestro* (Madrid, 1535), Giuliano Tiburtino's *Fantasie, et Recerchari a tre voci, accomodate da cantare et sonare per ogni instrumento*, Venice, 1549, and *Fantasie Recercari Contrapunti a tre voci di M. adriano & de altri Autori appropriati per Cantare & Sonare d'ogni sorte di Stromenti*, Venice, 1559.[2] Yet the continental influence did not go very far beyond the name and the basic formal structure. On the whole the English works are of English evolution. The earliest fantasia in England which I have been able to find is a piece called 'Fansy' by 'Mr Newman', contained in the famous Mulliner's Book[3] as an organ piece. There are other fantasias composed before 1600 for several instruments, for instance a fantasia a 3 and one a 6 by William Daman (d. 1593),[4] Thomas Wilson,[5] Alfonso Ferrabosco, sen.,[6] and the great William Byrd (1543–1623); students of Byrd's music may be referred to one of his earlier pieces, a fantasia for three strings[7] which exemplifies the earliest English chamber music at its best.

The fantasia a 3 by William Daman (d. 1593) must have enjoyed special popularity abroad, for it was given the honour of being printed in a continental collection.[8] It is more of an 'Ut-re-mi-fa-

---

[1] *A Plaine and Easie Introduction to Practical Musicke*, 1597, pp. 80 ff.

[2] See R. Eitner, *Bibliographie*.

[3] Add. 30513, written by Th. Mulliner, Master of St. Paul's Choir before the middle of the sixteenth century. Fantasias by early masters like Strogers (d. about 1585) and Wm. Munday (d. 1591) are also in the Fitzwilliam Virginal Book.

[4] The one a 3 is printed in the collection *Konincklyche Fantasien* (Amsterdam, 1648; now in Royal Library, Uppsala and Scheurleer Library, The Hague).

[5] Add. 36484.

[6] Add. 32377 (Cantus only). The subject of the first section of this fantasia:

occurs many times throughout the instrumental literature of the sixteenth, seventeenth and eighteenth centuries, up to Bach's famous E-major fugue (Wohltemperiertes Klavier, Vol. II). See also 'Et exultavit' by Taverner, quoted above, p. 81.

[7] Add. 34800. See *Collected Works* of W. Byrd, No. 17, Consort Music, ed. K. Elliott, 1971.

[8] In the already mentioned 20 *Konincklyche Fantasien*, Amsterdam, 1648.

sol-la', on the model used in the middle of the sixteenth century; the only progress compared with the older species being the introduction of much shorter note values, for the piece starts in breves and semibreves and works itself up to a lively second half with crotchets and quavers. A fantasia a 6 by the same composer[1] is less interesting.

Thomas Morley's only 5-part fantasia[2] (he wrote many in two parts) is kept in the traditional motet style. It is, however, unusually homophonic and bears certain traces of the influence of the vocal madrigal. This piece is not typical of the great master's instrumental compositions, which will be considered later on.

Thomas Whythorne (1528 – after 1590) wrote several instrumental fantasias which are contained in his *Duos or Songs for 2 voices* (London, 1590).[3] The purely instrumental pieces form the third part of this collection of duets. In the first part the composer leaves it to the performers to play the vocal items of his work on 'Instruments of Musicke that be of the like compasse or distance in sound', while those of the second part, also originally intended for voices, may be played on two treble cornets.

Technically these duos introduce a kind of practice which was very fashionable on the Continent during the sixteenth century. Such duets for voices or all kinds of instruments of equal pitch were a favourite form especially in Germany and Italy where they were called Bicinia. In all these pieces the two parts perform a concertant and fugal counterpoint. No difference appears to have been made between vocal and instrumental duos either in style or in form. In England the technique of the Bicinium was neglected until Whythorne and his far more important immediate successor Morley published their collections.[4]

Although Whythorne's compositions for two instruments have been condemned as very poor indeed by almost every scholar who has written about them,[5] they are interesting and important as one

---

[1] Oxford Christ Church, MSS. 979–83.

[2] Brit. Mus. Add. 37402–6.

[3] Copy in the British Museum.

[4] Whythorne himself refers to this fact in the preface to his publication (which, incidentally, was paid for by the author himself) where he says: 'Having understanding . . . that neither before nor since that I published in print Musick for 3, 4 & 5 voices, which is now almost 20 yeeres past ther hath not any of our nation published in print any Musick for 2 voices (as divers strangers in forrein countries have don heretofore).' See Thomas Whythorne, *Autobiography*, edited James Osborne (Oxford, 1961).

[5] P. Warlock, *Thomas Whythorne*, London, 1925; see also Ch. Burney, H. Davey and E. Walker in their books on the history of music.

of the earliest printed collections of instrumental music ever published in this country. They cannot be considered, however, as in any way essential or typical from the point of view of the development of chamber music in England, being weak copies of the continental masterpieces. True, they are contrapuntal compositions,[1] but they lack special characteristics, scale motifs up and down being the chief melodic feature.

It was the fantasia, even more than the vocal madrigal, which subsequently formed the main basis of the home-music which became so immensely popular towards the end of Elizabeth's reign. When the fantasia swept the homes of the new gentry and middle classes, the two historical sources of instrumental chamber music became equally visible: Church motet and dance tune.

[1] Whythorne calls them 'canons of 2 parts in one'.

CHAPTER IV

Church Motet and Dance Tune, the Parents of English Chamber Music

Such was the state of instrumental music at the beginning and during the first years of the Elizabethan age: a dualism in musical practice, resulting from a class division in cultural life – the growing power of a new class while the old one was still rather firmly entrenched. The early In Nomines and fantasias, both deriving from vocal Church forms and practices, contain the relics of the feudal age that formerly ruled supreme. Dance music, on the other hand, was derived from the tunes of the people and now progressed vigorously as the music of the rising merchant class.[1]

In spite of the considerable advance achieved in the struggle for greater independence of style in instrumental music, almost all the In Nomines and fantasias of the 16th century still showed important features of the vocal style of an earlier aristocratic society. Those which survived most obstinately were the long-drawn-out, motet-like melodic lines by which the neutral character of the Church motet was still maintained, and the device of 'overlapping' the sections, by which the formal structure of the whole was blurred. We have seen how even in William Byrd's piece clear-cut cadences were avoided by the technique of 'overlapping'. The 'eternal melody' of the Catholic age was still suggested.

At the same time dance music during Henry VIII's reign and part of Elizabeth's was chiefly practised in its genuine and pure form, as rhythmical music to which people really danced. The practice of dancing to regularly phrased yet tuneful melodies, continuing the age-old popular art of the minstrelsy, was thriving in the second half of the sixteenth century in England as much as anywhere.

During the last twenty years of that century the popularity of dance music broke all previous bounds. Practically the whole of Europe was held, as never before or since, in the spell of a rage for dancing. There, mankind was virtually racing through life in a whirl of gliding, stamping and hurrying rhythms. Innumerable editions of dance collections appearing year by year bear witness to

---

[1] Most composers of the time actually wrote *both* types of music, Church motets and dance tunes.

the consciousness of the newly-won freedom – too early, one is tempted to say, in view of the ordeals through which following generations had yet to pass.

Here is an example of such a 'dancing-dance' (time about 1570):

Example 22: Galliard for 5 instruments.[1]

In later Elizabethan England, dancing was cultivated with special gaiety, no doubt because the threat of the Counter-Reformation was more effectively checked over here than in other countries. With the defeat of the Armada the menace of a return of the dark ages seemed to have been finally removed. Dance music was even encouraged by some clergymen, such as Hugh Kinge who wrote a treatise in defence of music and dancing.[1]

Pictures as well as literary works of the time give evidence of the great popularity of dancing during the Elizabethan age. One recalls Sir Toby's exuberant variations on the theme:

'Wherefore are these things hid? Wherefore have these gifts a curtain before 'em? are they like to take dust, like Mistress Mall's picture? Why dost thou not go to church in a galliard, and come

[1] Brit. Mus. MS. Harley 2019 (date about 1575).

home in a coranto? My very walk should be a jig: I would not so much as make water but in a sink-a-pace. What dost thou mean? Is it a world to hide virtues in? I did think, by the excellent constitution of thy leg, it was formed under the star of a galliard.[1]

A particularly interesting category of dance tunes are those associated with the broadside ballad. According to William Webbe in his *Discourse of English Poetrie* (1586):

Neither is there anie tune or stroke which may be sung or plaide on instruments, which hath not some poetical dittie framed to the numbers thereof, some to Rogero, some to Trenchmore, to downe right Squire, to Galliardes, to Pavines, to Jygges, to Brawles, to all manner of tunes which everie Fidler knows better than myself.

The 'poetical ditties', to which Webbe refers were, on the one hand, the words of the black-letter broadside ballads which were printed in their hundreds and, though urban in origin, were carried to all parts of the country by ballad singers and pedlars; and, on the other hand, the sophisticated stanzas of the courtier, poet or dramatist such as Sir Edward Dyer, Sir Walter Raleigh and Christopher Marlowe, written to some of the same tunes. So familiar were these melodies that the music was seldom printed on the sheet, the name of the ballad being followed only by the title of the tune to which it was to be sung.

Scenes such as that described by Shakespeare in *The Winter's Tale*, where the pedlar Autolycus is selling ballads to the Clown and the two shepherdesses, Mopsa and Dorcas, at a sheep-shearing, must have been a common occurrence wherever crowds were gathered together. The enormous popularity of these ballads is demonstrated both by the great numbers of sheets that have come down to us, and by the repeated references that are made to them by characters in all stations of life throughout the dramatic literature of the age.

The tunes themselves had a similarly wide appeal and settings are found for virginals, lute, cittern, bandora, lyra viol; for viols and for mixed consorts. In the hands of the most famous composers 'Walsingham', 'Fortune my foe', 'Greensleeves', 'Rowland' or 'Lord Willoughby', 'The Spanish Pavan', 'Go from

---

[1] *Twelfth Night*, Act I, Scene III. This passage has been freely, though mostly incompletely, quoted (e.g. H. O. Anderton, *Early English Music*, 1920).

my window' and a host of others take on the form of a highly developed art in which the original melody serves as the strain upon which sets of elaborate divisions or variations were composed. Thus the same music was common property throughout the musical fraternity from the itinerant ballad singer to the court musician, although in performance the result must have been vastly different.

Gay melodies in popular style can be found among the galliards and almands of Anthony Holborne and John Dowland, two of the most famous composers of serious music:

Example 23: A. Holborne, *The Night Watch*.

Tunes such as "Mr. George Whitehead his Almand" by Dowland remind us of "Lucie Locket lost her pocket"—or even "Yankee Doodle":

These dances are completely homophonic, as may be seen in this typical galliard by Holborne (conclusion) (Example 24, opposite).

Dancing was inseparable from the people's life during the age of Elizabeth. Some sixteenth-century critics may have noticed 'a certain deformity and insolency of mind' among their fellow countrymen, dress, food and luxury in general may have been sumptuous; Italian extravagance and flamboyance may have been aped by the English; there may have been exaggeration, vehemence of action and licence of expression in pageantry and many stage plays; manners may have been naughty or the English

Example 24: from A. Holborne, Galliard for 5 instruments.

italianate 'a devil incarnate'[1] – the Elizabethan age was wonderfully and insolently alive. And hundreds of dance melodies still bear witness to this exuberant intensity of living.

The development of instrumental music so far discussed has been conceived as being based on the dualism of clerical and secular (middle-class) elements. During Elizabeth's reign this dualism gradually disappeared, and was succeeded by an astonishingly uniform and homogeneous musical life.

In particular, a new form of chamber music developed, to which all authoritative parts of the community contributed, and in which a singular *rapprochement* of styles was achieved. Fantasias and In Nomines were more and more secularised and influenced by the elements of dance music, and dance music itself was stylised, taking on many a feature of the complicated and contrapuntal fantasias and In Nomines. Dances and fantasias henceforth were only two aspects of one and the same musical era.

This amalgamation of two kinds of musical practice which had once seemed irreconcilable; this incorporation of the best elements of the art of the old age in the vigorous cultural drive of the new time, proved immensely beneficial to English chamber music. The resulting hybrid style gradually developed more and more in a secular direction, and the music became more typically instrumental and more independent.

In many spheres of musical practice the small man distrusts the so-called 'good music' which he has not the education to

[1] J. B. Black, The Reign of Elizabeth (1558–1603) in *The Oxford History of England*, Oxford, 1936, p. 237.

understand. At the same time sophisticated people regard the music of the masses as vulgar and over-simple, an atttitude that mostly springs from the upper-class standard of better and more complete musical education. In the middle ages up to the reigns of Henry VII and Henry VIII, the gap lay between clerical motets, the art of a feudal society, and the music of the popular minstrelsy.

Why did this gap close at the time of Elizabeth? How was it possible for an art that originated in the Church and another that arose out of popular activities to come together?

The answer is: because the Elizabethan age witnessed a remarkable unification of hitherto warring forces of society.

For one thing Elizabeth succeeded in rallying a large part of the population on the issue of resistance to foreign invasion and Spain's reactionary power.

National unity was further strengthened by the success of Elizabeth's policy on the constructive economic side, for example her patronage of commercial and colonial expansion and the encouragement which she gave to industrial development. Successes in these fields silenced the criticism and thwarted the opposition of the Catholics.

Furthermore the growing acceptance by the nation of the Anglican Church and the cultural *rapprochement* of town and country, described earlier, are clear indications of the unification of these leading cultural elements under Elizabeth's control.

It is true that there was within the state another 'opposition' class (apart from the Catholics). There were certain radical sections of the growing capitalist bourgeoisie whose creeds were expressed in the gradual spreading of Puritan doctrines. So with the defeat of Spain, the greatest enemy, and therefore England's entry on to the European stage of power, there came not only the height of national glory but also the young beginnings of a clash between state power and just this rising bourgeoisie (which could only end in revolution, since the state power was in form feudal and absolutist and therefore unsuitable to an expansionist bourgeoisie). However, Elizabeth's state power suited the bourgeoisie up to the great turning point of the Armada. The vital problems of foreign policy that confronted the country between 1558 and 1588 effected a temporary solidarity, and the struggle between absolutist-Anglican conservatism and Puritan ambitions was postponed.

The cultural life of the nation reflected its social and political unity. The cultural features of the different groups of Elizabethan society became assimilated to a high degree. Hence also the unity in the practice and production of chamber music.

But what was the position of the popular masses, especially the small peasants, manufacturing artisans, agricultural labourers, and shop-keepers? Did they cultivate an art of their own? If so, did they contribute to the development of chamber music which was from now on considered an accomplishment among 'Gentlemen and Merchants of good accompt'?[1] Or did a new split appear between official and popular cultural activities with the rise of the merchant monopolists to increasingly powerful positions in the country?

The answer to these questions reveals perhaps the most imposing feature of Elizabethan cultural life: an astonishing mutuality of influences between popular and official music.

It is true that the sixteenth century as a whole was a terrible one for many dispossessed peasants. But the free yeomanry played an important part in cultural life.

So it was a veritable two-way traffic reflecting the close bonds that existed between free yeoman and prosperous townsman in an age when the majority of the people of England still depended on the land.

On the one hand, then, the masses consumed the cultural fruits that came from the higher strata of society. On the other hand the new wave of musical activity in singing and playing in the second half of the sixteenth century proves most eloquently that the ordinary folk, especially the peasantry, were not only not incapable of creative thought, but a very important part of Elizabethan musical life. In turn the art of the higher regions of society was most strongly influenced by the vigour in the cultural activities of the common people, in their popular pageants, folk songs, and dances.

Aristocratic music lovers did not consider it at all beneath them to listen to or indulge in such activities, even though it may not have occurred often (as it did occur fifty years later) that a gentleman confessed: 'Even that vulgar and Tavern-Musick, which makes one man merry another mad, strikes in me a deep fit of devotion and a profound contemplation of the First Composer. [2] And a study of Elizabethan virginal music (e.g. the Fitzwilliam

---

[1] Introduction to *Musica Transalpina* by Nicholas Yonge, London, 1588.
[2] Sir Thomas Browne in his *Religio Medici*, 1642.

Virginal Book) reveals how very close the bonds between aristocratic or intellectual and popular music were. In Virginal music there are innumerable ballad tunes used by composers to build up sets of variations, dances and fantasias.

The influence of this popular music is most impressively documented in the general use of the popular idiom in the works of all composers, even the most intellectual and sophisticated, as the examples of Dowland and Holborne show.

So Elizabethan and early Jacobean chamber music, though it chiefly originated and was mainly practised in the circles of 'polite society', was not quite such an exclusive and aristocratic affair as is often imagined. If a man could afford any degree of luxury, musical instruments were among the first things he would acquire. Instrumental music, especially the smaller combinations, such as solos and duos, had a comparatively wide appeal among artisans, small producers, shopkeepers, and well-to-do yeomen, and continued to do so during the age of James I.

In the midst of all these activities stood Elizabeth's court. It combined, furthered, and co-ordinated all the productive forces which had been springing up in the cultural life of the country ever since the beginning of the Reformation. Musical life in particular profited from Elizabeth's broadmindedness in all matters of science and art. Apart from being personally fond of music, the Queen was a great organiser of musical activities in all quarters.[1] Her personal patronage of music and musicians is proverbial. This patronage did not indeed create the marvellous musical life of the end of the sixteenth century, but it assisted and advanced it enormously.

*

Among the old instrumental motets, fantasias as well as In Nomines, we find a tendency to take on more and more the elements of popular music – even dance music. The fantasias of Thomas Morley (1557–1603) provide the most lively instances of the secularisation of the instrumental motet. It is chiefly his two-part fantasias which we have to consider as representative of this process.

There are nine fantasias a 2 in *The First Booke of Canzonets* of 1595[2]

[1] See Hayes, *King's Music*, p. 55.

[2] *Nine Fantasias for Two Viols*, edited Edmund H. Fellowes (1928); *Neun Fantasien für zwei Viola da Gamba*, edited Nathalie Dolmetsch (1956), and a Facsimile edition of the whole volume, edited by John E. Uhler (1954).

and six in *A Plaine and Easie Introduction* of 1597.[1] Here an important advance has been made, not only beyond Whythorne's duos but also beyond the general style of the previous period. For the first time the 'overlapping' of the sections is, if not entirely given up, yet everywhere reduced in its veiling effect; after isolated attempts to the same end had been made by earlier composers such as Tye.[2] Each one of the small sections of the pieces expires on a clear cadence, before the next section starts:

Morley, 'La caccia' a 2 (1595).

Morley, 'La girandola' a 2 (1595).

The only trace of the earlier 'overlapping' here is that in most cases one of the two parts does not pause immediately after the final note of the cadence is reached, but holds the final note of its section while the other part introduces the new fugal theme, thus still bridging over the transition from one section to another.

Altogether Morley pays much more attention to cadences and clearly noticeable conclusions than any of his predecessors. In the *Plaine and Easie Introduction* he treats the problem of cadences in detail,[3] differentiating between 'middle closes', as 'commonle taken at the ende of the first part of a song', and 'finall closes', '. . . whereof such as bee suddaine closes belong properlie to light musicke, as Madrigals, Canzonetts, Pavins and Galliards, wherein a semibriefe will be enough to cadence upon, but if you list you may draw out your cadence or close to what length you will'. Other music is classified as 'grave music', including fantasias; here 'you

[1] *A Plain and Easy Introduction to Practical Music*, edited by R. Alec Harman (London, 1952). Facsimile edition (Farnborough, 1971).

[2] See above, p. 96.

[3] Pp. 132–144.

must in them come with more deliberation in bindings and long notes to the close'.

A similar tightening-up of the form appears in some works of Morley's contemporaries, such as Edward Blankes.[1] Here, too, the sections are differentiated from each other. Blankes' fantasia a 5, which seems to have been written before 1578,[2] thus being one of the earliest pieces of chamber music in England so called, is moderately vocal in outlook, being at the same time fairly homophonic rather in the way of certain contemporary madrigals. But in the middle of the piece, which is in common time, we find a short episode that is entirely homophonic and has 3/4 rhythm, clearly dividing two rather long sections:

Example 25: from fantasia a 5 by Edward Blankes.

An early In Nomine a 5 by William Byrd[3] has the last section in a coranto-like triple rhythm as against common time in the earlier sections (Example 26, opposite).

A similar arrangement of various rhythms can be found in the 5th duo of the *Plaine and Easie Introduction* by Morley.

Clarification of form seemed now to be the general aim of composers.

Thus a technique was being attacked that had been one of the chief characteristics of Church polyphony for centuries. It was largely by means of the technique of overlapping that musical art under declining feudalism was kept in such a state of complexity

[1] Add 31390, p. 31.

[2] See Catalogue of MS. Music in the Brit. Mus., Vol. III.

[3] Add. 31390, p. 44. Published in William Byrd, *Instrumental Works*, edited Kenneth Elliott. *Collected Works*, Vol. 17 (London, 1971).

Example 26: from In Nomine a 5 by William Byrd.

and turgidity, many highly ornamental voices winding around each other in slow-moving counterpoint. The psychological effects of this weaving of continuous close tissues of independent parts, impossible to disentangle from each other and from the whole, was one of neutrality and lack of definition (which does not mean that many of these pieces were not singularly beautiful and powerful).

The 'overlapping' had first appeared in some motets and other vocal forms of the thirteenth and fourteenth centuries. The Catholic Church, from that time, had to make a stand against Humanist and Renaissance tendencies in all spheres of spiritual life. These tendencies were always towards clarity of thought, enlightenment by education, and recognition of the rights of the individual. As against them, the Church cultivated mystical complexity in its art. The desire of the Church to keep in particular its music neutral and opaque became most noticeable in the choral works of the Netherlandish School towards 1500. Certain reforming tendencies can, it is true, be found again and again in this music, such as the use of secular melodies as cantus firmi in the motet (officially discouraged by the Catholic Church about the middle of the sixteenth century), and the elaboration of a more elegant and comprehensible melodic and formal structure, as for

instance established by Josquin des Près and his pupil Mouton
(but Josquin's intentions were counteracted by composers like
Gombert, De la Rue and others on the Continent, and by Taverner
in this country, also by Merbecke and Aston). Yet in spite of the fact
that such Renaissance tendencies even penetrated into the sacred
motet, the 'medieval' character of the motet was, on the whole
maintained throughout the sixteenth century. This was effected to
a high degree by avoiding cadences, in particular by the welding
together of the sections, i.e. by the 'overlapping':

The abolition of the overlapping of the sections in the motet
form represents an assault on the very stronghold of the music of
the old Church. After having developed forms of art of their own in
the dances of the first half of the sixteenth century, the young

bourgeoisie in England now took hold of the forms of the old age and transformed them while absorbing them completely.

Just as important as this process of growing clarity and transparency of the form is another interesting development, on the melodic side. Morley occasionally interrupts the continuous flow of the melody, cutting it up into little fragments:

Example 27: from a duo by Morley (1597).

We have already seen the beginnings of this technique in Robert Parsons' famous In Nomine a 5.[1] But Morley in his duo goes much further.

Morley's duos are on the whole far less monotonous in structure than those of his predecessors. Each melody consists of several more or less independent short sub-melodies. For instance in 'La Torello' (1595) the initial theme clearly consists of four little segments: a thematic lead (a), a cadence (b), a figure (c) corresponding to (a), and again a cadence (d):

Example 28: 'La Torello' a 2 by Morley (1595).

Compare this melodic structure with that of works of his forerunners, even of progressive composers like Parsons:

Parsons, In Nomine a 4[2]

[1] See above, p. 97.
[2] Oxford, Bodleian Library, MSS. D. 212–16.

Parsons, In Nomine a 4[1]

so the essence of Morley's advance in the spirit of the new age
becomes manifest. The whole atmosphere in Morley's duos is one
of greater freshness and popular simplicity:

Example 29: Morley, Duo III (1597)[2]

Eight instrumental versions of 3-part canzonets by Morley (1593)[3]
as well as several more pieces a 3 and 4 from the *Plaine and Easie
Introduction* (among them nine movements similar to Fantasias on a
vocal tenor to the words 'Christes crosse be my speed') are even
more lucid and popular. Some elements of the form of

---

[1] Ibid.

[2] *Plaine and Easie Introduction*, pp. 60–61.

[3] Add. 34800. The MS also contains 6 fantasies a 3 by Blankes, similar to Morley's but
without the freshness of the greater master. They bear more traces of Church music.

contemporary popular songs have been taken over, for instance the repetition of the last part of a piece.

Finally the treble melody becomes more important, being worked out more elaborately and strikingly than the other parts of the score. This happens even in Morley's polyphonic pieces:

Yet Thomas Morley's work itself was only a beginning.

Some composers before and about 1600 gave the fantasia form a further secular meaning by connecting it up with amusing non-musical subjects, sometimes even going so far as to play about with it in the form of programme music. John Baldwyne (d. after 1615), author of In Nomines and fantasias a 2 and 3 in Morley's style, wrote a fantasia based on the 'Coockow's' motif.[1] Munday wrote a fantasia which mixes contrapuntal elements with programmatic passages representing 'Faire Wether', 'Thunder' and 'Lightning',[2] Certain programmatic ideas also appear in Morley's duos, for instance in 'La Caccia' where a little motif is 'chased' over the whole scale in unusually long sequences;[3] similar instances can be found in some pieces by Tobias Hume (shortly after 1600).

*

How on the other hand popular dance music began to change into something much more artistic and stylised is most impressively shown in the works of Anthony Holborne (d. 1602). Much of the elaborate style of the In Nomines and fantasias has been incorporated in these pieces which were once famous on the Continent as well as in England.

Holborne published a collection *Pavans, Galliards, Almains and other short Æirs for five Instruments* (1599) which contains 65 items.[4] Throughout the collection a galliard follows a pavan, except in the last part which contains almains, rounds and gavots. Most of the pieces have literary, religious or fanciful names, such as 'The Tears

[1] Brit. Mus., Roy. MS. RM. 24, d. 2.
[2] *Fitzwilliam Virginal Book.*, Vol. I, No. III.
[3] From the Canzonets, 1595.
[4] Examples from Holborne's *Pavanas, Galliards, Almaynes, Corantes*, London, 1599, in Brit. Mus. h. 267 (printed music in photocopy), and P. Warlock's publication of dances by Dowland, London, 1926.

of the Muses', 'Paradizo', 'Infernum', 'The Image of Melancholy', 'Mens Innovata', etc.

Holborne's dances are strongly influenced by the style of the abstract fantasias of the day. There is nothing vulgar or strikingly obvious in them; they are lyrical, long-drawn and always highly civilised and elegant, avoiding literal sequences and too obvious analogies:

Example 30: from 'Amoretta' a 5 by Holborne.

The structure of the melodies is similar to that of Morley's themes with the natural differences necessitated by the form of the pavan; (the pavana consisting of several 'strains' each of which finishes on a full stop at a double-bar). There is first a 'thematic lead' (*a*), then a series of sequences which, however, are never mechanical and literal (*b*), and finally a long cadence (*c*):

Example 31: from 'Patiencia' a 5 by Holborne.

Sometimes the distinguished character of the melodies in Holborne's stylised dances appears most beautifully in a kind of melodic structure in which a thematic lead is repeated several times, again not literally but in extensions and rhythmical variations:

Example 32: from Pavan 41 a 5 by Holborne.

Here the originally neutral character of the thematic lead is enlivened through the insistent phrase repetitions. The melodic ups and downs are very carefully balanced; climaxes are reached slowly, to avoid either too dramatic or too obvious effects.

Even more intimately influenced by the technique of the *fantasias* is the *counterpoint* in Holborne's dances. All parts of the score are independent, making up a moderately polyphonic counterpoint, as opposed to the homophonic character of the pure 'dancing-dances' before mentioned.[1] Imitations are often used to create polyphony; they are mostly based on scale motifs:

---

[1] See above, p. 106. The German theorist Michael Praetorius expressed his surprise that there were left in England pavans to which people still danced. At that time the complete stylisation of pavans was already an accepted fact on the Continent. See Michael Praetorius, *Syntagma Musicum*, III, 1619, p. 24.

Polyphony in the dances is, however, not as dense as in the fantasias of the time, for the parts nearly always play on without breaks in their melodic lines, so that there is not as much scope as in the fantasias for imitations at entry and re-entry.[1]

Between 1580 and 1600 there was one particular vogue which illustrates very well the birth of the new style of secular music out of the unification of popular elements and aristocratic art. This was the sudden popularity of the "Browning," an instrumental form containing sets of variations on a certain folk tune. This song[2] is based on a simple rhythmical and melodic scheme.

Example 33: The Leaves be greene.

Composers produced complicated and artistic variations on this tune, weaving contrapuntal nets in all instrumental parts, including very lively passages and all kinds of polyphonic tricks. Among the composers of Brownings were John Baldwyne,[3] Elway Bevin,[4] William Byrd,[5] Henry Stoninge[6] and Clement Woodcocke.[7] Those by Byrd and Woodcocke are particularly fine and elaborate specimens of early chamber music.[8]

Baldwyne also wrote a set of variations which he called 'fantasia upon a ground',[9] thus opening for the viols the long series of grounds that were popular during the seventeenth century as music for bass viol. The technique of writing divisions over an *ostinato* bass was, however, in use before Baldwyne's time. By the

[1] An anonymous piece called 'Frayse Galliard' (Add. 31390. fol. 115b–116) is not really an instrumental composition but a transcription of a chanson by Clemens non Papa called 'Frais et Gaillard'.

[2] See Chappell, pp. 154 ff.

[3] a 3 (1600); Royal MSS. RM. 24 d. 2.

[4] a 3; ibid.

[5] a 5; Add. 31390; re-edited by Sir R. R. Terry, 1923.

[6] a 5; ibid.

[7] a 5; Oxford, Christ Church MSS. 984–8

[8] An admirable description of Byrd's Browning is found in E. H. Fellowes's biography of Byrd, 1936, p. 196. It is published in William Byrd, *Instrumental Works*, edited by Kenneth Elliott, *Collected Works*, Vol. 17 (London, 1971).

[9] Roy. MSS. RM. 24 d. 2.

third decade of the sixteenth century stock basses such as the *passamezzo antico* and *folía* had begun to make a fairly frequent appearance, particularly in lute music, in Italy, Spain and Germany.

*

So much for the *rapprochement* of styles and forms in chamber music towards 1600. This combination of styles characterises the work of the whole generation of composers between 1580 and 1615. There remains the other problem: how to explain the amazing intensification · of activity, particularly in the practice and composition of chamber music, and at the same time to account for the high general level of artistic value and the profundity of feeling that gave the musical life of Elizabeth's time and her successor's the character of a 'golden age'.[1]

One of the most conspicuous features of the time was that the general economic standards of the country were advancing. With rising prices and expanding markets commercial enterprise, large new manufacturing houses and commercial centres developed quickly. The East India Company established regular connections between England and the Orient. Virginia and other colonies were planted which gave England access to the riches of the new world. Wealth accumulated especially among the merchants and landed gentry who in due course laid the foundations of a new nobility. It became more and more essential for the citizen of the realm to form his life in accordance with the recently established ideal of the 'complete gentleman' as we know it from Henry Peacham's revealing description of a slightly later date.[2]

For a considerable number of citizens among well-to-do classes there was plenty of opportunity for repose, and inclination to enjoy it, and with the consolidation of economic welfare came increased demand for valuable musical instruments as items of elegance – a fact that itself strongly favoured the further extension of musical life. From the last decade of the sixteenth century onwards we find an increasing number of printed publications of music both vocal and instrumental.[3]

[1] A summary of recent research into the origin of sixteenth-century chord sequences can be found in John Caldwell, *English Keyboard Music before the Nineteenth Century* (Oxford, 1973).

[2] *The Compleat Gentleman*, London, 1622.

[3] A list of publications appears in Davey's *History of English Music*, pp. 157–159 and 168–169. We know of 2 publications of secular music before 1587 as against 88 from 1587–1630 (E. Walker, *History of English Music*, p. 56).

The co-operation of the new and musically educated general public in the development of musical life must have been astonishing, especially in London. Under the direct sponsorship of Elizabeth herself the influence of her Court and the vigour of its musical life greatly assisted this development. There was always a chapel at the Court that included the greatest musicians of the time, composers, singers, players, choir masters and teachers.[1] The houses of aristocrats and wealthy citizens such as Sir Christopher Hatton, Sir Robert Cecil, Sir Robert Sydney, Nicholas Yonge and many others closely imitated the musical life of the Court.[2] The musical activities of less prominent private individuals were in turn influenced by the stratum of society immediately above them; and so on down the social scale. The influence of fashion assisted the general blossoming of musical life in no small way; for by a process of conscious and unconscious emulation the musical aspirations of the aristocracy, the rich and educated bourgeoisie and the intelligentsia were transmitted to other social circles.

> Whenever anyone entered the house of a friend or a shop where he was compelled to wait instruments stood ready or hung on the walls to shorten his time of waiting.[3]

Henry Peacham desired of the complete gentleman:

> no more . . . than to sing your part sure and at the first sight; withal to play the same upon your viol or the exercise of the lute, privately to yourself.[4]

The growing popularity of instrumental and other secular music was occasionally regretted by certain men who were unable to

---

[1] Some of the great musicians who were employed at Elizabeth's court were: Byrd, Ferrabosco sen., Tallis, Weelkes, Parsons. Some were at the great churches; for instance, Morley and Cranford were employed as organists at St Paul's.

[2] Some very well-known musicians were in the service of private individuals, such as John Bartlett who mentions in his *Book of Airs* (1606) that he was in the employment of 'his singular good lord and maister, Sir Edward Seymour'. Michael East was in the service of Lady Hatton. See J. Pulver, *Biographical Dictionary*. Some noblemen were themselves active composers, such as Sir William Keith (d. 1581). He was one of the guardians of Mary, Queen of Scotland, during her minority; he retired into private life about 1570. He was reputed to be the wealthiest man in Scotland. A pavan a 5 by him is in Brit. Mus. Add. 36484 (bass part only). See also Hayes, *King's Musick*.

[3] W. Nagel, *Gesch. der Engl. Musik*, p. 165. For further quotations, see J. A. Westrup, *Domestic Music under the Stuarts*, Mus. Ass. Proc. 1941–2; also Davey, p. 156, and Crowest, p. 179.

[4] *Compleat Gentleman*, 1622.

follow the trend of the age. John Cosyn complains in the dedication of his *Musicke of Six and Five Parts* (1585) that

> ... the abuse of Musike may be great when it is made an instrument to feed vaine delightes, or to nourish and entertaine superstitious devotion.[1]

But such criticisms were exceptions.

*

Yet behind this improvement in the standard of living and the code of elegance there must have been a unique forward drive in all spheres of Elizabethan life. It was this general social impetus that made the composers produce with such ardour and vigour. First of all, the age of Elizabeth was quite generally an intellectually active age. Elizabethan England was filled with a spirit of enquiry, lively in its visions and energetic in the pursuit of its Renaissance ideals. If the Elizabethan had time for contemplation and repose, he certainly hated spiritual sloth. 'Otium animæ vivæ sepultura' (Sloth is the tomb of the living mind) – this assertion of an Elizabethan[2] is typical of many of his contemporaries as far as spiritual interest and activity are concerned. In Elizabethan and early Jacobean England the battle of ideas was lively and intense, not only among its politicians but also among its 'metaphysicals', poets and musicians.

There was certainly no element of stagnation in the Elizabethan conception of social life; on the contrary, there was a most determined desire for social progress throughout the second half of the sixteenth century and even beyond 1600,[3] and the citizens were prepared for any amount of sacrifice in their will to overcome all obstacles and dangers on the road to the fulfilment of this desire.

The age of Elizabeth was resolutely intent on developing all the forces and potentialities that had appeared on the ruins of medieval society. And it did not indulge in vague yearning and

---

[1] The only existing copy of this work is in Brit. Mus., k.8.b.6.

[2] Lawrence Keymis, Raleigh's companion in the Guiana Expedition; see also J. B. Black, *The Reign of Elizabeth* (1558–1603) in *The Oxford History of England*, Oxford, 1936, p. 239.

[3] J. A. Westrup is quite correct in stating that the intensity of musical practice and production did not decrease but continued during the early years of James I's reign. See his excellent paper on 'Domestic Music under the Stuarts', *Musical Association Proceedings*, 1941–2, p. 19 ff.

frustrated brooding – there was a very material foundation for the optimism of the age.

If sixteenth-century England had not yet seen the feudal order of the past completely demolished, it had secured a firm basis for the new mercantile and industrial forces who had written the ideal of individual freedom and expansion on their banners. Enormous prospects had opened up in the country's internal as well as its external development. Its thinkers, philosophers and artists alike did not, it is true, exclusively write and sing of the great *material* achievements of their society: of the flourishing cities, the pompous country manors, the glories of battle on land and at sea. But they were imbued with the same spirit of activity and optimism as the builders of the new realm themselves.

'The outgoings of the spirit are conditioned by its intakings, and the imaginative reaching of the man of letters [and art!] keeps pace with the widening horizon of his experience.'[1] And their music, too, reflects in vivid colours and patterns of sound the emotional richness of the age.

So there was unusually high quality and depth of feeling, beside great impetus and strength in Elizabethan and early Jacobean culture. The citizens were men of this world and of their day – passionately fond of their own time, and fully awake to the glorious possibilities of the future. The poets and artists were no exception, even though Elizabethan art and literature were capable not only of glorifying their heroes but also of expressing tenderness, and of exploring the profoundest depths of the human soul.

*

The emotional depth of the music has its counterpart in the 'musical philosophy' of the age.

Music during the time under discussion meant for the average citizen something very high and noble. The attitude of the Elizabethan musician and music lover, as already shown by Byrd, is expressed in innumerable sayings and writings of the time. The depth of musical feeling can be judged in many passages in Shakespeare:

> O but they say, the tongues of dying men
> Enforce attention like deep harmony:

[1] J. B. Black, *The Reign of Elizabeth*, p. 238.

Where words are scarce, they are seldom spent in vain;
For they breathe truth, that breake their words in pain.
He, that no more must say, is listen'd more
Than they, whom youth and ease have taught to glose;
More are men's ends mark'd, than their lives before:
The setting sun, and music at the close.

(Richard II)

Though the element of recreation and pleasure becomes more and more conspicuous in the dedications of publications in the second half of the sixteenth century, it was no superficial entertainment that the man of the Elizabethan age sought. Profound emotions resound in the works and thoughts of the century of the Reformation. Nobody found a clearer expression of the inner purpose of music during the age of Shakespeare than Thomas Morley, one of its best musical masters:

> Among so many brave and excellent qualities which have enriched that vertuous minde of yours, I know the same also to be much delighted with that of Musicke, which peraduenture no less then any of the rest hath beene to it as a ladder to the intelligence of higher things.[1]

The magical effect, the emotional power of the instrumental sound is expressed in many sonnets, several of which served the composers as favourite texts for the composition of madrigals. In them Orpheus and the supernatural power of his art are pictured again and again. Revelling in music, man might 'fall asleep or hearing die'.

At this time profound emotions are stirred by instrumental music:

> O softly singing lute,
> See with my tears thou time do keep.
> Yet softly, gentle strings,
> Agree with love that cannot sleep.
> (Madrigal from Pilkington's collection, 1624)

To his Lute

Thy pleasing notes be pleasing notes no more,
But Orphans wailing to the fainting ears;

---

[1] From dedication to *The First Book of Ballets*, 1595.

Each stroke a sigh, each sound draws forth a tear;
For which be silent as in woods before:

Or if that any hand to touch thee deign,
Like widow'd turtle still her loss complain.

(W. Drummond, 1616)

Slow, slow, fresh fount, keepe time with my salt teares;
Yet slower, yet, O faintly gentle springs:
List to the heavy part the musique beares,
   Woe weepes out her division, when she sings.
      Droope herbs, and flowres;
      Fall griefe in showres;
      Our beauties are not ours:
        O, I could still
  (Like melting snow upon some craggie hill),
     Drop, drop, drop, drop,
Since natures pride is, now, a wither'd daffodill.

(Ben Jonson, *Cynthia's Revels*, 1600)

For William Byrd good music is such a matter of importance that he wants it to be listened to again and again for it to be properly understood:

A song that is well and artificially made cannot be well perceived nor understood at the first hearing, but the oftner you shall hear it, the better cause of liking you will discover.[1]

In Ben Jonson's *Entertainment at Theobald's* of 1607 Genius, who had been struck dumb through his admiration of the Queen, cannot find suitable expression to tell his feelings. Rendered speechless by emotion he implores music to express his awe and homage.[2]

The musical artist at this time began to develop distinct signs of that excitability in his emotional life that later became – alas! – one of the permanent attributes of the professional musician. Shortly after 1600 Stephen Gosson speaks about 'musitians whose mindes are as variable as their arte'.[3] The musical profession, moreover, following the general development of professional life in the early

---

[1] *Psalms, Songs and Sonnets*, 1611, dedication.
[2] W. McClung Evans, *Ben Jonson and Elizabethan Music*, 1931, p. 6.
[3] *Playes Confuted in Five Actions*, see *The English Drama and Stage under the Tudor and Stuart Princes*, Roxburghe Library, 1869, p. 182.

stages of capitalism, became increasingly independent of Church and Court. 'Musician' as freelance, as private music teacher or even as composer was one of the new professions of the time about 1600. Richard Allison (d. after 1606), composer of *The Psalms of David in Meter*, 1599, an 'In Nomine',[1] and an amount of lute music';[2] calls himself 'gentleman practitioner' in the art of music;[3] he sold his music himself at his house 'in the Duke's place, near Aldgate'. John Farmer (d. about 1603), famous composer of madrigals, also of instrumental pieces, similarly calls himself an independent 'practitioner in the Art of Musique',[4] although he seems to have been in the employment of the Earl of Oxford as a music teacher for a short time.

This development of the profession, together with the new individualism in society, began to have a profound effect on the character of many musicians towards the end of the sixteenth century.

Naturally it would be going too far to characterise the musician of the seventeenth century as a neurotic of the twentieth century type. And yet at that time we hear, for the first time in the history of music, of strange, adventurous careers of musicians, of composers and instrumentalists who were highly strung and hot-blooded – as Dowland expressed it: 'aut furit aut lacrimat quem non fortuna beavit' (he who has been neglected by fortune either rages or weeps).

Some musicians even got into conflict more than once with the law. George Wither devotes a whole poem to these 'problem musicians'; a kind of poetical curtain-lecture:

For a Musician

What helps it those,
    Who skill in Song have found;
Well to compose
    (Of disagreeing notes)
By artfull choice
    A sweetly pleasing sound;
To fit their Voice,
    And their melodious throats?

---

[1] Oxford, Bodleian MSS. 212–16.
[2] Add. 31392.
[3] J. Pulver, *Dictionary*, p. 11.
[4] Ibid. p. 169.

What helps it them,
   That they this cunning know;
If most condemn
   The way in which they go?

What will he gain
   By touching well his Lute,
Who shall disdain
   A grave advise to hear?
What from the sounds,
   Of Organ, Fife or Lute,
To him redounds,
   Who doth not sin forbear?
A mean respect,
   By tuning strings, he hath,
Who doth neglect
   A rectified path.

Therefore, oh Lord,
   So tuned, let me be
Unto my word,
   And thy ten-stringed law,
That in each part
   I may thereto agree;
And feel my heart
   Inspire with loving awe:
He sings and plaies,
   The Songs which best thou lovest,
Who doth and sayes,
   The things which thou approvest.

Teach me the skill,
   Of him, whose Harp asswag'd
Those passions ill,
   Which oft afflicted Saul.
Teach me the strain
   Which calmeth minds enrag'd;
And which from vain
   Affections doth recall.
So, to the Quire,
   Where Angels musicke make,
I may aspire,
   When I this life forsake.

        George Wither, from 'Hallelujah' (1641)

Tobias Hume was one who led a strange life and spent his last fifteen years as a Poor Brother in the Charter House. Especially were the lives and activities of many masters either temporarily or permanently upset by the religious strife which began to destroy the peace of many people soon after 1600.

John Dowland (1563–1626) was among those whose lives were disturbed by religious difficulties. Whether or not it was the case, he believed his conversion to Catholicism prevented his securing a post at the court of Queen Elizabeth. On learning of the failure of his hopes he decided to travel abroad and led a somewhat restless life until, in Italy, an attempt was made to involve him in a popish plot to assassinate Queen Elizabeth. At this he took fright, fled from Italy and disclosed all details of the plot in a letter to Sir Robert Cecil. In 1598 he was appointed lutenist to Christian IV of Denmark, but was dismissed in 1606, probably on account of his having incurred heavy debts and overstaying his leave in England. On his appointment to James I in 1612 his restlessness seems to have been overcome and he remained in the King's Service until shortly before his death.[1]

Dowland has been described as in many respects an outsider in Elizabethan music. There are certain pessimistic tendencies in some of his compositions which are sometimes similar in outlook to those of Spenser, yet there is still enough that is typically Elizabethan in his work. 'Semper Dowland, semper dolens':[2] this is how Dowland himself names one of the pavanas of his most outstanding collection of instrumental works. This collection is entitled: '*Lachrimæ, or Seaven Teares*, figured in seven passionate Pavans'; it was published in 1604 and became so well-known that such poets as Middleton, Fletcher, Webster and Ben Jonson referred to it in their poetry.[3] Here is, indeed, a musical language of deep effects. In several respects Dowland's music is more developed than Holborne's. Apart from having more richly figured and more interesting and varied themes and counterpoint, the movement in general is more vivid. There are short, characteristic and expressive motifs like:

[1] Diana Poulton's *John Dowland* appeared in 1972 (Faber & Faber).

[2] 'Ever Dowland, ever doleful.'

[3] See also P. Warlock's edition, Oxford Univ. Press, 1926, with biographical Preface. There is also a pavan by Weelkes, the madrigalist, called 'Lachrimæ', obviously in admiration for Dowland. It is an expressive little piece, all in slow movements with long notes, yet rather more vocal in style. Brit. Mus. MS Add. 30480–84, also 30826–28 (fragments). Dowland's *Lachrimæ* is now published in facsimile (Boethius Press, 1974).

which are used to build up climaxes. Scale motifs are no longer important; other combinations of intervals prevail with figures which are often highly interesting. Melodies are still long-breathed, but not so smooth and abstract as in Holborne's pieces. Everything seems more personal and unusual. There are more dramatic moments brought about by sequences and repetitions of the above-mentioned expressive little phrases.

Example 34: from Semper Dowland, semper dolens: Pavan, by J. Dowland.

(a)

or long pedals, which appear, by their harmonic character particularly exciting, in view of the otherwise polyphonic style of the music:

(b)

The passionate rising and final relapsing of the bass line, together with the conclusion on the Dominant (D) which suggests a doubtful and anxious mood, make this piece, especially at the end, one of the most emotional of the whole period.

Dowland's 'Lachrimæ' are all built on the famous theme:[1]

There are only very few pieces in Holborne's collection which are on a similarly high level of emotionalism. A pavan by Holborne, called 'The Funeralls' flows on slowly in a sombre mood; all instruments move about in their lowest registers:

The bass has long and dismal breves:

[1] Even Orlando Gibbons pays homage to his great contemporary by quoting this motif in a fantasia a 5 (Oxford, Christ Church):

Only towards the end of this remarkable piece is there something like a mournfully sighing climax. In another obviously slow piece by Holborne, 'The Sighes', a galliard, the continual touching of the top-c, together with the slow upward movement of the melody, seems to express a programmatic idea:

Example 35: from *The Sighes*, galliard by A. Holborne.

The works of the great masters after 1600 show even more strikingly the character of the chamber music of the great age: intimate, elaborate, expressive, distinguished, delicate and, often passionate, yet neither vague nor morbid, but always active and of transparent beauty.

CHAPTER V

The Age of Plenty

We have watched the birth of instrumental music, with its new function in society and the rise of the new economic and social forces which made that birth possible. From the end of the sixteenth century instrumental music in England developed more and more on the lines and in the spirit of that particular practice which we are used to define as chamber music.

During the last years of Elizabeth's and nearly the whole of James I's reigns the production of chamber music – instrumental as well as vocal and instrumental combined – was a unique phenomenon in musical history. There was hardly any trace of an orchestral art such as was being created in contemporary Italy and Germany. Religious choral music, though still cultivated in this country on a magnificent scale was on the wane. Chamber music was decidedly the vogue, and that more purely instrumental than vocal. Even the vocal music was often in practice instrumental, for airs and madrigals written to verbal texts could be, and, indeed, were played on instruments just as often as they were sung.[1] It is true that more vocal music than instrumental was printed, but far more instrumental music than vocal survives in manuscript, and the sum total of instrumental music composed surpasses that of secular vocal music.

It was an age not only of instrumental music, but especially of instrumental group-music – a true chamber-music era. Of the instrumental pieces intended and composed for home consumption, music for groups of instruments is far more frequently found than music for virginal or lute or guitar alone. Music for lute and virginals, though still often heard at both Court and private performances, was only a comparatively small part of instrumental music as a whole. In spite of this fact, the public today tends wrongly to associate virginals rather than ensembles of viols with Elizabethan and Jacobean culture. It was not so much the

---

[1] Peacham actually asks of the 'complete gentleman' to be able to 'sing his part sure and at the first sight, withal to play the same upon the viol'. Very many vocal airs and madrigals are preserved as instrumental pieces. Gibbons' 'Silver Swan', for instance, can be found as an instrumental piece in dozens of collections. Again the reader is referred to titles like R. Allison's *An Howres Recreation in Musicke, apt for Instruments and Voyces* (1606).

soloist as the musical company in the private home that was the centre of interest in Elizabethan and early Jacobean England.

Private Musicke, as one important collection is called,[1] was indeed the art of the 'good family'. In 1599 Morley introduces the first edition of his *First Booke of Consort lessons*:

> ... newly set forth at the coast and charges of a Gentleman, for his private pleasure, and for divers others his frendes which delight in Musicke.

Two to six players, very rarely more, participated in such musical gatherings. The numerous contemporary pictures showing performances of chamber music all agree that participation was restricted to a few players. Nor was there an audience. In several dedications of printed collections of instrumental music it is emphasised that this art ought to be practised 'privately' by the players. The 'Clubs for Music Making'[2] are further proof of the particular character of English chamber music. Only a small number of selected listeners – if any at all – were supposed to be present at these performances.

The intimacy of the art is admired and referred to in contemporary poetry, e.g. in the Pilkington collection of 1605 addressed to the 'softly singing lute', the permanent companion especially of the young lover,

> Killing care, and griefe of heart.
>
> (Fletcher)

Contemporary poetry shows very clearly that during the Elizabethan and Jacobean age the individual always related the effect of music to his own intimate feelings; music was a private affair in its content as well as in its condition of practice.

So the country house of the gentry-nobility and the drawing-room of the average well-to-do citizen were the chief homes of musical activities.[3] Music at the courts of Elizabeth and James was music in the home of the monarch, the same in style and substance as in the home of the subject. Elizabeth was a keen instrumentalist

---

[1] Martin Pierson (Peerson), published 1620.

[2] Mentioned in P. Scholes's *Oxford Companion to Music*, London, New York and Toronto, 1939.

[3] See Warwick Edwards, 'The Walsingham Consort Books', *Music and Letters*, Vol. LV (April, 1974), pp. 209–214.

herself and liked to take part[1] or listen to, and be lost in, the 'concord of sweete sounde' provided by the great composers employed by her. There are not nearly as many examples of large gatherings of musicians for the purpose of pompous display under the Tudor kings as had been customary in the castles of medieval predecessors and still were in the homes of Spanish grandees. It is true that Elizabeth on certain occasions liked to show off before important guests at her palace with twelve trumpets, two kettle-drums, pipes and cornets which 'made the hall ring for half an hour together',[2] but the use of 'quiet' and elaborate music at her Court by far exceeded that of noisy drum and trumpet. James I maintained for a considerable time the practice of 'private music'; but in the course of his reign the 'Masks', and other ostentatious musical shows with their new conception of orchestra and public, came more to the fore.[3]

The development of the royal chapel from Henry VIII to the end of Elizabeth's reign is characterized by a reduction of brass and percussion and an increase of pure chamber music instruments. At Henry's court where there were already more lutes, viols and rebecks than at his father's, we count 4 lutenists, a virginalist, 3 rebeck players, 3 taborists, 1 harpist, 2 violists, a piper, 9 or 10 sackbut players, 4 percussionists and 16 trumpeters, the latter serving as 'waits' on occasions like big receptions, pageants and other functions. Edward VI's chapel in turn recruits further chamber-music instruments – another harpist, 6 violists, 2 flautists, 2 virginalists and 8 'players of interludes' as well as 2 'makers of instruments', while the taborist and 3 sackbutters are dismissed. Elizabeth adds a violist and dismisses another sackbutter, although she takes in a bagpiper for special purposes, and also 7 'musitions straungers' whose identity is not known. There were, of course, always singers and organists.[4] On the whole,

---

[1] According to John Playford (11th edition of *Preface to Skill of Music*, 1687) 'Queen Elizabeth herself was not only a lover of this divine science (music) but a good proficient therein', and she is said to have often 'recreated herself on an excellent instrument called the poliphant, not much unlike a lute, but strung with wire'.

[2] P. Hentzner, *A Journey into England in the Year 1598*, ed. 1757, p. 53.

[3] Brit. Mus. MS. Harl. 2034 contains a curious item of pre-Commonwealth court representative music, called 'The voluntary before the march', for drum solo, an array of very pompous rhythms, shakes and percussion-figures. Facsimile of the piece in Hayes's '*King's Musick*'. Hayes believes that the piece was used for regularisation in the army.

[4] Duncan and Crowest, *The Story of the Minstrelsy*, pp. 138 and 162. See also Hayes, *King's Music*, for music at the Court from Elizabeth to James.

it was safer to be a violist or other fiddler than a drummer or a trombone player.

1540 saw the arrival in England of six Italian viol players who came from Venice, Milan and Cremona, and who were taken into Royal Service as a complete entity. In 1555, the payments mention the use of *violons*, probably for the first time,[1] and by the middle 1560s they seem to have converted entirely to the newer instruments.[2] We know little about the use to which this band was put during the reign of Elizabeth, but the evidence suggests that they played dance music of the kind published by Anthony Holborne in 1599 where *violins* are mentioned as an option on the title page, and were heard at banquets, balls, masques and disguisings. For a very different type of music they are again given as an alternative to viols on the title page of John Dowland's *Lachrimæ or Seaven Teares* (1604). By 1605, the band, now expanded to nine, was being used regularly in court masques to provide dance music and, in this role, was occasionally increased, as in Ben Jonson's *Pleasure Reconciled to Virtue* (1618) to as many as 'twenty-five or thirty',[3] though the basic strength remained below 15 until the Civil War. Dance music possibly used in the court masques can be found printed in William Brade's *Neue Liebliche Branden* (Hamburg, 1617) and John Adson's *Courtly Masquing Ayres* (London, 1621). These show, as do several lists of instrumentalists from the 1630s,[4] and references by Mersenne[5] to the similar French band, that these groups always played in five parts: one violin, three violas (tuned in unison, but graded by size), and *bass violin* (tuned a tone below the modern 'cello). Double basses and continuo instruments were apparently not used at least until after the Restoration. The music they played for the masques, by such composers as Robert Johnson, Alfonso Ferrabosco jun., William Lawes and Simon Ives is all in dance form, sprightly in character, and with a strong polarisation between treble and bass. Those dances for the antimasque sections are characterised by very short contrasted sections, making a 'patchwork' structure, intended to convey the grotesque nature of the choreography. Those for the

[1] Henry Cart de Lafontaine, *The King's Musick* (London, 1909; repr. New York, 1973), p. 9.
[2] See *The Musical Antiquary* (London, 1909/10; repr. Farnborough, 1968), pp. 56 ff.
[3] See *A Book of Masques* (London, 1967), pp. 232–234.
[4] See, for instance, Lafontaine, op. cit., pp. 76–77.
[5] M. Mersenne: *L'Harmonie Universelle* (Paris, 1636; trans. R. E. Chapman, The Hague, 1957), pp. 244–248.

main dances are usually of an alman type, with two repeated sections, often with an extra triple time strain to follow.

Musical establishments of prominent people were private. Sir Henry Unton had a violin, a cittern, a flute, a lute, a pandora and a bass viol functioning at his marriage in 1580.[1] The inventory at Hengrave Hall, Suffolk, showed in 1602 and 1603 that the following instruments were in use (apart from a few waits' instruments like sackbuts, cornets and a serpent), 6 violins, 6 viols, 7 recorders, 4 lutes, 1 bandora, 1 mute cornet, 1 cittern, 3 oboes, 1 bassoon, 2 flutes, 2 virginals, 1 portable and 2 large organs.

All this shows the general character of the musical practice during the 'golden age' – music for the player rather than music for the listener. It must also be remembered that according to the acknowledged code it was 'good manners' to be able to perform upon as many instruments as possible. Numerous representatives of the nobility and gentry are known to have been able musicians.[2]

We may perhaps digress to ask why contemporary Italy developed its musical life in a direction so completely different from that of England. In Italy large orchestral groups competed in producing harmonic mass effects that were at the same time dazzling and exciting. Violins, trumpets and trombones carried the full chords of great 'sonatas' and 'canzonas' through the halls of palaces and churches. In Italy even chamber music itself was a medium through which composer and performer alike harangued their contemporaries, passionately expressing the storm that raged in the Italy of the conquering Counter-Reformation. During the fourteenth and fifteenth centuries rising merchant capitalism released intellectual forces hitherto unknown; it was carried by a revolutionary élan which in Italian spiritual and artistic life made itself felt down to the seventeenth century. The magnificent humanist-revolutionary Renaissance tradition in Italy as the artistic expression of the Italian burgherdom which despite economic and political defeats was still powerful in the sixteenth and seventeenth centuries, formed the basis for the great innovations in Italian music around 1600. Thus arose the 'stilo rappresentativo' and the intense melodic life in the 'Nuovo Musiche', the concreteness of expression, the dynamic contrasts and the passionate fervour permeated secular as well as sacred

---

[1] Galpin, p. 176, see also picture plate LIV.
[2] Examples mentioned by Westrup, *Domestic Music*.

music in Italy from madrigal to opera and to the new instrumental *canzoni* and *sonate*.

Simultaneously the people's music, carried along by popular movements that swept Italy again and again like rising waves, exercised a rejuvenating influence on the music of the great masters. That their works were lifted up to true greatness was due to the expressive and sensuous melodic life of popular *canzonetti*, *villanelli* dance movements from which they could draw. Opera no' less than instrumental music around 1600 relied on popular sources.

For certain reasons sacred music in Italy in the second half of the sixteenth century received a particular stimulus from Jesuitism.

The Catholic Church of the Counter-Reformation had developed a weapon in Jesuitism by which it strove to acquire new and immense material and spiritual power. Jesuitism was the most forceful expression and the most active factor in the changed policy of the Church of the Counter-Reformation which endeavoured to accommodate itself to capitalism and to exploit its enormous potentialities for the aims of the Catholic Church. Thus the Catholic Church, by supporting bourgeois interests, tried to regain its former position of universal power. The Catholic Church, especially from the time of the papal revival under Sixtus V (1585–1590) onwards, employed every means of violent expression to accentuate her aims. Music was to show the might of Papism in radiant colours. It was to attract men and at the same time bewilder them and startle them into submission – a procedure of which pieces like Giovanni Gabrieli's famous and almost expressionist 'O Christe' are vivid examples:

Example 36: from the Christmas Motet *O Jesu mi dulcissime*, for two choirs, Venice, 1615.

Jesuitism sought to use the highly-developed revolutionary art of Italian burgherdom for its aims – which did not prevent Italian philosophers, writers, artists and musicians from opening up paths of their own – going far beyond the aims and purposes of the Catholic Church or even countering it, as did Giordano Bruno, Campanella, Copernicus and Galilei.

Late Renaissance music, too, the truly 'modern' art of Monteverdi and other early seventeenth-century Italian composers, is marked by innovations of an almost prophetic nature, and, with its eloquence and persuasive power, constitutes a counterpart to English music (from which it certainly differs, on the other hand, in some important aspects).

In the music of Elizabethan and early Jacobean England the features which determined Italian music played a subordinate part.

The sonatas, canzonas and symphonias of the Gabrielis, Monteverdi and the others compare with English chamber music as paintings compare with drawings. Not the massive effect of deep and ardent colours, but rather the tender beauty of independent and delicately devised melodic lines, is the pride of early English chamber music. The current vogues in instrumental part-writing clearly show this pre-occupation with line as against mass colour effects.

Elizabethan and Jacobean music is not entirely uninfluenced by Italian elements of style; although it is not so much the instrumental fantasia as the vocal madrigal and the canzonet of the Morley and Weelkes type which show traces of Italian models (Gastoldi, Luzzaschi). But these influences and similarities appear small when compared with the vital differences of the two national styles as characterised above.

The name 'consort', meaning a consortium of several individual players, appeared for the first time in English music about the middle of the sixteenth century. The chief characteristic of the consort is that it is a combination of several instruments, each with its peculiar distinguishing quality of tone. Morley's *Consort Lessons* of 1599 were written for a combination of a treble lute, a pandora, a citterne, a bass viol, a flute and a treble viol;[1] four MS. part-books for treble viol, flute, cittern and bass viol, now known as the Walsingham Consort Books, still exist, in which the name Daniell Bachiler frequently occurs,[2] the four surviving Cambridge MSS.[3] for lute, recorder, cittern and bass viol contain a number of works, some of which are closely related to pieces which appear in Morley's *Consort Lessons*; in Anthony Holborne's *The Cittharn Schoole* (1597) 'six short Aers Neapolitan' for cittern and three unnamed instruments by his brother William are added; and in his *Pavans, Galliards, Almains, and other Short Aeirs* (1599) 'Viols, Violins, or other Musicall Winde Instruments' are specified. John Adson's *Courtly Masquing Ayres* for 5 and 6 parts are intended for violins, consort viols and/or cornets (1621), Philip Rosseter's *Lessons for Consort* (1609) count on the same instrumental combination as Morley's. Charles Butler explains the consort in his *Principles of Music* of 1636:

[1] See also above, p. 139, where Sir Henry Unton's consort is described.
[2] Warwick Edwards, 'The Walsingham Consort Books' in *Music and Letters*, Vol. LV, April, 1974, pp. 209–214.
[3] Ian Harwood, 'The Origins of the Cambridge Lute Manuscripts', *Lute Society Journal*, Vol. V, 1963, pp. 32–48.

The severall kinds of Instruments are commonly used severally by them selvs: as a Set of Viols, a Set of Waits, or the like: but sometimes, upon soom special occasion, many of bothe Sortes are moste sweetely joined in Consort.[1]

Butler's contemporary Walter Porter includes in his collection of airs and madrigals of 1632:

Toccatos, Sinfonias and Ritornellos, after the manner of Consort Musique. To be performed with the Harpsechord, Lutes, Theorbos, Base Violl, two Violins or two Viols.

The German composer and theorist Michael Praetorius gives a particularly picturesque description of the English consort. According to him:

several persons with all sorts of instruments, such as clavicymbal or large spinett, large lyra, double harp, lute, theorbo, bandora, penorcon, cittern, viol de gamba, a small descant fiddle, a traverse flute or recorder, sometimes also a quiet sackbut or racket, sound together in one company and society ever so quietly, tenderly and lovely, and agree with each other in a graceful symphony.[2]

Such groupings of a variety of instruments are known to have been much favoured in English chamber music. They became a definite practice some time about 1575. True, we know of many examples of performances of several instruments with heterogeneous sound qualities throughout the sixteenth century. Apart from the above-mentioned pageant at Westminster Hall in 1502,[3] there was a dinner-music for Henry VIII (1547), which had 'players on the flute, rebeck and virginalls, making the sweetest melody'.[4] Yet before 1575 such variety was mostly the casual result of gatherings of musicians; no particular combinations of instrumental sounds were demanded. One engaged whatever instrumentalists or singers happened to be available, without

[1] Butler, p. 94.
[2] *Syntagma Musicum*, III, p. 5 (1619): 'ein Consort ist Wenn etliche Personen mit allerley Instrumenten, als Clavicymbal oder Grossspinnet, gross-Lyra, Doppelharff, Lautten, Theorben, Bandorn, Penorcon, Zitterne, Viol de Gamba, einer kleinen Discant Geig, einer Querflöit oder Blockflöit, bissweilen auch einer stillen Posaun oder Racket zusammen in einer Compagny vnnd Gesellschaft gar still, sanfft und lieblich accordiren, vnnd in anmutiger Symphonia mit einander zusammen stimmen.'
[3] See above, p. 57.
[4] Galpin, p. 84.

prescribing the use of any particular ones. Often we find the vague indication that 'all sorts of instruments' may be used if those originally meant are not available, as for instance in works by Whythorne and Holborne. This 'ad libitum' permitted in instrumental combinations in Elizabethan days is valid also for works of English chamber music of later dates; recorders and viols in particular are known to have been freely substituted for one another down to the second half of the seventeenth century. But the essential principle was that a *variety* of instruments was to be employed. Only in the works by Morley, Rosseter and Dowland is preference given to a certain combination. Here we find, for the first time, something like real orchestration.

In all the combinations of instruments noted above, the fact strikes us that they all include instruments of equally moderate dynamic strength. Lutes, viols, recorders, cithers, pandoras, harps, dulcimers and clavichords all go perfectly well with each other. This is confirmed by Francis Bacon who gives his opinion on orchestration in one of the most famous passages in *Sylva Sylvarum* (1627):

> And so (likewise) in that Musick which we call Broken Musick or Consort Musick;[1] some Consorts of Instruments are sweeter than others; (A Thing not sufficiently yet observed): As the Irish Harp, and Base Viall agree well: The Recorder and Stringed Musick agree well: Organs and the Voice agree well, &c. But the Virginalls and the Lute; Or the Welsh Harp and the Irish Harp; Or the Voice and Pipes alone, agree not so well. But for the Melioration of Musick there is yet much left (in this Point of Exquisit Consorts) to try and enquire.[2]

A famous example of the attention which was sometimes paid to the balance of tone is found in the funeral music for James I, where though the numbers of players was considerable only lutenists and violists were employed (and one lone singer). We never find, say, trumpets and recorders playing together. There are a few instances in which several different instruments of equally *powerful* sound

[1] 'Broken Consort' or 'broken music' means just this combination of various instruments in gatherings of chamber music where the sound is 'broken' into various components. The name became more and more frequent during the seventeenth century when other forms of consort appeared, so that the original species of 'broken' consort had to be characterised as different from the others. It must be stressed, however, that the exact meaning of this term is still being discussed.

[2] *Sylva Sylvarum*, Century III, No. 278.

were made to perform together, such as the music in *Silenus* (1613) where the consort consisted of pipe, tabor, violin, 2 bass violins (celli), 2 sackbuts, 1 mandora and 1 tenor cornet.[1] Even in this combination of loud instruments the basic character of the consort is maintained, namely the differentiation of the parts from each other and the strongest possible independence of the individual melodic lines, effected by allocating them to instruments of very different sound qualities.[2] A similar combination appears in a picture of Henry VIII's time, given in Galpin's book; here a trumpet, a large harp, a bassoon, a pipe and a tabor are seen together.

[1] Galpin, p. 281; more examples ibid.

[2] Here are a few general remarks about the instruments in common use in England during the sixteenth and seventeenth centuries. In several cases the history reaches back into antiquity, but long, detailed studies would be inappropriate in this context. The *harp*. From the twelfth century onwards the harp shows a triangular shape consisting of the soundbox, down the centre of which the strings are attached; the neck with the 'harmonic curve', which holds the tuning pins; and a fore-pillar. In the middle ages the small harps then in use played an important part in the musical life of Europe. Though flourishing mainly in Celtic cultures during the sixteenth and seventeenth centuries, the wire-strung Irish harp and the gut-strung Welsh harp had many renowned players, some of whom, particularly those from Wales, became admired musicians at the Tudor and Stuart courts. Towards the end of the sixteenth century the need for diatonic tuning began to cause problems. The *arpa doppia* with a double row of strings, invented in Italy, was the first attempt to provide accidentals. Later, small hooks were placed beside the tuning pins and, subsequently, small metal plates which, moved by hand, could sharpen the strings. Later still, a system of pedals was invented whereby modulation could be achieved while playing still continued. The *lute*. A pear-shaped body consisting of a number of curved ribs; a thin soundboard with a carved rose; a neck on which movable gut frets are tied; and a turned-back peg-box with lateral pegs constituted an instrument which dominated the European musical scene for some 250 years. From the late fifteenth century till near the end of the sixteenth, the lute was strung with six gut courses. Of these the highest could be either single or double while all the rest were double. These were attached to a bridge fixed to the soundboard. The most commonly used sizes were as follows (all mentions of pitch in this note must be regarded as nominal): Treble: d to d″ or c to c″; Tenor: G to g′ or A to a′; Bass: C to c′ or D to d′. The term 'Treble lute' as used by Thomas Morley in his *Consort Lessons* is somewhat misleading since a Tenor lute in G is in fact needed. Although some early writers mention a seventh course, music involving this addition only began to appear during the last twenty years of the century. Indications for the use of a seventh, and subsequently for an eighth course can then frequently be seen. The limit of the number of courses used with the renaissance tuning was reached with ten, but on the baroque lute, they were eventually increased to fourteen. In some cases the lower diapasons were accommodated in a second peg-box prolonged above the neck. The terms archlute, theorbo lute, *arciliuto* or *liuto attiorbato* were used by different writers to differentiate among the various types of double-headed instruments. The *theorbo*, introduced into England by Inigo Jones in 1605, was essentially an instrument for thorough-bass accompaniment, although some solos were written for it. It was a double-headed lute in the tenor register, in the renaissance tuning (until the eighteenth century, when some players altered it to the D minor tuning), with thirteen or fourteen courses. Its distinguishing characteristic was the fact that the first course, or the first and second courses, were tuned an octave lower than those of the lute proper. The four-course guitar or *gittern*

was well known in England during the sixteenth century, though comparatively little written music has survived, possibly because it was often used in a popular or strumming fashion. In Spain it existed side by side with the six- or seven-course vihuela, a member of the same family dedicated to 'art' music. It had several different tunings, one, described by Juan Bermudo in *Declaracion de instrumentos musicales* (Osuna, 1555) was reached by removing the two outer courses of the vihuela, leaving, in the A to a' tuning d g b e'. In Miguel de Fuenllana's *Orphenica Lyra* (1554) music for a five-course instrument, with the top course only of the vihuela removed, appears for the first time. This type of instrument became known as the Spanish guitar. Eventually, in both its four- and five-course forms it displaced the vihuela in Spain and became one of the most popular instruments of the seventeenth century in other parts of Europe. When Francesco Corbetta, a famous Italian virtuoso of his time, took his place among the musicians at the court of Charles II the guitar became the rage in fashionable circles of the day. The *orpharion* was a flat-backed, wire-strung instrument in normal tenor lute tuning. Six or seven courses were normal during the sixteenth and early seventeenth centuries. It is mentioned as an alternative to the lute on the title pages of a number of song books of the time. In company with the lute, the number of diapasons continued to grow, and when they reached eleven or thirteen some were accommodated on a second head. In this form, in England, the orpharion appears to have acquired the name 'stump'. The *pandora* or *bandora* is a six- or seven-course instrument, the sound-box having a scalloped outline. The back is flat, and the neck is longer than that of the lute and accommodates more frets, which are of metal. The wire courses are double and the tuning is either C D G c e a or G' C D G c e a. It was invented by the London viol maker, John Rose, in 1562, and remained in use until the late seventeenth century. The *cittern* is a small flat-backed instrument with a shallow sound-box of pear-shaped outline. It has four main wire courses, usually of two strings each, although in some cases a third is added to the lower two and occasionally to the first. The strings pass from a peg-box, often sickle-shaped, over a raised bridge, and are attached at the lower end of the body, below the level of the soundboard. Though tunings varied, they were always re-entrant, with the fourth course higher in pitch than the third. This is shown, for example, in the tuning used by Morley in the *Consort Lessons*: b g d' e'. It enjoyed a considerable popularity and, though its music is more limited than that of the lute, some of the foremost composers of the time wrote, or adapted, music for it. In common with other plucked stringed instruments it acquired additional bass courses. Though generally played with a plectrum, some of the solo music requires the use of the fingers. The *psaltery* (*psalterium*) originated in the Near East, and was known in the West from the twelfth century onwards. Of trapezium shape, with wooden frame and soundboard, it has no neck. The two- or three-string courses are stretched over the soundboard from side to side. These are sounded with two quills, one in each hand. Although the psaltery was the ancestor of the virginal and harpsichord it continued in use throughout the time these instruments flourished. The *dulcimer* is of a similar type to the psaltery, but is sounded with two small hammers. Still known as the *cimbal* in Eastern Europe it remains an important folk instrument to the present day. The *cymbal*, mentioned by Butler (see below) belongs to this family. The *viols*, bowed instruments held on or between the knees, have already been dealt with (p. 94), the name *viola da gamba* being associated, in particular, with the bass of the family. The *lyra viol* is distinguished from the other viols only by the intervals of its tuning. With the development of the viol as a solo instrument, to be played without accompaniment, the execution of chords with a bow presented a problem since the constituent notes must lie on adjacent strings. A number of different tunings were invented in order to facilitate the placings of a maximum number of chords in such positions with manageable fingering for the left hand. A small bass or large tenor was generally used. It became the solo bowed instrument *par excellence* during the seventeenth century and may even have rivalled the popularity of the lute as the century advanced. The music was written in French lute tablature. The use of the *violin* in England has already been mentioned on p. 142. The *virginal*, sometimes called a 'pair of virginals', is a keyboard instrument of the harpsichord family, with a unit of mechanism called a 'jack' which

The fact that in the consort the parts were to be distinguishable from one another is in itself clear indication that the purpose of the artist was to draw delicate and elaborate lines with all the instrumental voices. Subjective emotionalism, and that later individualism of the eighteenth-century concert style, was as yet not so far developed in this art as to make the treble melody the carrier of the emotional message, and to reduce the other parts to the function of mere accompaniment or 'basso continuo'. It cannot be denied, however, that the treble melody was becoming more and more important in the whole harmonic structure of English music, even though Elizabethan and early Jacobean chamber music remains essentially polyphonic.

It must be emphasised that this differentiation of the parts was made possible only by the fact that each instrument in the consort

---

activates the strings with a plucking device. In sixteenth-century England, nomenclature was far from precise, but the instrument now known by this name is the simplest member of the family, with an oblong case and single manual.

Among the wind instruments that were in use at the time in question the *pipes* were still prominent. They were whistle-flutes with 3 holes; usually associated with the medieval tabor, the pipe was an open-air instrument of little relevance to chamber music, where its place as a high-pitched woodwind instrument was occupied by the descant recorder. For the state of the *organ*, during the seventeenth century more and more often accompanying string instruments, I have to refer the reader to Grove's list of books dealing specially with the history and varieties of this instrument. *Shalm* (shawm, schalmei, i.e. calamus-reed) is, like the old *oboe* (hautbois, hobois), a reed instrument with a conical bore and a curious shrill tone, slightly nasal but of extraordinary strength, much greater than the oboe. The shalm had a special appendix-like mouthpiece. There were complete families (sets) of bass, tenor, contralto and treble shalms, like the viol, violin and recorder families. The oboe usually occurred only in treble and rarely in tenor pitch. The *waits* or wait-pipes which were treated in the first chapter are of the shalm family and often identical with shalms. *Sackbut* (sagbut) is the forerunner of the modern trombone, usually played in a band with *cornets* and *trumpets*. *Flute* about 1600 had a twofold meaning. In many cases it meant the cone instrument which was cross-blown and held from the right to the lips (later usually called German flute or flauto traverso and flute traversière). But this flute proper was not nearly as much in use as the *recorders*, which were blown into from the top, had 6 to 7 holes, and formed a family of treble, alto, tenor and bass pitch. The sound of the recorders, too, is distinguished from the German flute, for the recorders have a very clear and 'u'-like sound quality which always reminds one of certain high organ registers. On some parts of the scale cross-fingering is needed to ensure an exact distinction between a tone and a semitone. The list of instruments, as just described, is taken from Charles Butler's *Principles of Musicke* (1636), which contains those in use at the time: 'harp, bandora, orpharion, cittern, gittern, cymbal, psaltery, dulcimer, viol, virginal, pipe, organ, shalm, sagbut, cornet, recorder, fluit, wait or hobois, and trumpet'. It is curious that this list does not include violins, which were increasing in popularity, or the lute. Though its hey-day in England was past it still played a far from inconsiderable part in musical life of the time. (For further information on all these instruments see Grove's *Dictionary of Music and Musicians*, Sixth Edition, 1978, where articles by leading experts will be found. Otherwise Butler's list seems fairly complete.)

had a clearly defined tone colour of its own.[1] Modern flutes, violins, pianofortes, clarinets, etc., react to any playing that is not 'made up' with expressivo, vibrato, rubato, cantabile, sforzato and all the other refinements, by uttering completely dead sounds. Only the subjective interpretation of the artist, coupled with the accentuation resulting from the different way of bowing, makes the sound of the modern instrument breathe and live with passion and colour. The old instruments, viols, recorders, virginals and lutes are of such strong instrumental personality in themselves that they sound best and most convincing when they are played in a restrained, quiet and objective way. Their beauty lies in their 'acoustic material', not in their capacity to reflect in a thousand details the psychology of the tortured individual in nineteenth- and twentieth-century society. Play an early seventeenth-century In Nomine à la César Franck and you will get a grotesque caricature, a hysterical mockery of the original.

In view of the essential nature of old English chamber music it is not difficult to understand why the violins played such a small part in its presentation. It took a complete change in the social outlook of the whole country to establish the popularity of the violin in the second half of the seventeenth century.

In all the consort music which we know the careful elaboration of the polyphonic lines is the most striking feature. But this artificiality is by no means based on intellectualism. The innovations which we noted in the Morley period; freshness and a new transparency of melody, and clarity of formal design, are everywhere noticeable in the music of the 'golden age' and are carried to a high stage of development.

The classical work of the period is Morley's *First Book of Consort Lessons* of 1599, a collection of works 'by divers exquisite Authors', to be performed by the six instrumental parts mentioned above. This precious work is partly lost; we know of the existence of most parts,[2] but even this torso gives us an idea of the simple melodic beauties of the work. Morley himself refers in his foreword to the predominance of the melodic element in the consort:

[1] See also Chapter III, p. 94, and Roger North, *Memoires*, p. 105.

[2] Brit. Mus.: flute part; Royal College: viol part. Burney attempted to add the other parts; the full score, with the other four parts composed by Burney in the style of the time, is contained in Brit. Mus. MS. Add. 11587. The bass part, too, has turned up in a Quaritch Catalogue (1935, No. 1051; the price of the bass viol part was then £425!), where reference is made to the existence of the pandora part in the Huntington Library, San Marino, California, which has also the flute part of 1611 (a reprint of the work appeared with

I recommend the same to your Seruants careful and skilfull handling, that the wants of exquisite harmony, apparent, being left unsupplied, for breuitie of Proportions, may be excused by their melodious addi(ti)ons, purposing hereafter to give them more testimonie of my Loue towards them. . . .

The other works for consort of the same period are equally rich in melodic beauties and harmonic charm. Holborne's *Cittharn School* (1597), which includes, among other movements, pieces for cittern, treble viol, tenor viol and bass viol; Rosseter's *Lessons for Consort*, 'made by Sundry Excellent Authors' (1609),[1] the manuscript Walsingham Consort Books,[2] and the Cambridge University Library Consort Books.[3] Richard Allison, in *The Psalmes of David in Meter* (1599),[4] gives the instruction that the psalms may be sung to 'the Lute, Orpharyon, Citterne or Base violl, severally or altogether', and in Sir William Leighton's *Teares or Lamentations of a Sorrowfull Soule* (1614) some of the songs are accompanied by the same group of instruments as those used in Thomas Morley's *Consort Lessons*. Tobias Hume's *Poeticall musicke* (1607),[5] though chiefly vocal, contains 16 instrumental items; and so on to Adson's *Courtly Masquing Ayres*, composed in five and six parts, for violins, consorts and cornets, which contains a number of charming pavans and galliards. In Tobias Hume's *Ayres* of 1605, where there are items for the 'Leero Viole with two treble viols, or two with the Treble', the harmonic element is slightly stronger, as the character and tuning of the lyra viols necessitate. R. Allison's *Psalter* for one voice with four viols, lute and cithern (1599) may be mentioned here too, although it is essentially a vocal work.

The parts of the consort are written as much in accordance with their peculiarities as instruments as possible. The lute part in Dowland's 'Lachrymae', for instance, supplies a chordal struc-

---

additions in 1611). The pandora part is in Oxford Christ Church, the cittern in Oxford Bodleian. The lute part is lost, but a MS. in Cambridge University Library contains the lute part of about a third of the work; it may serve as a guide to the whole. See edition by S. Beck, New York, 1959.

[1] Only two part-books have survived; cf. I. Harwood, 'Rosseter's Lessons for Consort', *The Lute Society Journal*, Vol. VII (1965), pp. 15–23.

[2] See Warwick Edwards, 'The Walsingham Consort Books', *Music and Letters*, Vol. LV (April, 1974), pp. 209–214.

[3] See Ian Harwood, 'The Origins of the Cambridge Lute Manuscripts', *The Lute Society Journal*, Vol. V (1963), pp. 32–48.

[4] Scolar Press Facsimile (1968), edited by Ian Harwood.

[5] Scolar Press Facsimile (1969), edited by Frank Traficante.

ture. At the same time we do not find in Dowland's lute parts, nor in other consorts of the time, parts for plucked instruments having long sustained notes, but long notes are always broken, by means of ornamentation. Dowland's lute part is a kind of short score of the other parts, yet adding decorative passages and rhythmicising certain bars.

The general elegance and distinction of the parts in the consorts are commended by the continental collector Besardus in his *Thesaurus Harmonicus* of 1603, where he speaks with obvious delight of 'those English consorts of a certain kind which are extremely sweet and elegant'.[1]

The careful elaboration of every single one of the parts of the instrumental score soon led to the establishment of an instrumental solo style. The 'stylo rappresentativo' in early seventeenth-century Italian instrumental music is also based on solo performance. But the essence of the Italian instrumental soli was, just as much as in orchestral music, the expressive and passionate gesture, while in English chamber music the instrumental solo was only the logical outcome of the whole style which treated all the individual melodic lines so elaborately. So combinations of lute and bass viol, bass lute with treble viol, bass viol and recorder, virginal and bass viol, and also lyra viol solos were familiar features of the music of the time. Lute with bass viol was an especially favourite combination. There are pieces for lute and bass viol in Pilkington's *Ayres* (1605), and Maynard's *XII Wonders of the World* (1611). A beautiful example is Dowland's *Adieu for Master Oliver Cromwell*.

On the other hand, although these pieces were melodically elaborate and richly figured, they were never clumsy or over intricate, even when written for the full consort of five or six parts. On the contrary, it must be emphasised again that clarity of structure was consciously and carefully preserved. Forms and melodies were made easy to scan and to comprehend; it is not difficult to see why; there might so easily have been a 'mess' of intricate parts which would have prevented the player from making any particular part heard – an overcrowded and incomprehensible polyphony. It is true that polyphony was the particular English way of building up musical forms for chamber combinations. But the jig-saw puzzles of fifteenth-century Church motets were not favoured in the Anglican England of 1600.

[1] 'Prout sunt illi Anglicani concentus suavissimi quidem, et elegantes', Cologne, 1603.

Rhythmical clarity, too, prevailed in these pieces. The use of the delicate polyphonic medium of the broken consort entails a natural risk of complexity. Therefore for the sake of simplicity the broken consort exploited to a large extent dance and similar forms, with their clear metrical and rhythmical schemes, and fantasias and In Nomines were left to other chamber combinations. The broken consort, small as well as larger ensembles, was given airs, pavanas, galliards, allemands, 'lessons' and variation forms. The 'lessons' in the works of Ferrabosco, Rosseter, Morley and others are pieces of easy rhythmical structure, originally presumably intended for educational purposes, with melodies easy to play, though not necessarily built in the way of existing dance types. Variations on themes already cultivated by composers of the end of the sixteenth century were more and more favoured, especially by viola da gamba and lyra viol players for whom were written many 'grounds' (simple subjects on the bass, either 4 or 8 bars in length) with 'variations' or 'divisions' (variations, 'dividing' the notes of the theme into broken chords, passages and other ornamental figures).

The viola da gamba became more and more the leading instrument after 1600, so that it occasionally trespassed upon the domain of the virginal, as in *Parthenia Inviolata*[1] of c. 1614; a collection of pieces for virginal solo in which the viola da gamba goes with the virginal bass all the time.

The last consequence of these tendencies was the evolution of solos for one melody instrument capable of producing double or treble stoppings without co-operation of lute or virginal. In Hume's *Ayres* of 1605 we find pieces 'for the Leero Viole to play alone'; there are 18 dances by Thomas Ford for lyra viol solo; there are some pieces for lyra viol alone in Corkine's *Ayrs* of 1612, and also Ferrabosco's *Lessons* contain items for one lyra viol.

English instrumental music in general was recognised to be paramount in many continental countries at the beginning of the seventeenth century, and English string playing in particular was very highly esteemed at this time. English music and musicians found their way to Germany, Denmark, Holland, France and also Italy. String music by William Brade, Thomas Simpson, Alfonso Ferrabosco, John Dowland, Thomas Morley, Peter Philips and many others was printed in continental collections such as

[1] Parthenia means virgin as well as 'virginal' ('belonging to a maiden'), inviolata means untouched as a virgin, as well as 'composed with viol'.

Matthysz's *T'uitnement Cabinet*, Amsterdam 1646, *Konincklyche Fantasien*, Amsterdam 1648, Füllsack-Hildebrand's *Ausserlesene Paduanen vnd Galliarden*, Hamburg 1607, David Oberndörffer's *Allegrezza musicale*, Frankfurt 1620, Thomas Simpson's *Taffel-Consort* and *Opusculum*, Hamburg 1621 and 1610, Brade's *Newe ausserlesene liebliche Branden*, Hamburg 1617, Schaeffer's *Amœnitatum musicalium hortulus*, Leipzig 1622, and others. English instrumentalists, especially string players, were particularly favoured in the bands and chapels of Northern German towns and Courts. The chapel of the Berlin electoral Court was transformed from a 'Kantoreigesellschaft' (choral company) into a chamber orchestra under the influence of English string players. The violist Price founded and directed a 'small chamber music' in Stuttgart between 1616 and 1630; the same musician continued this practice in Dresden after 1630. In the chapel of Düsseldorf-Neuberg where there were only three players permanently active, only once (in 1618) was a new musician engaged: an English violist and lutenist.[1]
Of the English musicians who went to Germany to be enthusiastically received and at once put into high and important positions some were political and religious refugees; for instance Simpson, Brade, Norcome, Valentine Flood, Rowe, John and Clement Dixon and Jack Jordan. At least three among those mentioned were really great composers; Thomas Simpson, William Brade and Peter Philips. Among those who went to other continental countries were Maynard, Dowland, Thomas Cutting, and Norcome, who went to Denmark and Belgium.

*

Besides the broken consort (that very genuine and characteristic form of English chamber music) and string solo playing, *combinations of instruments of the same family* were used in sixteenth- and seventeenth-century musical England. Such combinations were also called 'consorts' but only from the second quarter of the seventeenth century onwards. Naturally the independence and individuality of the parts of the ensemble was less strongly maintained than in the broken consort. But in view of the particularly tender and clear quality of tone of some families of English instruments, the delicate polyphonic character of the music was preserved or in certain combinations only slightly modified.

[1] Details in the author's *Die mehrstimmige Spielmusik*, 1934, p. 56.

Robinson's *Schoole of Musicke* (1603) contains 'toys' (as certain forms of light music were called) and a fantasia for two lutes. Duets are found in nearly all the manuscript lute books of the time. The already mentioned collection by Ferrabosco (1609) includes lessons for '1, 2, and 3 viols tuned lyraway'; so does Hume's work of 1605. There are many more works for three lyra viols. Butler talks of a 'consort of waits' as already mentioned.[1] In *Gorboduc*, a drama of early Elizabethan time,[2] there is a pantomime before each act; a consort of violins plays before the first act, cornets before the second, flutes before the third, hautboys (for the appearance of Furies) before the fourth, and drums and flutes before the fifth act.

In this kind of consort for groups of instruments of the same family the ordinary *viols* offered the best possibilities for the peculiar type of polyphony that was demanded by Elizabethan and early Jacobean society. Throughout the seventeenth century there is altogether a most conspicuous preponderance of stringed instruments in the chamber music of this country, and the viols certainly represented the main contingent of stringed instruments. Viols were combined into ensembles of three, four, five, and six players; the popular 'chest of viols'[3] often consisted of two trebles, two tenors and two basses, or of one treble, one tenor and one bass. These two combinations carried a large body of chamber music in England down to the second half of the seventeenth century. As late as 1676 Thomas Mace, famous musical theorist, wrote thus in his *Musick's Monument* in protest against the rapidly encroaching violins: 'Your best provision (and most complete) will be a good chest of viols, six in number, 2 Basses, 2 Tenors, 2 Trebbles, all truly proportionably suited'. The consort for viols became the favourite art of one particular type of cultured and musically educated family.

Compositions for this kind of chamber music ensemble appeared in a never ending flood. The amount of works printed, comparatively small, shows however, that the 'music for viols' was intended for but a comparatively small section of the musical public and not for the mass. Other combinations of chamber music, chiefly the accompanied solos, but also several kinds of broken consort, were more widely used than the pure viol

---

[1] See above, p. 142.
[2] 1562; see Davey, p. 221.
[3] More about the chest of viols and music for viols may be found in Hayes' book.

ensemble. Only three collections of fantasias for a consort of viols appeared in print between 1597 and 1638: Gibbons' 9 fantasias a 3, circa 1620, East's *Third Set of Books* (1610) and *Seventh Set of Books* (1638) with fantasias a 2–5. A few single pieces appeared in vocal collections, such as two of Byrd's best pieces, a fantasia a 4 and another one a 6, which are contained in *Psalms, Songs and Sonnets* (1611). On the other hand, 13 collections for mixed combinations (in some of them the choice of the instruments is left to the player) for 2 to 6 parts appeared in print during the same period, not counting many vocal collections containing single instrumental items. The bulk of the music for viols was passed on from one group of players to another by copying; up to the present day the music for viols is preserved almost exclusively in MS. copies.

Seventeenth-century English music for viols includes some of the best compositions of one of the greatest periods of chamber music in all ages and countries. We may profitably consider this wonderful body of work in some detail.

It will be necessary to deal with this music from two angles: first, its instrumental style, which at last establishes itself, in this period, as the antithesis of that of the religious vocal motet of old; and secondly, its great intrinsic value, for early seventeenth-century music for viols is the crowning achievement, the climax of the entire development of instrumental music in this country.

In the development of its formal structure, the 'music for viols' was the field for experiment which played an important part in determining the instrumental forms we use today.

The *fantasia* is the chief form used in writing for viol ensemble. The fantasia, freest and most abstract species of early English instrumental music, was shown to be strongly influenced by the vocal motet of the sixteenth century. The motet consisted of a number of successive sections each of which was built up on the contrapuntal development of one thematic subject. Each of these subjects was based on whatever melody of the Gregorian Chant happened to go with the particular sentence of the biblical text that was needed in the service. The instrumental fantasia was shown to be, exactly like the vocal motet, a succession of polyphonic sections; the only difference between the motet and the earliest instrumental fantasias was that the thematic subjects of the fantasia were never based on Gregorian melodies but invented by the composers. Morley defines the fantasia in the *Plaine and Easie Introduction*:

The most principall and chiefest kind of musicke which is made
without a dittie is the fantasia, that is, when a musician taketh a
point at his pleasure, and wresteth and turneth it as he list,
making either much or little of it according as shall seeme best in
his own conceit. In this may more art be showne then in any
other musicke, because the composer is tide to nothing but that
he may adde, deminish, and alter at his pleasure. And this kind
will beare any allowances whatsoeuer tolerable in other
musicke, except changing the ayre & leaving the key, which in
fantasie may neuer be suffered. Other things you may use at your
pleasure, as bindings with discordes, quicke motions, slow
motions, proportions, and what you list. Likewise, this kind of
musick is with them who practise instruments of parts in greatest
use, but for voices it is but sildome used.[1]

Thomas Morley, we found, carried the fantasia form a step
beyond the 'instrumental motet' stage by discarding the device of
overlapping the sections. The sections became detached from each
other; thus the formal structure of the fantasia became clearer and
much easier to understand.

Now the various sections in these early fantasias (those by
Thomas Morley and many of his contemporaries such as Elway
Bevin,[2] John Baldwin[3] and (possibly) the virginalist John Bull) were
still based on motifs of fairly similar character throughout the
piece. Therefore the general impression made by most of these
fantasias is one of a thematic uniformity almost as constant as in
the vocal motets, even though Morley's fantasias, as we have seen,
were much livelier in style than the vocal motets, and even though
we have already recognised in Morley's fantasias important
changes towards formal clarity such as the abolition of overlapping.

Yet bolder innovations were introduced by Morley's successors.
The earlier generation of composers merely carried out a clearer
separation of the sections from one another. The momentous new
advance of the composers of the generation that succeeded Morley
was the introduction of *variety* into the fantasia form. The sections
were no longer based on subjects of more or less similar character
and equally moderate speed, but on definitely different types of

---

[1] Pp. 80 ff.
[2] Oxford, Bodleian, MSS. D. 212–6.
[3] Brit. Mus. Roy. MS. RM. 24, d. 2 (dated 1595–1606).

themes. Christopher Simpson's description of the fantasia of a somewhat later date depicts this new achievement very clearly:

> In this sort of Musick the composer (being not limited to words) doth imploy all his art & invention solely about the bringing in and carrying on these fuges according to the order and method formerly shewed. When he has tried all the several ways which he thinks fit to be used therein, he takes some other point, and does the like with it, or else, *for variety*,[1] introduces some chromatic notes, with lighter humour like a Madrigal, or what else his own fancy shall lead him to; but still concluding with something which hath art and excellency in it.[2]

Variety was introduced in response to the demands of the time. The changeability of the mind and temper of the new human being, his need to expand, to fit himself into new and changing situations, was one reason for the new mobility and variety in art. Another reason was that it became part of the function of early seventeenth-century music even more than of any sixteenth-century art to offer an antidote to the increasing feverishness of economic life, at any rate in London. In music the increasing restlessness of the age is reflected in the desire for variety. Monotony, anything that savoured of the uniformity of the medieval motet, had to disappear.

A fantasia by Thomas Lupo (1587–1628)[3], one of the most important composers of the new generation, shows this significant advance:

Example 37: Fantasia for three parts by Thomas Lupo.[4]

[1] Author's italics.

[2] *A Compendium of Practical Musick*, 1667.

[3] Englishman, of Italian descent; fl. 1605–15. This fantasia like most of Lupo's numerous fantasias a 3 are in Oxf. Bodl. MS. E. 437–42. His four, five and six part fantasias are mostly in Oxf. Christ Ch. MS. 2.

[4] Oxf. Bodl. MS. E. 437–42.

The first section (the sections in Lupo's fantasias are numbered) is based on two subjects that appear successively. One of these starts in minims and slides into faster movement:

The other one is built on a quaver figure (tenor part):

After thorough fugal exploitation especially of the second subject the following simple motif introduces the second section:

It is developed in sequences throughout the score. The third section has a theme that suggests folk-song influence, especially as it is (like the whole section) almost entirely homophonic:

The fourth section stands on this motif:

It is carried through all parts in a very syncopated manner which veils the arsis and thesis of the bars and gives the section the air of an extremely busy polyphony, while the fifth and last section returns to straight 4/4 rhythm with clearly marked accents on the main beat of the bars:

Most of Lupo's fantasias are similar to the one just analysed, in that they introduce a variety of musical ideas.[1] The same principles of form appear in the numerous fantasias by the composer Giovanni Coperario. While most of Coperario's 5 and 6 part pieces are either transcriptions or imitations of his vocal madrigals, his 3 and 4 part fantasias are important here, especially regarding their formal structure. The number of sections in the three- and four-part pieces even exceeds that in Lupo's fantasias. Coperario's fantasias are full of variety; of changing musical pictures which pass by in constant succession. The idea of the 'musical kaleidoscope' never forces itself upon the mind with greater insistency than when one listens to a fantasia a 3 by Coperario.[2]

Thomas Ravenscroft, writer on music and collector of rounds and catches,[3] left a number of fantasias for viols which amply illustrate the same principle. In fantasia No. 3 a 5, for instance, the first section introduces a warm and singable subject and stricter counter-subject at the same time.[4]

Example 38: from fantasia a 5 by Thomas Ravenscroft,

(*a*) first section:

[1] Lupo wrote about 82 fantasias a 3–6. The above fantasia a 3 is No. 8 of his three-part pieces; the numbering of this and other pieces by seventeenth-century composers is taken over from the author's *Die mehrstimmige Spielmusik des 17 Jahrhunderts*, where a detailed list of these works is given (including all sources).

[2] Coperario's real name was John Cooper; he was a Londoner and only italianised his name as Italian music and musicians became more fashionable. He lived from 1570 to 1627, for a long time as musician at the royal court. Seventy-four fantasias a 3–6 are known to be by Coperario. Oxford, Christ Church, MS. 2, and Roy. Coll. of Music, MS. 1145 contain most of his fantasias.

[3] Ravenscroft's chief theoretical work is called *A Brief Discourse of the True (but neglected) use of Charact'ring the Degrees . . . 1614*. It is a most peculiar book. All his 5-part compositions are published.

[4] The simultaneous introduction of two themes at the beginning of a fantasia is also one

The second section, based on this motif:

(*b*) second section:

which appears numerous times in all parts of the score, produces a curious effect which suggests a man trying again and again to climb a ladder and always falling back. The third section of this amusing piece is homophonic and only a few bars long; the theme is:

(*c*) third section:

The fourth section climbs down the ladder in all parts:

(*d*) fourth section:

The fifth section displays long melodic lines, all in minims and semibreves:

(*e*) fifth section:

of Lupo's favourite features. Here is an example (from a Lupo fantasia) of a section based on a *couple* of themes:

Fantasia No. 6 a 5:

Both themes are developed together or rather against each other. This device was used by a number of other composers.

The variety in all these pieces is unlimited. No rules or customs seem to prescribe a definite order for all the small movements that are piled up; the whole production blossoms forth unchecked, in a sort of festival of happy creation. Many more composers could be mentioned such as J. Bassano (d. 1630),[1] J. Bennet (d. after 1614),[2] W. Cobbold (1560–1639),[3] Nath. Giles (1558–1633),[4] J. Gibbs (d. about 1640),[5] J. Mundie (d. 1630),[6] J. Milton (father of the poet, 1562–1647),[7] and others; all of their fantasias and In Nomines convey the same impression, that of general joy and triumphantly creative effort.

However, in the midst of this abundance of types and characters certain preferences are beginning to be shown, certain habits to be found: some types of sections occur again and again. For instance restful sections in minims and semibreves, like the fifth section in the piece by Ravenscroft just shown, appear in many pieces, mostly in the second half. Another very common feature is the conclusion of a fantasia with a lively polyphonic section. The fantasias by the great composer Alfonso Ferrabosco, jun. (1578–1628), excel in such striking conclusions:[8]

Example 39: from fantasia No. 1 a 4 by Ferrabosco (conclusion).

[1] 4 fantasias a 5 in Oxford, Christ Church MSS. 716–20.
[2] 1 fantasia a 5 in Add. 17786–91.
[3] 1 In Nomine a 5 in Add. 18936–9.
[4] 1 Miserere a 2 in Roy. MSS. RM. 24, d. 2.
[5] 1 In Nomine a 5 in Oxford, Bodleian MSS. D. 212–16.
[6] 5 In Nomines a 5–6; 1 fantasia a 5 in Add. 37402–6.
[7] 5 fantasias and 1 In Nomine a 5–6 in Oxford, Christ Church 423–8.
[8] 37 fantasias a 4–6 by Ferrabosco are known; among them 5 In Nomines. Chief MSS. containing his works are Oxford, Christ Church MS. 2 and Dublin, Marsh's Library MS.

(poco rit.)

This example shows, however, that a new element is entering the fantasia. The piece ends in a climax; and to conclude a piece on a particularly effective and convincing note (a long pedal just before the end is another one of Ferrabosco's favourite devices) is an architectonic principle. This implies that more of the element of emotion and drama, of personal expression, is wanted in chamber music. We shall have to deal later with this new tendency; it is symptomatic of the rapid advance of individualism in art. In its effect upon the formal structure of the fantasia, this new element leads to an extension of the previous limits of variety: very soon the connecting-up of sections of varying character begins to approach *dramatic contrast*. The juxtaposition of very different or even antagonistic types of sections is something deeper, something more emotional than the simple enumeration of little pictures which have no inner relationship with each other. It is this 'light-and-shade' expressionism that has so often reminded people of Rembrandt's art and induced scholars to call seventeenth-century music 'baroque', a term otherwise applied to painting and architecture of this and the following century.

Alfonso Ferrabosco jun.'s numerous works are among the first in which stress is laid on expression based on contrast. The evolution of greater dramatic strength is Ferrabosco's chief

Z. 3.41–12; also Brit. Mus. Add. 29996 and Egerton MS. 3665 (Tregian score). The composer was in the service of the Crown as was most of this widespread and famous family of musicians. See G. E. P. Arkwright, 'Notes on the Ferrabosco Family' (*Musical Antiquary*, July, 1912).

contribution to instrumental music in England. This is how it is done. Take, for instance, fantasia No. 17 a 4. The opening section is an extensive, gay and lively fugue:

Example 40: from fantasia No. 17 a 4 by Ferrabosco:

(*a*) first section:

It moves about in crotchets and minims and concludes on a cadence on D. The second section hurries in with quite an exciting combination of an augmentation and a diminution of the first subject, deliberately outdoing the first section in vigour and intensity:

(*b*) second section:

This section soon concludes in F; another section starts, introducing a strongly ornamental duo of the alto and tenor viols, all in quavers and semiquavers:

(*c*) third section:

It leads into an equally lively concert of the two other parts, and finally into a complete symphony of four intricate instrumental lines. Here the architectonic conception becomes clearest, for a pedal that stretches over eight bars forms the crowning climax of the whole piece.

Another fantasia by Ferrabosco, No. 3 a 4, begins with this bright and happy theme:

Example 41: from fantasia No. 3 a 4 by Ferrabosco.

After a tuneful development of this cheerful subject, a contrasting section appears, all in long notes, definitely calming down the gay excitement of the first. Yet the excitement returns: the third and concluding section takes up the thematic material as well as the general behaviour of the first section.

We give the whole fantasia.[1] It is one of the best of its kind.

It should be noted that Ferrabosco's innovations are in no sense due to the Italian origin of the Ferrabosco family, for he was born in England and grew up in the atmosphere of London's musical life, under no specifically Italian influence.

Orlando Gibbons (1583–1625) in most of his fantasias, and William Byrd in at least a few of his latest instrumental compositions, go yet a step beyond Ferrabosco. The various sections have different time signatures; the order of their arrangement is, at the same time, by no means casual: they are arranged according to a well-devised plan; simultaneously the sections grow in extension to real miniature *'movements'*.

Gibbons – we shall have to recognise him as the greatest master of the fantasia of the period – was singularly consistent in the application of his architectonic principles. Among his main instrumental works are two collections of three-part fantasias, one containing seven, the other nine pieces. From the point of view of formal development his seven fantasias a 3 (and one a 4) 'with the greate dooble base',[2] and also some of the 3-part pieces in his printed collection[3] are most interesting. In all these pieces, some of which are of much greater length than earlier fantasias, we find at

[1] See Appendix, Example I.

[2] 35 fantasias (among them 5 In Nomines, including the 'Cries of London') are known to be written by Gibbons. The 7 a 3 and 2 a 4 (all with double bass) are in the Marsh Library (Dublin); the one a 4 is reprinted by Fellowes (Stainer and Bell) and two a 3 in my edition of three-part fantasias (Baerenreiter). See also above, pp. 3 ff. The old double bass is the violone which has the contra-A as its lowest string.

[3] 9 fantasias a 3 (either 2 trebles and bass, or bass with tenor and treble viols), probably printed 1620 and reprinted in Matthysz's collection of 1648; later by Fellowes (Stainer and Bell, 1924).

least four complete movements. They all begin with a fugato section of moderate speed:

Examples 42 and 43: from fantasia No. 2 a 3 and fantasia No. 1 a 4 by Orlando Gibbons:

from fantasia a 3 :   (*a*) first section:

from fantasia a 4 :   (*a*) first section:

A section of the galliard type follows:

fantasia a 3 :   (*b*) second section:

fantasia a 4 :   (*b*) second section:

succeeded almost invariably (either immediately or after another short fugato) by a melody in common time of definite folk-dance character (the melody from the 4 part fantasia is taken from a contemporary Morris Dance):

fantasia a 3 :   (*c*) third section:

fantasia a 4 :   (*c*) third section:

This section usually leads back to a fugato which is of the same nature as the first section and often also thematically related to it; sometimes a finishing touch is provided by a coda in which the movement slows down considerably.

Externally this form is influenced by the dance-suite which had grown out of the 'couple' (pavan plus galliard)[1] and was at this time (about 1610–20) mainly cultivated by German composers such as Schein, Peuerl, Groh, Otto and others. A strong similarity between Gibbons' form and the Italian 'chain-canzona' also exists, especially in the fantasias with the double bass. The chain-canzona consisted of 10 to 20 little sections, each only two or three bars long, rarely more; it represented the final breaking-up of the motet form in the radical Italian way and was sponsored by most of the great composers of the period, Giovanni Gabrieli, Massaino, Grillo, Rossi and others. However, the evolution of the Gibbons fantasia seems to me to have come about chiefly as a logical development of the genuinely English fantasia form whose development we have been following from its origins in the middle of the sixteenth century.

Gibbons is master of the art of contrast; the way he mixes tragic and gay often reminds us of Shakespeare. In Gibbons' instrumental works the technique of contrast is a clear expression of a desire to get away from the 'epical evenness' of the medieval motet; to unite the parts of the piece in a dramatic unified whole. For to connect two movements of opposite character means to *unite* them, by giving them a functional relationship to each other.

We realise that an important factor, perhaps indeed the main motive force, of this urgent development of style was the subjective desire on the part of many composers to *communicate* their individual problems and ideas to the world. In earlier centuries most music was imbued with the non-individualist spirit prevailing in medieval life. In the seventeenth century the individual imagination of the composer is allowed (and even desired) to take its free and independent course. The work of art now begins to take shape as a self-contained whole or organic unity of divers kinds. The composer submits a course of mental and emotional experiences to the public. The contents of such a course of events are more and more subordinated to the *general* trend of the *whole* work. It should be clear, however, that Ferrabosco's and even Gibbons's pieces represent but a first and modest step on the

[1] See above, p. 78.

road towards real 'dramatic consistency' as it was achieved, for
instance, in Purcell's works. We admire in early seventeenth-
century music qualities in which it differs essentially from classical
music. There is still much reserve in the tidy sectional structure
even of the most advanced composers of the Gibbons-Ferrabosco
era. Yet the development which is taken up by Purcell and finally by
the great Vienna classics begins with our masters of the Jacobean
age and their Italian contemporaries, and there are more indications that the music of this time points in that direction. In
the English development they can be summarised under two
headings: (1) the sections of a fantasia become more and more
independent of each other; at the same time they are grouped in a
way that puts them into closer relationship to each other and to the
piece as a whole; (2) the number of sections diminishes while the
sections themselves grow in length.

The first tendency points more and more towards the sonata
form in which the sections have become independent movements,
arranged according to a definite order (allegro-adagio-allegro, or
adagio-allegro-adagio-allegro). The second tendency points to the
'fugue' in the modern sense; the thematic material is unified more
and more until there is only one subject to a whole movement, and
the former 'sections' of the fantasia become the 'developments' of
the fugue.

A fantasia a 6 by William Byrd offers a perfect example of the
first tendency. It is one of the last works of the master, and it is quite
as elaborate as those of Gibbons, but it is less militant and more
amiable and 'human'. The piece in question is in C-minor and
consists of three movements. The first is an adagio-like fugato that
is full of warmth and intimacy, recalling Byrd's lovely d-minor
'Lullaby':

Example 44: from fantasia a 6 by William Byrd.[1]

(a) first section:

A more popular episode of the gigue type follows:

(b) second section:

succeeded by a 3/4 movement that resembles a minuet as well as a galliard:

(c) third section:

[1] From *Psalms, Songs and Sonnets*, (1611); reprinted by Fellowes (Stainer & Bell). Altogether there are 22 fantasias a 3–6 by Byrd, including In Nomines and the Browning (see E. H. Fellowes's already mentioned book on Byrd) as well as 2 Pavans and 1 Galliard. The 'Lullaby' was re-edited by Fellowes in 1925 (Stainer & Bell).

A short coda takes up the mood of the adagio beginning. Here the form of the later sonata is definitely prepared, especially by the introduction of the 'da-capo' element in the concluding coda. Several fantasias (called 'Ayres') by the composer Thomas Holmes (son of John Holmes)[1] strongly resemble those by Byrd and Gibbons. The beginning returns at the end, and in the middle the changing little movements are grouped round an imaginary centre.

The second tendency (the unification of the thematic material) is shown in several fantasias by Ferrabosco. In fantasia No. 16 a 4 the opening theme:

is quoted again and again throughout the piece. The above mentioned fantasia No. 17 a 4 keeps one subject all the way through, although it appears in several variations and the sections differ greatly in kind.[2] Fantasia No. 10 a 3 by Lupo also returns to the opening subject:

in every section. This subject is, incidentally, very common in this music, as it 'turns on' the movement with the crotchets running into quavers. Gibbons, Ferrabosco, Coperario and others all use this subject in some form or other.

In the fantasias of several masters we see the number of sections dwindling down. Some of Tye's In Nomines indeed had only two or three sections, and few-section compositions were long-section compositions. This layout was rare at his time; but after 1600 fantasias that consist of two sections only become quite a normal occurrence. The one-section fantasia, i.e. the new 'fugue' tentatively handled by Bull, Lupo and Ferrabosco is taken over and further perfected by John Jenkins, the chief master of the following generation. For the time being we can watch the two tendencies as described above growing rapidly: one, the establishment of a cyclical form of several more or less independent movements, and

[1] All in Brit. Mus. Add. 40657–61.
[2] See above, p. 166.

the other, the creation of single long movements based on one subject only. Both aim at the unification of the work of art.

Returning to Gibbons and his nine printed fantasias a 3, we find a similar tendency to unify their thematic material. Some of them consist of four independent and strongly contrasting section-movements. Yet in No. 7 of the set the sections are put into closer inner relationship to each other by using similar themes for all of them. The likeness of the thematic material in all the four sections is really conspicuous.

Example 45: from fantasia No. 7 a 3 (from the printed set).

Section 1 is in 2/4:

(a)

section 2 in 3/8:

(b)

section 3 again in 2/4:

(c)

section 4 also in 2/4:

In addition to this tendency to unify the thematic material we notice again the attempt to balance the formal structure as a whole. The end rather recalls the beginning; so again we approach the vital formula A–B–A which became so absolutely dominating in the eighteenth century, determining the sonata, arias, scherzo, minuet and all the other key-forms known today. Furthermore, Gibbons certainly admitted violins instead of treble viols.

As in other fields Gibbons' advance in the field of form shows him as an independent personality gifted with greater courage and deeper understanding than most of his contemporaries. There is a certain atmosphere of struggle in Gibbons' works. Orlando Gibbons does not evade the problems of his time; he tackles them in a bellicose way; he assaults them. His instrumental language – and the expressionistic formal structure of his fantasias is part of it – is proof of this. It recalls the most dramatic moments in his vocal works. It is very striking how Gibbons always becomes particularly dramatic and passionate when setting to music texts which expose the wrongs of human life. It was the wrongs of his own age which Gibbons interpreted in: 'What is our Life?', 'Oh, Lord, how do my woes increase', 'O Lord, in thy wrath', 'Why art thou so heavy oh my soul?'

We also think of the emotional beauty in the composition of the concluding words of the 'Silver Swan', most famous of Gibbons' madrigals:

> Farewell, all joys; o death, come close mine eyes.
> More geese than swans now live, more fools than wise.

Again and again he tries subconsciously, we fancy, to achieve in his music that classical unity which made Elizabethan society appear to the seventeenth-century 'merry England' and the lost paradise. In this endeavour, which is at the same time heroic and tragic, Gibbons resembles Beethoven – we do not hesitate to make this comparison: it can be substantiated in detail, for instance by the analysis of Gibbons' fantasias and Beethoven's last quartets. Beethoven's age was, of course, an age of far greater tension, owing to the far-reaching social developments of this era of the industrial transformation and the French Revolution. Moreover a study of Beethoven's works shows that at his time the spiritual emancipation of the individual had progressed much further than in the time of Gibbons. But essentially the comparison, we believe, can be made.

*

Thus we have seen how the development of the *formal* structure in the fantasias foreshadows the final achievements of the Vienna classics.

In *melodic* development we shall find that the progress towards a proper instrumental style is even more striking.

The melodic material of the sixteenth century chiefly relied on scale progression, step by step, rather than on characteristically shaped and striking themes. The proximity to the vocal age was still very noticeable in the instrumental works of the sixteenth century. But truly instrumental patterns appear with increasing frequency in the fantasias of Elizabethan and Jacobean composers. Such an interesting instrumental figure as Ferrabosco's:

Example 46: from fantasia No. 3 a 4 by A. Ferrabosco.

which, as everyone will agree, is far removed from the vocal age, is essentially a seventeenth-century achievement. Such figures became indeed part of the natural instrumental language of the time. With the increasing valuation of the subjective element in the art as a whole, the development of marked and personally-shaped themes progresses. Here are some more instances of such striking melodic ideas:

Example 47:

(*a*) William White, fantasia a 6[1]

<hr />

[1] Oxford, Christ Church MS. 2.

(*b*) Wm. White, fantasia a 5.[1]

Example 48: from fantasia No. 13 a 4 by A. Ferrabosco.

This new individualism in the melodic element begins to permeate all sections of the fantasia – we say 'begins', for only the latter part of the seventeenth century sees its full unfolding.

The example by Ferrabosco shows that as part of the evolution of characteristically shaped themes a process of *metrical clarification* was going on. Already in Morley's pieces we have seen a division of the themes into two or four corresponding phrases which were in the nature of question and answer. More so in Ferrabosco's and Gibbons' themes:

Example 49: from (*a*) fantasia a 3 (No. 3 with the double bass)[2] by Orlando Gibbons:

(*b*) from fantasia No. 7 a 3 (1620), by Orlando Gibbons.

[1] Ibid.

[2] MS. in Dublin, Marsh's Library and Oxford, Christ Church MS. 419–22. The piece is one of Gibbons' greatest works, incidentally one of his longest. In the same series of 3-part fantasias there is a piece (No. 7) with the same subject in opposite movement:

This theme seems to have been used by other composers of the time, too. In the Fitzwilliam Virginal Book, new edition, Vol. II, p. 489, there is a fantasia for harpsichord or virginal by Giles Farnaby, built on a very similar subject:

Melodies of this kind are obviously influenced by dance music with its metrical clarity.

The popular element is still prominently displayed in early Jacobean chamber music. We find that in the fantasias not only are existing popular themes taken over and developed, but the spirit of folk-music is embodied also in newly-composed pieces, just as it happened earlier in the music of Henry VIII's court. The popularity of such folk tunes as the Browning in chamber music is proof that English chamber music about 1600 and some time after had still retained its vigour and soundness. Several popular melodies in Gibbons' pieces have already been mentioned; here are some more:

Example 50: (*a*) from fantasia No. 7 a 3 (with double bass), by Orlando Gibbons.

(*b*) From fantasia No. 3 a 3 (with double bass), by Orlando Gibbons:[1]

They all show how the great master in particular relied on the directness of popular melodies in order to achieve the classical forcefulness in which his works excel.

Another feature of the melodic element in chamber music of the early years of the seventeenth century is its increasing liveliness. It is very rich in purely instrumental features – again a comparison between an average melodic line of the sixteenth century with a typical one of the Jacobean fantasia will be instructive:

[1] This episode from fantasia No. 3 (with double bass) is a Dutch tune called 'de Rommelpot', popular in England at the beginning of the seventeenth century (as were other Dutch melodies which were probably introduced here by the English soldiers who fought for Dutch freedom and by the numerous English actors who toured Holland during that time). This melody also occurs as one of the three voices in a Quodlibet Round (No. 70) in Ravenscroft's *Pammelia* (a collection of contemporary rounds published in 1609–11); there it appears as a 'country dance'.

Example 51: (a) Preston, In Nomine a 4[1] (about 1575):

(b) J. Ward, fantasia No. 6 a 4[2] (about 1615):

The three-part and four-part pieces of most composers are of especially great animation and complexity, while those a 5 and 6 mostly rely on calmer movement, although they are similarly based on polyphonic rather than on homophonic conception. Very small note values such as demi-semi-quavers are introduced. At the same time quite unvocal jumps become more and more frequent:

Example 52: from In Nomine No. 2 a 6,[3] by John Ward:

The quick note-repetitions which were so new in Tye's time[4] are now well-established. Moreover, long sequences of fast instrumental figures appear:

Example 53: from fantasia No. 9 a 3 (1620), by Orlando Gibbons.

Generally the 'sequence' becomes a more and more frequently employed technique for the building-up of melodic developments; notably the fantasias by the composer Chetwoode largely depend on the employment of sequence,[5] this important feature of the music of the past 350 years.

[1] Oxford, Bodleian MS. D. 212–16.
[2] Oxford, Christ Church MS. 2. Ward (d. 1640) was an ingenious composer of madrigals and instrumental works. He was partly in the service of Mr Fanshawe, remembrancer of the exchequer of Ware Park, Herts, and Warwick Lane. Twenty-seven fantasias by Ward are known.
[3] MS. Oxford, Christ Church MS. 2.
[4] See above, pp.96 f.
[5] Fantasias and other instrumental pieces by Chetwoode in Brit. Mus. MS. Add. 40657–61.

There is one more important instance of the advance of the instrumental style. The compass of the part grows. Not only that sometimes passages run over two complete octaves:

Example 54: from fantasia No. 2 a 3 (with the double bass), by Orlando Gibbons.

but the actual extension of the scale is widening. While in earlier instrumental music the highest notes were g″ and a″, we now find many instances of b″, c‴, and even d‴ being used in treble or descant viol parts by Gibbons, Thomas Holmes and others. In Gibbons' often-mentioned fantasia a 4 No. 1 (with the double bass) the top part even climbs as far as e-flat‴: at the other extreme Gibbons' use of the double bass (violone) in some of his fantasias enables him to introduce contra-A; there are many examples of the employment of this note in such fantasias.

In the music of the best composers of the period the 'freedom' of the writing is the same in all parts of the score. The melodic material is more or less the same in all instruments. The means to achieve polyphony is *imitation*. One part introduces a motif, theme or melody which is imitated or literally repeated by the other parts that enter the score one by one. All parts achieve in this way equal mobility and equal rights. A highly instrumentalised, 'concertante' polyphony is the result; it is the chief characteristic of English instrumental music compared with that of other nations. Episodes like this one:

Example 55: from fantasia No. 8 a 3 (1620), by Orlando Gibbons.

are found only in English chamber music.

If it is seen as part of the whole panorama of European musical history in the seventeenth century this highly-evolved polyphony (which is ultimately an offspring of the old Netherlandish polyphony) might appear backward in the face of such 'futuristic' achievements in the contemporary scene as the Italian monody, basso continuo, stilo rappresentativo:[1]

Example 56: from *Concerti Ecclesiastici* by Ludovico Grosso da Viadana, 1615.

[1] The Italian 'monody' represents the victory of expressive melody over medieval constructivism. One melodic line, either vocal or instrumental, and produced by one performer only, replaces the intricate counterpoint of earlier sixteenth century schools.

The 'basso continuo' represents the victory of functional harmony over 'horizontal' line. From 1600, a permanent harmonic background accompanies even complicated polyphonic structures: first in Italian music, later in all European music. All the contrapuntal happenings in the score are thus given a harmonic meaning. The harmonies of the basso continuo are performed on instruments capable of producing *chords* (such as organ, harpsichord, theorbo or harp). The chords to be performed by the player of the basso

A - mo-re tu-o lan-gue - o, a - mo-re tu-o lan - gue-o

And yet the English composers from about 1600 and after exhibited characteristic qualities of initiative and adventure as the promoters of an instrumental style, and they evolved an instrumental technique embodying these features. That is one of the enduring contributions of this country to European music of this and later times.

In a few fantasias a 5 and 6 by Ferrabosco, jun., Thomas Lupo, and also William White,[1] the compact polyphony of the fantasia seems to be broken up by the introduction of concertante solo parts which here and there come to the foreground of the ensemble. This technique anticipates indeed certain elements of the later 'concerto grosso', if only in those few isolated examples by the composers mentioned. In the concerto grosso of the Handel type, single instruments occasionally have livelier passages to perform than the orchestra. The following episode, which is taken from a fantasia a 6 by Thomas Lupo,[2] even shows some features of the later solo concerto (Example 57, overleaf).

The two bass parts dominate the whole piece which sounds like a concertino for two bass viols accompanied by four higher-pitch viols.

Yet it can be stated quite definitely that not Italian influence but rather an established English practice is behind this curious development. For these virtuoso solo episodes are mostly found in the bass parts of pieces. In view of the preference that was given to the bass viol in the musical life of the time it is only natural that

continuo are indicated in the form of figures and accidentals above the notes of the bass part – a kind of musical shorthand.

The 'stilo rappresentativo' is another achievement of Italian composers about 1600. It means the expressive and dramatic recitativo which replaces the neutral flowing of the voice parts in earlier Church music.

[1] All in Oxford, Christ Church MS. 2. William White is chiefly known from three fantasias a 5, and seven a 6; chiefly in Oxford, Christ Church MS. 2. Little is known of his career.

[2] Oxford, Christ Church MS. 2.

Example 57: from fantasia for a chest of viols (2 trebles, 2 tenors, 2 basses), by Thomas Lupo.

sometimes the bass viol took a more prominent part in the score, for the simple reason that it was often easier to find a really good player on the bass viol than on the treble or tenor viols. If we remember that many fantasias were written for particular players we understand the varying demands on the technical skills of the executants so that certain parts emerge almost as solos.

Occasionally in pieces by Gibbons and Byrd the treble part dominates and reduces other instruments to the function of accompaniment. But for the time being such 'homophonic' episodes are rare. In general the polyphonic character of this music is little contested by homophonic arrangements. It is, as already stated, the most 'genuine' polyphony of the time throughout Europe.

Real Italian influence on English instrumental polyphony at the beginning of the seventeenth century is felt only in certain minor and purely external features. Arising out of the monodic style of the Florentine and Venetian schools a trio combination of two trebles and one bass became the great fashion in Italian chamber music. The two trebles were equally busy and equally important as concertante and expressive melodic instruments; they were supported by the bass which provided, as basso continuo, a continuous harmonic background of chords all along throughout the piece. Now this arrangement of two sopranos and one bass was taken over by some English composers, in particular by Coperario, Gibbons and Lupo. But there was no question of importing, with the instrumentation, the 'vertical' harmonic conception as against the native 'horizontal' polyphonic idea. The three parts were just polyphonic lines as in all English music; only the external form was Italian. An interesting compromise between the Italian trio-sonata and the English polyphonic style is found in a fantasia by Lupo in which three treble parts of equal pitch and importance perform a polyphonic concerto.[1]

Once again, the musical life and production of this country, especially the progressive instrumental polyphony, was so closed in itself, so healthy and independent that – at least for the time being – it could resist all the splendour and all the allurements of the new art that came from the south.

This polyphonic activity and achievement does not so occupy the composers as to prevent them from developing instrumental expressionism and emotionalism in yet another direction, the *harmonic*. On the contrary, the depth of sentiment which we found in earlier English music, reached new intensity in early Jacobean

---

[1] Oxford, Christ Church MS. 2. Re-edited by the author (Baerenreiter). Almost the identical music is set at different pitches for 3 tenors and 3 basses; cf. *Musica Britannica*, Vol. IX).

chamber music, largely owing to the exploitation in an intensely conscious way of the emotional possibilities of the major and minor keys.

The full and lively polyphony of the score when built up on one of those radiantly gay themes in which this music is so rich becomes a feast of optimism and brightness as in some pieces by Ferrabosco and Gibbons. A pavana a 6 by Gibbons[1] is a particularly beautiful example of such 'radiant major'. How deliberately some composers contrived their polyphonic textures with a view to utilising these qualities of major and minor is shown by the fact that chord motifs were often chosen as chief subjects in fantasias. William Cranford's first fantasia a 6[2] has such a theme:

Example 58: from fantasia a 6 by William Cranford.

On the other hand, the emotional implications of the minor mode were no less recognised by composers. A fantasia a 4 by John Bull may serve as an example of the ability of some masters to create musical lyrics in an extremely tragic mood.[3]

This is the place to mention Richard Deering (d. 1630) whose fantasias[4] were well known at their time and indeed are among the best. Deering's always moderate musical diction avoids too heavy

---

[1] Published by E. H. Fellowes (Stainer & Bell).

[2] Brit. Mus. Add. 39550–4. Bass part is missing; here added tentatively by the author. Cranford who flourished during the first quarter of the seventeenth century left about 15 fantasias and In Nomines most of which are in Dublin, Marsh's Library and Brit. Mus. Add. 39550–4.

[3] Oxford, Bodleian MSS. F. 568–9 and Christ Church MS. 2 (here no name is given). See Appendix, Example II. The other bass part exists in Brit. Mus. Add. 17792–6.

[4] An almaine for strings by Deering was re-edited by Sir R. R. Terry, 1925. Further instrumental works by Deering are to be found in Add. 39550–4 (8 fantasias a 5), Add. 17786–91 (2 fantasias a 6), Add. 17792–6, and Dublin, Marsh's Library (1 a 6; the copy in

accents yet shows most beautifully the early English sense of
brightness and radiancy of colour. Again it is especially the minor
(usually a-minor) which Deering employs. Here is at least one
example of the simple yet masterful art of Richard Deering:

Example 59: from fantasia a 5 in a-minor by Richard Deering.

Dublin is anonymous, the one in the British Museum incomplete). In the *Musical Quarterly*,
XXVII, No. 1, 1941, pp. 36–41, there is an article on Deering's fancies for viols by Ch. W.
Hughes.

Towards the end of the 'golden age', that is to say, between 1615 and 1620, expressionism by harmonic and tonal means became more intense. Chromatic harmonies appear and there is a curious liking for long chains of modulations. In this respect, more than in any other, a moderate influx of Italian modernism has to be recognised at this stage. While chromatic progressions were already cautiously used by Thomas Morley and with more intensity Dowland,[1] modulations such as were now used were new in English chamber music.

In Ravenscroft's fantasia No. 5 a 5,[2] easily the master's most outstanding instrumental composition, the third section has chromatic lines in all parts:

Example 60: from fantasia No. 5 a 5 by Thomas Ravenscroft.

The long first section of a fantasia by Thomas Tomkins (1573–1656),[3] also an ingenious piece, is built on a chromatic subject (Example 61, opposite).

While such chromatic progressions do not necessarily mean a definite upsetting of the key, even though they bring about, by their very nature, a quick change of chords and relationships, some

[1] E.g. Dowland's 'Forlorn Hope' (fantasias for the lute). Here as elsewhere in seventeenth-century music, suffering and disappointment are expressed by chromatic progressions. In Cambridge University Library.

[2] Brit. Mus. Add. 39550–4.

[3] Oxford, Bodleian MS. c. 64–9; reprinted by Stainer & Bell; ed. Fellowes. 21 fantasias are known to be by Tomkins. Tomkins, who was W. Byrd's pupil, was organist at Worcester Cathedral and later at the Royal Chapel. He is chiefly known as composer of *Songs of 3, 4, 5 and 6 parts* which were printed in 1622 (re-edited by Fellowes in *The English Madrigal School*). A detailed study on Th. Tomkins by D. Stevens appeared in 1967.

Example 61: from fantasia a 6 by Thomas Tomkins.

composers deliberately aim at breaking up the tonal uniformity of the pieces. Thomas Tomkins, a great and daring composer who had an unusual technical skill at his command, wrote a fantasia a 3[1] in which he modulates from C-sharp minor through B-minor, A-minor, G-minor, F-minor, E-flat-minor back to C-sharp-minor, the key from which he had started, and in steady progress on to A-minor where he stays:

Example 62: from fantasia a 3 by Thomas Tomkins.

John Ward modulates in fantasia a 5 No. 1,[2] a piece in A-minor, first to E-flat-major, then from sub-dominant to sub-dominant through A-flat, D-flat, G-flat, B, and E to A-major; the rest of the piece is in A-major.

Here is the point where the classical unity (and security) of the old English polyphonic style was breached for the first time. Through the element of harmonic expressionism Italian influence – and with it experiments and even speculation – gained a foothold in English music. In the next chapters we shall have to inquire why this had to happen. What a wise man was Morley, who with

[1] Oxford, Bodleian MS. D. 245–7.
[2] Brit. Mus. MS. Eg. MS. 3665.

prophetic foresight had stated quite definitely that 'leaving the key in fantasie may never be suffered'! Now, twenty years after Morley, the search for the new and startling begins; the old rules of moderation and restraint are left. 'Newness' is demanded for the first time; as John Adson puts it in his work in 1621:

> There are three Vertues (Goodnesse, Truth and Newnesse) which, as they embolden a Worke, and make it an unblushing Offspring at the Noblest Altar: So doe they also preserve from Taxation the Presenter; and from disparagement the Protector.[1]

However, such experiments do not occur until the end of the classical age of English chamber music. Indeed, as one age grows out of the previous, they herald the next; they are definitely outside features and do not affect the general character of the music of the period, which is best seen as something complete in itself, and quite unique. Within this unity of the whole body of production the subjective characters of the composers yet found full individual expression. There is no end to exploring all this wonderful music, to counting up all the beauties and ingenuities which are found in the works of the distinguished and aristocratic Holborne, the witty and serene Morley, the restrained, melancholic Coperario, the vigorous Ferrabosco, the concentrated musical thinker, Gibbons, the profoundly human W. Byrd, the innovator Tomkins, and all the other men, all true masters, White, Ward, Cranford, Edward Gibbons, Ravenscroft, and many more who, like the great madrigalists Wilbye, Weelkes and Farmer can only be mentioned here as composers of fine stylised dance music. Pavans, galliards, allemands and other dance tunes, incidentally, occupied a secondary place compared with the fantasia in the music for viols; dance styles cannot therefore be discussed at length now, although

---

[1] *Courtly Masquing Ayres*, Dedication. Morley was also the first to warn his pupils not to exaggerate such 'newness' and that at a time when the question of Italian influence in this country was still only of secondary importance compared with the end of the seventeenth century: 'The composers of musick who otherwise would follow the depth of their skill . . . are compelled, for lack of maecenates, to put on another humour and follow that kind whereunto they have neither beene brought up, nor yet (except so much as they can learne by seeing other mens works in an unknown tounge) doe perfectlie understand ye nature of it, *such be the newfangled opinions of our countrey men, who will highlie esteeme whatsoeuer cometh from beyond the seas, and speciallie from Italie* (author's italics), be it never so simple, contemning that which is done at home, though it be never so excellent' (*A Plaine and Easie Introduction*, p. 179).

the dance repertory contains such pearls as Ferrabosco's 'Dovehouse Pavin'.[1] Much must be left to the exploring initiative of the music-lover; this review being intended but to draw public attention to these thirty years of glorious achievement as a whole.

[1] Collections of dance music for viols are in the great libraries of London and Oxford. I mention the contents of Brit. Mus. MSS. Add. 15118, 17792–6, 34800, 30480–4, 37402–6, 30826–8, Oxf. Bodl. Mus. School E 415–8; composers represented in these MSS. and also in the Oxford libraries and not mentioned here yet are: Cormack, Robert Johnson, Joseph Lupo, and Robert Taylor.

CHAPTER VI

The Crisis

The student of early English chamber music, holding a general review of the musical life of this country, cannot but be struck by the ominous change which takes place between 1620 and 1642. England fails to keep pace with other countries in the development of chamber music. The slowing-up, which we had occasion to notice in reviewing the first twenty years of the century, becomes exceedingly obvious after 1620. The appreciation of chamber music is no longer universal, nor is artistic achievement maintained on the level reached in Elizabethan and early Jacobean times.

It may well strike us as tragic that the classical unity of style and approach that distinguished the art of the first two decades of the century was so soon broken down. The old cleavage reappeared – the gap between the 'music of the many' and the 'music of the few' which the age of Elizabeth had for a time succeeded in bridging. From about the beginning of the second quarter of the century the stream of production divided and flowed in two very different directions: on one side towards intellectualism, complexity and speculation, as represented chiefly in the music of the Court and the Anglican Church, on the other side towards facility, superficiality and obviousness, as shown in the music of the public.

We must try to discover why this cleavage took place.

Once more we have to recall the spirit of the sixteenth century. The culture of Elizabeth's court was the culture of the nation at large. Close ties united the Court with most of the other sections of higher society, for the political, economic, and cultural aspirations of the Crown expressed those of the young English society as a whole.

Signs of a clash of interests between the Court and parts of the new bourgeoisie had already appeared during Elizabeth's last few years. Such signs of disagreement reappeared again and again during James's reign and open conflict broke out under Charles I.[1] The Crown and the royalist gentry, the representatives of absolutism and monopoly, rallied to their side all the forces of

---

[1] For the whole development the reader is referred to R. H. Tawney's *Religion and the Rise of Capitalism*, and Christopher Hill's *The English Revolution*.

stagnation and retrogression, while the stand of the bourgeoisie and parliament to maintain themselves against Charles's increasingly aggressive demands, in the end united all the forces interested in breaking the feudal bonds.

> The issue was one of political power. The bourgeoisie had rejected Charles I's government, not because he was a bad man, but because he represented an obsolete social system. His government tried to perpetuate a feudal social order when the conditions existed for free capitalist development, when the increase of national wealth could only come by means of free capitalist development.[1]

At the same time Charles endeavoured to bring about a new Anglican sacerdotalism, a relationship between the Church and the country's economic and political regime which to an increasing degree made the Anglican Church an instrument for appropriating to the Crown the dictatorial powers of the pre-Reformation Catholic Church.

In the cultural life of the country the Court rapidly became isolated. A screen of glass seemed to surround it and its grandees; they could well see what was brewing outside, but were unable to influence events. The society of the striving and blossoming new England was not represented in the life at Court. The Court itself increasingly lost touch with public life. Cultural in-breeding in the circles round Charles was the logical consequence.

Not that this close atmosphere killed art altogether. On the contrary, Charles was no less ambitious and fond of display than his father; he took a certain Neronic interest in matters of art. The Court attracted a considerable number of artists and musicians.

> The Puritan austerity drove to the King's faction all who made pleasure their business, who affected gallantry, splendour of dress or taste in the lighter arts. With these went all who live by amusing the leisure of others, from the painter and the comic poet, down to the rope-dancer and the Merry Andrew. For these artists well knew that they might thrive under a superb and luxurious despotism, but must starve under the rigid rule of the precisians.[2]

The masques at the courts of James and Charles offered more

---

[1] Hill, p. 56.
[2] Macaulay, *History of England*, ed. 1889, I, p. 51.

than enough room for all kinds of mummeries, from the pastoral-idyllic to the piquant-obscene. A large instrumental apparatus was frequently employed to produce pretentious orchestral effects in these masques which were to a high degree imitations of Italian entertainments.[1] The melodic substance of the music in the masques was, however, usually slender, now that the great days of Ben Jonson were past. They were just two-part tunes of treble and bass conceived on the simplest possible lines.[2] There was a curious atmosphere of forced merriment and spurious simplicity about the tunes contained in the masques of Charles's court, particularly between 1630 and 1640.

This was just the trouble. Those men of art who had a deeper understanding of the trend of society under Puritan influence were the more bewildered at the character of Court life. This irresponsible flippancy must have appeared disgusting to such genuine artists and thinkers as were close enough to observe it without being too close to criticise it.

Court and Anglican Church were united like the Siamese twins in their reactionary cultural policy. Laud's very ability and success in advancing and consolidating Charles's aims in Church policy largely contributed to the deepening of the antagonism between Church-cum-Court on the one side and the main body of society on the other. The Church in particular became the more reactionary the keener the attacks on it grew. More and more elements of the cultural 'defence-system' of the Catholic Church of the previous century were dug up by the Anglican clergy. Not only did many paintings and carvings which had escaped the zeal of the Anglican Reformation 100 years before, return to the churches, but the musical side of the service took on more and more traits of Catholic ornamental splendour. Sir Richard Terry was the first to observe that the Church composers of the first quarter of the seventeenth century reintroduced polyphony into religious music – that rich and complex art which was so strongly denounced by Cranmer and other Anglican reformers of the sixteenth century.

---

[1] About the Court masques, see E. J. Dent, *Opera*, 1940, p. 144.

[2] The British Museum contains a large number of masque tunes; see Add. 10444. Here are some titles: 'The beares dance', 'Wiches dance', 'The Haymakers Masque', 'The Furies', 'The Gipsies Masque', etc. For identification see A. V. Sabol, *Songs and Dances of the Stuart Masque* (Providence, Rhode Island, 1959) and the Introductory Note by Peter Holman to the Scolar Press Facsimile edition of *The Description of a Maske, Thomas Campion 1607* (1973) and *The Discription of a Maske, Thomas Campion 1614* (1973). I understand from Peter Holman that the two parts mentioned above are not complete but only skeletons of five-part pieces. Some of the complete versions appear in collections by Brade, Adson and others.

Catholicism and Anglicanism approached one another closely. In 1641 the Anglican Church issued a collection of tunes and motets by Anglican and Catholic authors (Barnard collection) which were taken over bodily into the Anglican service, with the one alteration that English words were written to them. No clearer proof of the retrospective attitude of the Church need be offered.

So polyphonic music once more had the official blessing of Crown and clergy. It was intended, just as in the middle ages, to symbolise the continuity that the clergy wished to preserve, and to bring back the atmosphere of mysticism that the rising rationalism threatened.

Polyphony became a symbol of the 'good old times' which were to be kept alive against the rising flood of bourgeois Puritanism. Is it surprising that during the years before the Civil War, Church and Court and the high-society circles around them patronised polyphonic music more than ever before, and to an increasing degree? And not only music of the past was performed – quite a number of composers were willing to write new works in the required polyphonic style of the Church.

In such an atmosphere polyphony became over-intricate, exaggerated, and finally decidedly retrogressive. Partly for this reason, and partly because of its association with an increasingly obsolete social tradition, the new-old idiom became discredited in the minds of the public. It cannot be denied that many composers at Court and Church tried to give their best in this hopelessly muddled and confused situation. But no fresh air blew on them from outside; the old forms were used, with complications and ornamentations, and left in an advanced stage of baroque refinement. Court and Church music (if we forget for the moment the le-roi-s'amuse style of the masques) adopted mannerisms, even at the hands of the very best masters England had at the time. There was little living inspiration or public admiration for these men. They found themselves in a vacuum. Towards 1640 Court music reached an astonishing state of introversion and involution, like some creeping plant writhing fantastically in a confined place.

It is true, the encouragement of an obsolete style was unable to obscure the talents of such an eminent musician as William Lawes; but at the same time it was absolutely incapable of creating as healthy a general musical life as Elizabeth's time had called into being.

Some of the instrumental music of Thomas Ford (Foord,

1580–1648),[1] in so far as it was composed after he joined the chapel royal in 1626,[2] reflects the state of intellectualism and over-development which had been reached under Charles I. Let us take, for instance, a piece a 4, presumably for viols, called 'Ayre' – in reality, a hybrid, something between a fantasia and a pavan. Its scholasticism is almost mathematical.

An elementary subject in breves:

Example 63: (a)

is introduced in one part, while the subject, executed in quavers, serves to weave an extremely difficult contrapuntal texture in the three remaining parts:

(b)

---

[1] One fantasia for 2 bass viols, and 6 fantasias for 5 viols are known to have been written by Ford at a comparatively late date, also the ayre a 4, which is discussed here. Oxford Bodleian Library C. 59–60 contains the piece for bass viols; Royal College MS. 1145 the 6 fantasias (in this MS. one part is missing but can be added from Brit. Mus. Add. 17792–65 where the pieces are complete though anonymous). The ayre is in Brit. Mus. 40657–61. Ford's *Musicke of Sundrie kindes* (1607) in addition to the 11 four-part ayres and a dialogue for two voices, contains a number of dance movements arranged for 'two Basse-Viols, the Liera-way' (Scolar Press facsimile, 1971). Ford's Almaine a 3 in Oxford Christ Church is particularly attractive.

[2] Before this time he was musician to Prince Henry of Wales.

When the first part finishes its figure in breves as shown above another part, the tenor, takes over the same subject, also in breves, but a tone higher, while again contrapuntal lines in quavers – based on the initial figure – circle round (these are always highly syncopated and lacking rhythmic clarity and vitality):

(c)

The bass part follows next with the five-notes subject, another tone higher; this time the other voices move about in minims, and the counterpoints also rely on the five notes of the chief motif which are, however, thrown about in varying order:

(d)

The five breves wander through the parts down and up the scale, while the other parts indulge in a polyphonic performance that is sometimes neck-breaking. There is a 'semi-colon' on the dominant; in the following second half the spectacle of the initial subject threading its way through the score is repeated, this time in semibreves. The counter-subject that builds up the polyphony is itself derived:

(e)

it had already occurred during the first part (in crotchets):

(f)

The main motif, this time in crotchets, concludes the piece, leading up to a short fugato in all parts.

The listener can but admire the intricacy of the polyphonic result, but this music makes no attempt whatsoever at popular appeal. This work makes today a most exciting piece for consorts of viols, but its essence is intellectual construction. Yet we do not by any means desire to deny to Ford's music interesting qualities. The restriction to one thematic subject is an especially noteworthy feature; Ford really tries to plan a piece of considerable length by developing it out of one or two seminal motifs. In this way this technique is progressive. Moreover, the same Ford had proved in his earlier works that he could also write tuneful airs; these bore no traces of Court style, however, and had no relation to it.

John Withy[1] and William Simmes,[2] as well as some less-known composers of the Chapel Royal who worked chiefly during the years preceding the Civil War, can be counted as Thomas Ford's spiritual relatives, though not perhaps so given to extremist practices.

Charles Coleman (d. 1664) was appointed a Court musician as early as 1625, and in that capacity enjoyed considerable fame in his

---

[1] Fantasia and In Nomine by Withy in Oxford, Christ Church MSS. 473–8; 23 fantasias for 2 bass viols and one for treble and bass in Oxford, Bodleian Music School C. 59–60 and 28–30. A number of dance tunes a 3, also in the sophisticated Court style without being anything but average art are in Brit. Mus. MSS. Add. 29283–85 and 31423.

[2] Simmes wrote 7 fantasias a 5 (Oxford, Christ Church MSS. 716–20).

time. His numerous compositions[1] are kept in a conservative style, and yet are fresh and intellectual. There is a certain drive in a beginning like this:

Example 64:[2]

(Rather fast)

Coleman wrote a suite in five parts for the royal wind musicians[3] which was performed on great occasions at Court. There are many other instrumental suites in two parts in *A Musicall Banquet* (1651) and *Court Ayres* (1655) which appeared during the Interregnum.

There was, however, one real genius among Charles I's composers. We must now turn to him and his work, for it is certain to

---

[1] Most of them are found in Lbm Add. 18940–4, Add. 31423; Christ Church, Oxford 353–6, 367–70, 379–81, 61–6, 1011, 1022; Bodleian, Mus. Sch. E. 410–4, 431–6.

[2] Christ Church, Oxford, 423–8.

[3] *Four Pieces for Sackbuts and Cornets*, transcribed and edited by Anthony Baines and arranged for brass quintet by Edrich Siebert (O.U.P. 1962).

outlast the music of the whole period, and to conquer the hearts of chamber-music lovers whenever and wherever it is awakened from its centuries-long slumber.

William Lawes (1602–1645) was certainly one of the outstanding musical personalities of the whole century. Being a pupil of Coperario, one of the best composers and teachers of the time, he was able to join the Chapel Royal as a boy and remained in the royal service until 1645 when he fell at the siege of Chester. Out of sheer loyalty to his master, William Lawes[1] supported the Royalist cause and died fighting a losing battle. Lawes was an unusually alert and ingenious musical thinker. He was adored by his friends and admired by those few musical amateurs who could grasp the spirit of his art. When his colleagues wrote elegies mourning his death (among them were his famous brother Henry, Simon Ives, D. Cobb, Capt. Edmund Foster, John Hilton and others) his keenness and versatility of mind were repeatedly referred to. As Cobb put it:[2]

> Dear Will is dead. Will Lawes whose active brains
> Gave life to many sweet harmonious strains,
> Whose boundless skill made music speak such sense
> As if't had sprung from an intelligence.
> In his just proportioned songs there might you find
> His soul convers'd with heav'n with his mind,
> And in such language rhetorick never knew. . . .

We have seen how some composers of late Jacobean time, such as Tomkins, Ward and Holmes, began to affect mannerisms. We found the beginnings of a search for the uncommon, for the out-of-the-way, which always appears where the healthy social impulse is fading. There were also certain signs that some products of Italian modernism were employed which were foreign to the original character of English chamber music. We further had to recognise that polyphony which in the last analysis is derived from the old Netherlandish masses and motets, still dominated instrumental music in this country, if in a very refined style.

These tendencies are manifest in Lawes' works. It was only owing to Lawes' great capacity and daring that something quite extraordinary blossomed in spite of such contradictory tendencies.

---

[1] M. Lefkowitz, *William Lawes* (London, 1960).

[2] Poem and composition in MS. Add. 34071; here the other elegies are also found, except the one by Hilton which is in Add. 11608.

Lawes' music is the most personal of the whole century. Many
features of his music are hard to explain and place by any critical
standard, and in the development of seventeenth-century music
this peculiar art of Lawes' led nowhere. In spite of numerous
progressive and even experimental elements contained in it, it is
the termination of a development, an end, not a beginning.
Posterity, however, must recognise in his work a singular
combination of such conflicting qualities as Court splendour,
hyperculture, profound sentiment, a kind of waywardness and a
prevailing amplitude of style, a breadth which is part of the grand
tradition of a grand time.

Lawes' compositions are very numerous, and instrumental
fancies and airs form the greater part of his life-work. His most
widely known work, the *Royal Consort*, is at the same time his least
sophisticated composition. The *Royal Consort* was an important
collection of 67 airs – almands, corants, sarabands, pavans and airs
(one is called 'echo') – intended for use and performance at Court.
Two 'setts', in D minor and D major, each divisible into three
Suites, survive in autograph; Suites 7 to 10 are in A minor, C
major, F and B flat. One source called the collection the Great
Consort.

Lefkowitz showed that the original version was for two violins,
tenor, and bass department probably consisting of a bowed bass
and two theorboes. Because, according to one source[1] 'the middle
part could not bee performed with equal advantage, to bee heard
as the trebles were, Therefor the Author involved the Inner part in
two breakinge bases'.

The new ensemble consisted of the two violins as before, and the
two theorboes as before, the theorboes having exactly the same
unfigured bass part. But the original bass and tenor music was
divided up between two divisions, hence the term 'breaking bases',
and new material that had not previously formed part of the
harmony. The two trebles are 'concertante', which is to say that
both are equally lively at equal pitch crossing and recrossing each
other. These two parts are melodically already rather erratic and
out of the old English tradition; they often make sense only when
heard together with the whole score and seem quite odd when
played alone:

[1] Bod. Mns. Sch. D.236.

Example 65: (For two treble viols, theorbo, dividing bass and breaking bass; about 1630).

William Lawes Almand from 'Royal Consort'

The parts are sometimes bizarre; but the bass is usually fairly simple, relying on easily comprehensible scale progressions, or on fourths and fifths up and down. It obviously holds the composition together, countering the extravagance of the other parts and of the harmonic structure as a whole. Most of the pieces keep to the traditional metrical dance scheme of two or three independent strains, each consisting of eight, twelve or sixteen bars. These two features – the harmonic base and the conventional dance form – explain the comparatively wide popularity of the *Royal Consort*.

There are true highlights in the *Royal Consort* which is altogether well worth reviving.

A second group of instrumental pieces, consisting of about 28 fantasias, pavanas and In Nomines a 5–6[1] and also a very large number of three and four part 'Ayres',[2] displays many more unusual features. Here we miss the restraining influence which the familiar dance rhythms and simply conceived bass lines exercised in the *Royal Consort*. The *Royal Consort* was at least semi-homophonic, being based on the two melodic parts and a more or less harmonic bass. But the second group of Lawes' pieces is very polyphonic indeed.

In these pieces (all of them for viols) we find a great variety of impressive and individual themes. Some are nostalgic in character:

Example 66: from fantasia No. 1 a 5, by William Lawes.

Others display a manly vigour:

Example 67: from fantasia No. 2 a 6, by William Lawes.

All show Lawes as a genuine artist, capable of giving convincing artistic realisation to the most contrasting emotions. But even more remarkable than this talent in the invention of new and interesting themes (which after all he had in common with men like Gibbons and Ferrabosco) is the adventurous spirit that characterises the *developments* in these pieces. Lawes builds up developments and climaxes out of very unusual, even eccentric figures. The ballad tunes of the 'golden age' have disappeared. Concessions to popular taste will be sought in vain in this music. Lawes' *Royal Consort* is indeed of a different character, but his fantasias as mentioned here can no longer be described as appealing to the musical public at large.

The motif in the just quoted

---

[1] Add. 29410–5.
[2] MSS. Add. 40657–61 and 18940–4.

fantasia a 6 is later changed to

This is what happens when this queer new figure is developed polyphonically:

Example 68: from fantasia No. 2 a 6, by William Lawes.

And yet such difficult contrapuntal combinations appear quite normal if compared with what comes after:

(b)

Here the language becomes very strange; certain bars seem really daring, such as bars 48, 49, and 50. Quite often it happens that a new voice comes in on a violently dissonant note (bar 48 and others). At the same time we see that Lawes has taken a curious liking to chords of the seventh, even unprepared ones, and for the first time the vital dominant-seventh appears (bars 45 and 51), if not yet used to strengthen the tension of the dominant leading to the solution in the tonic.

In his harmonic adventures Lawes goes very far, considering how early the date (about 1635?). Another fantasia a 6 contains the element of harmonic extravagance already in its initial subject:

Example 69: from fantasia No. 7 a 6, by William Lawes.

This is great music. The complete fantasia may serve as an example of Lawes' art.[1] In the last years before the Civil War Court life was still brightened by such fantasias and pavanas for viols. But the golden age is hastening to its close. Lawes and his fellows write not as a glorious company, but as individuals, as isolated experimentalists. Their music is introspective, personal, subjective.

The noonday of spontaneous and happy creation is well past. A sun is setting, and just as long, eccentric shadows invade the countryside at sunset, so now strange beauties, mysterious and otherworldly, invest the art of the English Court.

The third and last group of Lawes' works – (a) fantasias for violins and organs, and (b) harp consorts – is even more personal than the other two. It comprises works for three to seven instruments (violins, theorboes, viols and harps or organ in various combinations). In these pieces the harp or organ parts are mostly neither basso continuo parts nor ordinary polyphonic single lines, but very elaborate scores in themselves.[2]

The fact that violins are used in these fantasias by Lawes needs explanation, too. In their external appearance these pieces follow the tradition of the consort, mixing tone colours of various classes of instruments. Here is music that was intended for an unusually ambitious court, not for the private home of the wealthy citizen as at the beginning of the century. The old, quiet viols will not do any longer. Lawes needs the strength of the violins which at the same time are more in agreement with the rapidly spreading Italian fashion, and he also needs their greater compass, for he employs all means and all instrumental ranges to achieve his ends.[3]

[1] See Appendix, Example III.

[2] The use of written-out organ parts with solo passages is common to English music up to the Restoration, and the practice is not unknown in contemporary music abroad such as in the canzonas by Guarmi (1611) and Frescobaldi (1628), and a sonata by Marini (1628).

[3] A considerable number of fantasias by Jenkins, Coperario, Ferrabosco and Locke have also organ parts; but these are only short scores, extracts from the viol parts and intended for performance *ad libitum*, without being necessary to the score. They add no new counterpoint to the string parts. A number of examples of the use of violins in England before 1620 can be found (for instance, Holborne's collection; see Chapter IV). See also Scholes, *Oxford Companion,* and Hayes, *Musical Instruments.* O. Gibbons is said to have used violins in some fancies (Dart, *Music and Letters,* Vol. XXXVII, 1956); the same applies to Dowland's *Lachrimæ or Seaven Teares* (1604) and Campion's *Maskes.*

Without doubt these pieces are Lawes' most interesting compositions. Some of them are magnificent in their structural proportions, and moving in their emotional content. It is true that the extravagance and oddness of Lawes' melodic lines nowhere else in his work appears more conspicuous. The parts move violently as though the old rules of counterpoint as exemplified by Morley had never existed. But in the polyphonic result they always add up to a convincing whole.

A fantasia for two violins, viola da gamba (bass viol) and organ will probably give a better idea of Lawes' art than any description.[1]

It seems justified to compare Lawes' twisted melodies and unusual harmonies with the stylised, long-shaped figures of El Greco, the painter. El Greco's life-work also represents the last stage of a great tradition. Notwithstanding the greatness of these men, their art sometimes came somewhat near to preciosity. But their works express both the exclusiveness of unpopular aristocratic surroundings and the loneliness of great artists trapped in them.[2]

However, of decisive importance is the fact that both artists are creators of great genius. Thus Lawes in reality stands between two ages. He was musically trained and active as a composer within the framework of a past age, yet he was well aware of the great innovations that were gaining ground all around him. He continued the entire long tradition of refined chamber music of court and aristocracy, and yet he employed in his works more and more modern elements of expression.

William Lawes, like Bach, not merely represents 'the end' of a tradition but in many respects he constitutes a 'new beginning', even though the style and content of his music were not immediately carried on by composers of his time.

---

[1] See Example IV in Appendix.

[2] How far ahead of his time Lawes' discordant harmonies were is shown by the fact that theorists who were considered progressive remained reserved and sceptical whenever dissonances were under discussion. 'A Discord', says Charles Butler in his *Principles of Musick* of 1636, 'is a jarry noiz of two permixed sounds offending the ear' (p. 48). Later on he goes into details:

'Discord are the Perfect and Imperfect Second,
the Perfect and Imperfect Seventh,
the Tritonum and Semidiapente . . .'

'Yet a discord, as in Œconomi, so in Musick, is sometimes allovable, as making the Concord following the sweeter: but neither in that nor in this is it too bee held too long . . .' (p. 51).

William Lawes is omitted in Butler's list of noted contemporary composers (p. 48).

These last Ages have produc'd very many *Able*, and most *Excellent Masters* in *Musick*; *Three only (of which) I will Instance in, in This Particular*; because They were as *Voluminous*, and *very Eminent* in *Their Works*, viz. Mr. *William Lawes*, Mr. *John Jenkins*, and Mr. *Christopher Simpson*.

These Three Famous Men, although *Two of Them* be laid *asleep* (or as we say, *Dead*) yet by *Their most Singular and Rare Works, They Live*; and may so easily be *Distinguished, the one from the other*, and as *Exactly known, which is which, as if they were present in person, and should speak Words*.[1]

A number of compositions by another great composer, John Jenkins (1592–1678), are in the same spirit as those of Lawes. But as the real importance of this master lies in the output of his last fifteen years of life his works will be discussed in a later chapter.

❋

So much for the state of such chamber music as was sponsored by Court and High Church. In the meantime the music of the general mass of the population also underwent a crisis – a crisis that proved even more serious for the future of English music. It arose from the aims and peculiarities of the English merchant class.

The cavaliers, among them many highly cultured, somewhat morbidly refined noblemen whose scions Peacham still calls 'plants from Heaven', were the main support of the Court and particularly the Church. On the Court side also were the greatest of the landowners with many of their tenants, and the conservative, clumsy, and uneducated country gentlemen of remoter parts of the country. The vast mass of Englishmen were against the outmoded order which Charles was bringing back. Their common resentment drew close together citizens of all classes, from the wealthy merchants, empire-builders, and navigators, to intellectuals, members of the growing middle-class professions, and above all, the small producers, and those independent yeomen who formed the backbone of Cromwell's army. In spite of their separate interests, which found expression in the formation of all their party movements, Presbyterians, Independents, Levellers, Diggers and others, they were united in the desire to check the encroachments of the Crown, and in the hope that after victory was won, each would find the way clear to achieve its own ends. It is true, this

[1] Thomas Mace, *Musick's Monument*, 1676, p. 151.

union did not last for ever. It lasted, however, as long as was necessary.

The religion of economic expansion was Puritanism which, while proclaiming its ideals in the language and the symbolism of the Old Testament, became the guiding spirit also in all matters of art. Puritanism was more than a philosophy – it was a rigid form of social organisation. Struggling against constant and growing attempts to establish royal and ecclesiastic privileges, Puritan determination and self-discipline grew in strength. Puritanism was at that time also the leading spiritual force aspiring to material progress; in every sphere it combated obscurantism, out-of-date prerogatives and social, religious and cultural reaction in the form of the revived mysticism of the Anglican Church. At the same time, it stood for the independent relation of the individual to God.

It drew strength and revolutionary impetus from the masses of the English people, who were stirred by the conviction that they were God's chosen people.

In 1649 the 'Rump' in the Commons passed a resolution declaring 'That the people are, under God, the original of all just power. . .'.[1]

We do not need to idealise the bourgeoisie of the seventeenth century, but it is possible to say that just because they were the historically progressive class of this time, they could not fight for their own rights and liberties without also fighting for the rights and liberties of humanity as a whole.

The Puritans and the masses fighting on their side were filled with truly revolutionary ardour; their deepest emotions were stirred by poets like Milton in whose works visions of the liberty of all men were set forth with prophetic conviction in the poetical language of the Bible.

But the 'Commonwealth', the form of state power of the Puritan bourgeoisie of 1649–60, was a class power: after victory was won the dominant factor in matters of art and culture was not the people but early capitalism which held political and economic sway. Therefore intellectual and cultural aims during the Commonwealth were shaped to the interests of the bourgeoisie.

The middle classes of the first half of the seventeenth century moulded themselves and their children to this pattern:

a picture grave to sternness, yet not untouched with a sober

---

[1] A. L. Morton, *A People's History of England*, London, 1976, p. 251.

exaltation – an earnest, zealous, godly generation, scorning delights, punctual in labour, constant in prayer, thrifty and thriving, filled with a decent pride in themselves and their calling, assured that strenuous toil is acceptable to Heaven. . . .[1]

. . . thinking, sober and patient men, and such as believe that labour and industry is their duty towards God.[2]

From gradual beginnings the demand for economic freedom permeated English cultural life. Under the influence of Puritanism the attitude of a great number of citizens towards philosophy, science and art became *utilitarian*; seventeenth-century English philosophy began to despise 'vague' utopianism and 'hot-headed' speculation. Instead, the ideal of pious sobriety and divinely ordered commercial realism was advanced more and more consciously by the philosophers.

The beginning of this process in the philosophy of art is to be seen in the writings of Francis Bacon. To him art is useful. Gone the magic beauty, the profound emotionalism that Elizabethans adored in music and poetry. Now the 'Muses . . . ought to be the leaders and conductors of human life, and not the handmaids of the passions'.[3] Art is useful, as useful to state and commerce as science. Bacon found 'no work so meritorious as the discovery of arts and sciences that tend to civilise the life of men'. This is the attitude of a political scientist, and a new phenomenon in the development of æsthetics.

The philosophy of music in particular undergoes an amazing change within a decade or two. Music begins to be analysed with regard to its potential value in relation to daily work and the development of industries and state institutions. Ardour gives way to cool, scientific detachment in the references to music in contemporary writing. Less and less is heard of the element of beauty, the imponderables of music; more and more of its usefulness as a means of providing recreation after work. For in this part of its function it helps to make man fit and disposed to resume his civil duties. He is stronger and more useful after having had a half-hour's dose of music. A *Treatise against Stage Playes* of 1625 is full of the utilitarian spirit.

Recreation . . . signifieth to renew, to repair, to recover, to

---

[1] R. H. Tawney, *Religion and the Rise of Capitalism*, 1926, p. 211.
[2] Petty, quoted by Tawney, ibid.
[3] *Advancement of Learning*, p. 114.

restore, or to refresh eyther the body or the minde, or both, when they are impaired, overworne, wearied, or spent in the imployments of mens lawfull callings . . . and refreshed may chearefully returne to their lawfull callings againe and therein serue Got faythfully.

Different kinds of recreation are permissible:

First some little rest from labour as, if the reapers in harvest time may sit downe and rest themselves for one quarter of an hour, they will return more freshly to their worke againe. . . . Secondly, foode, meate and drinke which refresheth man comfortably and maketh him fitter and more able to performe the duties of his calling. Thirdly, Sleepe reneweth man and refresheth him greatly that he is thereby as if he had not beene wearied before. Fourthly, some change of labour quickeneth man that his former weariness is forgotten. Fiftly, Musick is a chearfull recreation to the minde that hath beene blunted with serious meditations. These and such like are holy and good recreations, both comfortable and profitable.[1]

Charles Butler, too, thinks of non-Church music as something that is 'most seasonable in the time of Feastings: wen men meete together to be merry, and to enjoy the fruit of their labours'.[2] Thomas Mace, author of *Musick's Monument* of a somewhat later date (1676), has music laid out in his mind in two categories and two categories only: 'sober-civil Musick' and 'solid-divine Musick', the art of the Church.[3]

Less and less is said of music being a 'ladder to the intelligence of higher things'.[4] More and more frequently music appears in company with such useful inventions as food or exercise. W. Perkins, in his *Cases of Conscience* (1631), says that athletics, fencing, music, chess, 'and all of this kind, wherein the industry of the mind and body hath the chiefest stroke, are very commendable'.[5] In *Salomon's House* Bacon grants a statue to 'the inventor of music'; he grants another one to the inventor of gun-powder.[6]

Music is recommended to doctors as an excellent medicine for

---

[1] Roxburghe Library, 1869, p. 241.

[2] *Principles of Musick*, p. 124. It should be noted that Butler is anti-Puritan, despite his theories on music.

[3] *The Highways of England*, 1675, p. 25 (advertisement for a new book of Mace's).

[4] See above, p. 127.

[5] H. Davey, *History of English Music*, 1921, p. 244.

[6] *New Atlantis*, ed. H. Osborne, 1937, p. 43.

various kinds of patients. 'Musica mentis medicina', written by an early seventeenth-century copyist as postscript to an instrumental air a 3[1] becomes the motto of many a writer on music. Even such humanists as Peacham look at music from a sober and practical point of view: Music

> . . . is a principall meanes of glorifying our mercifull Creator, it heightens our devotion, it gives delight and ease to our travailes, it expelleth sadnesse and heavinesse of Spirit, preserveth people in concord and amity, allayeth fiercenesse and anger.

The passage ends with the familiar recipe for the pathologist: '. . . and lastly, it is the best Phisicke for many melancholy diseases'.[2] Charles Butler, too, expresses the view that 'music is a medicine for those complaints which arise out of hard labour'.[3] Herrick's 'To Music, to becalm his Fever' reflects this conception of the art:

> Charm me asleep, and melt me so
>   With thy delicious numbers;
> That being ravished, hence I go
>   Away in easy slumbers.
>   Ease my sick head,
>   And make my bed,
>   Thou power that canst sever
>   From me this ill:
>   And quickly still:
>   Though thou not kill
>   My fever.
>
> Thou sweetly canst convert the same
>   From a consuming fire,
> Into a gentle-licking flame,
>   And make it thus expire.
>   Then make me weep
>   My pains asleep;
>   And give me such reposes,
>   That I, poor I,
>   May think thereby,
>   I live and die
>   'Mongst roses.

---

[1] Brit. Mus. MS. Add. 36484.
[2] *Compleat Gentleman*, ed. 1634, p. 104.
[3] *Principles of Music*, 1636, p. 123.

> Fall on me like a silent dew,
>   Or like those maiden showers,
> Which, by the peep of day, do strew
>   A baptism o'er the flowers.
>   Melt, melt my pains,
>   With thy soft strains;
>   That having ease me given,
>   With full delight,
>   I leave this light;
>   And take my flight
>   For Heaven.

Music is thought of as an excellent means to find husbands for young girls:

> A thing . . . frequently used, and part of a gentlewoman's bringing up, to sing, dance, and play on the Lute, or some such instrument, before she can say her Pater Noster, or Ten Commandments. 'Tis the next way their parents think, to get them husbands, they are compelled to learn.

However, the very same gentlewoman, 'now being married, will scarce touch an instrument, they care not for it'.[1]

Some Puritans, even the most militant, are very eloquent in the recommendation of 'sober-civil' music, as an ally in the dissemination of utilitarian doctrines. Of all writers on music John Milton subscribes to this view most frankly and radically:

> Sometimes the lute or soft organ stop waiting on elegant voices either to religious, martial or civil ditties, which, if wise men and prophets be not extremely out, have a great power over dispositions and manners to smoothe and make (them) gentle from rustic harshness and distempered passions. The like would also not be unexpedient after meat, to assist and cherish nature in her first concoction, and send (their) minds back to study in good tune and satisfaction.[2]

The effect of utilitarianism thus established in musical life and musical philosophy, was twofold. For one thing there was the practical issue – to guide working people in conformity with the ideal of the 'godly discipline' of *laborare et orare*. For another (and this was,

---

[1] Robert Burton in *The Anatomy of Melancholy*, 1621, III, pp. 135 and 204. See also Westrup, *Domestic Music*, for more examples (pp. 28 ff. and 32).

[2] From a letter to Master Sam Hartlib. Complete collection, Vol. I, 1739, p. 139.

as will be shown, the decisive factor) music, handled by piously-sober merchants and manufacturers, became *useful*, to those whose slogan it was – as Baxter put it – that 'every penny which is laid out . . . must be done as by God's own appointment'.

Puritanism, conscious of its mission as herald of new forms of life in the development of human society, was bound to consider profound as well as (in many cases) religious music an obstacle to the realization of just these forms of life. It zealously turned against anything which could not be adjusted to its system of hard work and religious strictness, as well as against everything which might strengthen the old aristocracy and its 'Cavaliers' and propagate their mentality. The leaders of the Commonwealth supported the cause of the early bourgeoisie, precisely those land-owning early capitalists whose attitude to life and ideological make-up has been described. In order to make their victory secure Cromwell's Independents applied radical measures in musical life too.

Did such an attitude assist the continuation and further evolution of great music? The answer is in the negative. As England slowly took over the political and economic hegemony in the world, she lost *pari passu* her musical leadership. A new spirit had invaded the cultural life of the nation. It worked like yeast in the minds of the thinkers of the day. Many were perplexed, and many undecided; doubtfully groping theories were put forward in the first half of the seventeenth century. The Puritans themselves were not quite sure which secular music ought to perform what secular function. But they were in agreement that somehow or other music ought to fit into their own pattern of social life.

Although it would be wrong (for reasons that will be discussed presently) to put all the blame for the degeneration of English music on the shoulders of the Puritans, we cannot absolve them from some responsibilities. The chief cause for criticism lies in their simplification of the music of the church service; the interdict on the use of the organ in church, passed by Parliament in 1644; and the closure of cathedral choir schools which not only affected the training of boys' voices, but produced a temporary hiatus in an important source of musical education in which so many of the finest musicians had previously been trained. When, after the Restoration in 1660, the Chapel Royal was re-established, the scarcity of trained boys' voices was noted by Matthew Locke:

. . . after the opening of His Majestie's Chapel the orderers of the musick were necessitated to supply superior parts of music with cornets and men's feigned voices, there being not a single lad for all that time capable of singing his part readily.

The violence of the Parliamentary soldiers in destroying organs after the interdict against their use is often written of as if this were the usual way in which they were disposed of. Certainly there is evidence of this happening in some cases,[1] but in John Evelyn's *A Character of England* (1659) a different way in which they were dealt with is described. This little book is a translation of a letter from an unknown Frenchman to an unknown 'Lord' in France, full of dire complaints against the regime. Evelyn, in the preface 'To the Reader', admits that much of the criticism is justified and he decides to translate and publish it 'not to reproach, but to instruct our Nation'. On p. 30 of the letter the following statement occurs:

> . . . they have translated the *Organs* out of the *Churches*, and set them up in Taverns, chanting their *Dithyrambicks*, and bestial *Bacchanalias* to the tune of those instruments.

In the margin of this passage, in the copy of the book in the British Museum, the words 'Musick Houses' are written in what appears to be a contemporary hand.

The reduction of the number of court musicians who held posts under Charles I, the disbanding of the Chapel Royal and the dismissal of many organists from churches, cathedrals and university chapels, undoubtedly threw a number of musicians out of steady employment, but it seems clear that, in many cases, provision was made for them after their employment ceased. His salary as a Gentleman of the Chapel Royal was paid to Henry Lawes for three years after its closure. This is made clear in a letter from him to the Receiver General preserved in Brit. Mus. Add. MS. 33965, f. 58 and 58ᵛ.[2]

The closure of the theatres also brought with it lack of employment for the theatre musicians, and 'The Actors Remonstrance or complaint for the silencing of their Profession' (1643) was particularly bitter on this point:

> Our Musicke that was held so delectable and precious that they scorned to come to a Tauerne under twentie shillings salary for two houres, now wander with their Instruments under their

[1] See also J. Pulver, *Biographical Dictionary of Old English Music* (1927) p. 284.
[2] *A General History of Music* (1789. Dover Publications Reprint, 1957, Vol. 2, p. 321).

cloaks, I mean such as haue any, into all houses of good fellowship, saluting euery roome where there is company with 'Will you haue any musicke Gentlemen?'

Nevertheless, Charles Burney,[1] though in general hostile to the Puritans, in writing of music during the Interregnum, says 'yet it seems to have been more zealously cultivated in private during the usurpation, if we may judge by the number of publications, than in the same number of years, at any former period'. This statement is borne out by the number of secular music books which came from the firm of Playford alone during these years:

1651   *The English Dancing Master, or Plaine and Easie rules for the Dancing of Country Dances, with the tunes to each dance* (104 dances). New and enlarged editions in 1652 and 1657.

Orlando Gibbons', Fantasies, of Three Parts.

Michael East, The Seventh Set of Bookes. Wherein are Duos for two Base Viols . . . Also Fancies of 3, Parts for treble Viols, and a base Violl. A reprint of a work of 1638.

Musick and Mirth, presented in a choice collection of Rounds and Catches, for 3 voices.

A Musical Banquet, in three books, consisting of Lessons for the Lyra Viol; Allmans, and Sarabands, Choice Catches and Rounds, etc.

Select Musicall Ayres, and Dialogues, For one or two Voyces, to sing to the Theorbo, Lute, or Basse Violl. Composed by John Wilson, Charles Coleman, Henry Lawes, William Webb, Gentlemen, and the Second Booke of Ayres, Containing Pastorall Dialogues For two Voyces, to sing either to the Theorbo, Harp-sicon or Basse Viol.

Musick's Recreation on the Lyra Viol (another edition in 1661).

Catch that Catch can, or A Choice Collection of Catches, Rounds and Canons by John Hilton (New edition, 1658).

About 1652   *A Book of new lessons for the Cittern and Gittern.*

---

[1] See Adrienne Simpson,' Richard Mathew and The Lutes Apology', *The Lute Society Journal*, Vol. VIII, 1966, pp. 41–7.

1653　　*Ayres and Dialogues for One, Two and Three voyces by Henry Lawes.* First book (second and third books 1655 and 1658).

1655　　*An Introduction to the Skill of Musick, in two books; first a brief and plain introduction to musick, both for singing and for playing the Viol, by J. P.; second the Art of setting or composing musick in parts... formerly published by Dr Tho. Campion, but now republished by Mr Christopher Sympson* (second edition 1658, third edition 1660).

　　　　Court Ayres: or Pavins, Almains, Corants, and Sarabands, of two parts, treble and basse; for Viols or Violins.

　　　　The Art of Setting or Composing Musick in parts; Dr Campion's second edition, with large annotations thereon, by Mr Christopher Sympson.

1656　　*Matthew Locke, his Little Consort, of Three Parts, containing Pavans, Ayres, Corants and Sarabands, for Viols and Violins.*

1657　　*Ayres and Dialogues To be Sung to the Theorbo-Lute, or Basse Viol by John Gamble.*

1659　　*The Division Violist or an introduction to playing upon a ground, by Christopher Simpson.*

Another book, Richard Mathew's *The Lute's Apology for Her Excellence*, printed in 1652, is interesting, not for the quality of the music, which is poor, but for the fact that the unique surviving copy was in the library of Sir William Boteler (d. 1656), a noted Parliamentarian, who was elected one of the five members for Bedford County under the 'instrument of Government'. Manuscripts of music from this period are also numerous.

That music was cultivated in both the Universities is clear. Degrees were given at Oxford and Cambridge. John Wilson (a confirmed Royalist) took his D.Mus. at Oxford in 1645 and became Professor of Music in 1656. We also learn from Anthony à Wood of the existence of a number of musical clubs in Oxford. In *Music and Puritanism*[1] Scholes lists four that are mentioned in his Diary:

1. The important weekly club carried on for profit by Ellis, late organist of St John's College.

[1] Percy A. Scholes, *Music and Puritanism* (1934), p. 24.

2. A weekly club carried on in his rooms by Narcissus Marsh, M.A., Fellow of Exeter College, and moved to St Alban's Hall when Marsh became its Principal.

3. A weekly club carried on in his rooms by Thomas Janes, M.A., of Magdalen College: he himself, 'practised much upon the Theorbo lute'.

4. The 'Scholastic Musicians', meeting every Friday in various colleges.

Of the Presbyterians and Independents of Oxford he also wrote, in 1659:

They encouraged instrumental musick, and some there were that had musick meetings every week in their chambers.

Less is known about musical activities in Cambridge, and no Professor of Music had ever been appointed there. Nevertheless, on two occasions during the Interregnum the University is known to have been requested to confer degrees in music. The first was in 1651 when Charles Coleman was recommended for the degree of Doctor of Music by the Committee appointed in that year to reform the University. He took the degree on 2 July.[1] The second occasion was when Cromwell himself wrote, in 1658, to 'Our trusty and well-beloved the Vice-Chancellor and Senate of Our University of Cambridge', asking that Benjamin Rogers 'be admitted and created Bacheler in Music in some one or more of your congregations in that our University'.[2]

In the *Amanda* of Nicholas Hookes, B.A., printed in 1653, there is a poem, addressed to 'Mr Lilly, Musick Master at Cambridge',[3] which suggests that an active musical life was carried on in Cambridge during these years. The following lines start towards the end of the second stanza:

> Your well spoke *viol* scornes *tautologie*,
> And I in truth had rather hear you *teach*
> O' the *Lyra*, then the rarest *tub-man* preach:
> In's holy speeches he may strike my eares
> With more of Heav'n: you with more o'th spheres.

[1] See H. Davey, *History of Music* (2nd edition, 1921) p. 276.

[2] Thomas Carlyle, *Oliver Cromwell, Letters and Speeches* (1845), Vol. IV, pp. 197–8.

[3] Reprinted Elkin Matthews (1923). Possibly the 'Mr Lilly'' is the John Lillie whose name occurs in a number of sources of music for Lyra Viol. See Frank Traficante, 'Music for the Lyra Viol: The Printed Sources', *The Lute Society Journal*, Vol. VIII, 1966, pp. 7–24; and 'Music for Lyra Viol: Manuscript Sources', *Chelys*, Vol. 8, 1978–9, pp. 4–22.

I've heard your *base* mumble and mutter too
Made angry with your cholerick hand, while you
With hastie jirks to vex and anger't more
Correct its stubbornnesse and lash it o'r:
I've heard you *pawse*, and dwell upon an *aire*,
(Then mak't i'th' end as loth to part it were)
Languish and melt away so leisurely,
As if 'twere pity that its Echo die;
Then snatch up *notes*, as if your *viol* broke,
And in the breaking every splinter spoke:
I've seen your active hands vault to and fro,
This to give *grace*, that to command your *bowe*;
As if your fingers and your *Instrument*
By conspiration made you eminent.
    We have good *Musick* and *Musicians* here,
If not the best, as good as any where:
A brave old *Irish Harper*, and you know
English or *French way* few or none out-go
Our *Lutanists*; the Lusemores too, I think
For Organists; the Sack-buts breath may stink,
And yet old *Brownes* be sweet; O'the *Violin*
Saunders plays well, where *Magge* or *Mel* han't been,
Then on his Cornet brave thanksgiving *Mun*,
Playes in *Kings Chappel* after Sermon's done:
At those *loud blasts*, though he's out-gone by none,
Yet *Cambridge* glories in *your self* alone:
No more but thus, he that heares only you,
Heares *Lillie* play, and Doctor Coleman too.
    You in the swiftness of your *hand* excel
All others, my *Amanda* sings as well,
No *Musick* like to *hers*; I wish in troth,
That we with her might *play in Consort* both;
Might I my self, and you my friend prefer
You with her *voice* should *play*, and I with her.

In spite of the closure of the theatres, public entertainments with music began to return to London. In 1656 Sir William Davenant presented the first English 'opera', *The Siege of Rhodes*, with music by Henry Lawes, Matthew Locke, Henry Cooke, Charles Coleman and George Hudson. He subsequently produced *The Cruelty of the Spaniards in Peru* in 1658 and *The History of Sir*

Francis Drake in 1659. These entertainments took place 'Daily at the Cockpit in Drury Lane'. Davenant is often referred to as the father of English opera.

It is also recorded that a number of masques were performed at private functions at such places as the Middle Temple and at schools for young ladies.[1]

The taverns where music was provided, or 'Musick Houses', mentioned in Evelyn's *A Character of England* (1659) were, it appears, becoming a fairly common feature of the London scene. Samuel Pepys records in his Diary how, in this same year, he listened to an entertainment in the 'Musick Room' at the Mitre in Fleet Street. Although he does not mention an organ, it appears that, at a slightly later date, many taverns in London and the close-by river resorts, provided themselves with instruments, including organs, and gave regular, well-organised, musical entertainments.

In the past, statements have been made that the Waits of many cities were suppressed but, as Percy Scholes states:[2]

> We know the London Waits continued, for the authorities in 1642 ordered that though (undoubtedly owing to the Puritan views on Sabbath-keeping) their Sunday playing at the Royal Exchange should be discontinued, they should 'perform the said service every holiday hereafter at and for the same time accustomed'. The city records of Norwich show the Waits as receiving their stipends throughout the Commonwealth, new Waits appointed, instruments repaired, the Waits ordered to attend the Mayor to Church, the Waits lent to the neighbouring town of King's Lynn, and so forth. And we find the Waits of Newcastle-on-Tyne receiving 12d. for playing at the celebration of Midsummer Day (1657) and employed to play before the door of the Puritan Mayor whilst he entertains Cromwell, passing through the city (1648) on his return from Scotland.

Concerning musical education at this time it is clear that the closing of the choir schools reduced the opportunity for musical education in a number of places. Nevertheless many of those who had been employed as organists set themselves up as teachers as also did some of the Gentlemen of the Chapel Royal. Henry Lawes is known to have become a very successful teacher of singing, and Playford in his *Musical Banquet* (1651) provides a list of eighteen

---

[1] See Scholes, ibid., p. 32.
[2] Scholes, ibid., p. 27.

eminent teachers 'For the Voyse or Viols' and nine 'For the Organ
or Virginall'. Many letters, diaries and other documents of the
period give details about lessons they have received from various
distinguished musicians. Private tuition in 'Musicke, Playing on
Instruments' could be obtained, among other subjects, at Sir
Balthasar Gerbier's academy, set up in 1649 at Bethnal Green.
Some musicians, such as John Jenkins, appear to have passed
through the whole period in their capacity as private teachers in
distinguished households without their lives being seriously in-
terfered with.

A very common method of instruction in the musical profession
in England was by means of apprenticeship. That this practice was
carried on through the Interregnum is shown, for example, in the
Minutes of the Sessions of the Middlesex County Records for the
years 1657 and 1658.

A project which, had it come to fruition, would have put
England into a leading role in musical education in Europe was the
proposal, put forward in a petition, signed by five of Cromwell's
household musicians, on 19 February 1657 or 1658, to the Committee of the Council for the Advancement of Music, for the 'erec-
tion' of a 'Corporation or Colledge of Musitians in London'.[1] This
is a curious document with some contradictory statements and, in
a period when private music was obviously flourishing, the
threatening cry that, without such an organisation 'the Science
itselfe, must dye in this Nacion' is odd. Scholes analyses this
petition with great care and adds the comment, 'England now saw
the appointment of the only "Government Committee for the Advancement of Music" she has ever known'.[2] Unhappily nothing
more was heard of the Committee or the petition and no such
college was to appear in England until the opening of the Royal
Academy of Music in 1823.

As for individual musicians, and writers who collaborated in
producing musical entertainments who had previously been active
in the Royalist cause, we find little evidence of their being subjected
to harsh treatment, and that only if their activities persisted to a
dangerous extent.

John Wilson is a notable case. As has already been seen, he was a
fervent Royalist and yet took his D.Mus. at Oxford in 1645 and was
made Professor in 1656. In 1657 he published his *Psalterium*

---

[1] Public Record Office. State Papers, 18, Vol. 153 (No. 123, fol. 254).
[2] Scholes, ibid., p. 23.

Carolinum. The Devotions of his Sacred Majestie in his Solitude and Sufferings. Musick for 3 voices and an Organ or Theorbo, By John Wilson, D^r. and Musick Professor of Oxford. This would appear to have been somewhat provocative, yet no action at all was taken against him and he continued in the Chair at Oxford until after the Restoration.

Christopher Simpson joined the Royalist army in 1643 and suffered many hardships. Later he came under the patronage of Sir Robert Bolles, teaching the children of the family and taking charge of the household music. He had no difficulty in publishing his books.

James Shirley became a Roman Catholic after his appointment as a master at St Alban's Grammar School. He was a dramatist of some distinction and appears to have led a comfortable life until the closure of the theatres in 1642. He fought in the Civil War on the Royalist side, yet we find his name as the author of the masque *Cupid and Death*, with music by Matthew Locke and Christopher Gibbons, an official entertainment given, at Cromwell's command, for the Portuguese Ambassador.

Sir William Davenant's activities in the Royalist cause, both during and after the Civil War, led to his having twice been imprisoned in the Tower, the second time being from 1650 to 1652. Yet, apparently without interference, he opened his successful productions of 'opera' in 1656. After further Royalist activities he was again imprisoned in 1659.

Evidence of Cromwell's own love of music both in his own home and on public occasions, is plentiful. John Hingeston, Master of the Music, George Hudson, David Mell and William Howes had all previously been in Royal service. Cromwell himself even liked to listen to Latin motets by such an outspokenly Catholic composer as Richard Deering, and these motets were performed with an organ and other instruments by Hingeston and his pupils.

Sir John Hawkins, in his *General History of the Science and Practice of Music* (1776),[1] states that Hingeston also taught music to Cromwell's daughters. At the wedding of one, there was an orchestra of forty-eight and a wind band of fifty.[2] At the wedding of the other, two pastorals, or musical dialogues, with words by Andrew Marvell, were performed.[3]

---

[1] Footnote, Chapter CXXI.
[2] Appendix to the *Fifth Report of the Historical Manuscripts Commission*, p. 157.
[3] See article on Andrew Marvell in *Dictionary of National Biography*. The texts of the two

Many official occasions are described at which Cromwell had music provided for the entertainment of his guests, or at which music was provided in his honour. For example, in 1654, one of the Dutch ambassadors described an occasion of state when:

> . . . The music played all the while we were at dinner. The Lord Protector then had us into another room, where the Lady Protectrice and others came to us: where we had also music, and wine and a psalm sung which His Highness gave us. . . .[1]

On 8 February 1653, a feast was given at the Grocers' Hall in honour of the Lord Protector, at which the Lord Mayor was present:

> . . . his Highness, having retired himself awhile upstairs . . . came down to dine in the great hall . . . being entertained, besides cheer, with music, voices and trumpets . . . his Highness departed being played out by hautboys and other loud music (*Mercurius Politicus*, No. 191).[2]

A perhaps less creditable aspect of Cromwell's love of music appears in the frequently told tale of how, with the consent of the Fellows, he had the organ removed from Magdalen College, Oxford, and set up in Hampton Court Palace.

At regular intervals in his funeral procession groups of three drums and three trumpets were placed. His musicians 'Mr John Rogers, Mr Thomas Mallard, Mr William Howe, Mr David Mell, Mr Thomas Blagrave, Mr William Gregory, Mr William Hudson, Mr Hinkston, Master of the Music' followed in the procession.[3]

Although, as has been shown, all the evidence testifies to the abundance of music that was written and performed during this period – a healthy sign in one way – changes were beginning to show themselves among the characteristics which had made English music great. Important among these was the question of polyphony. This must have divided the musical world of England as Moses' sword divided the Red Sea. It was associated with ornament, luxury, distraction of the mind, and High Church. We have

---

pastorals can be found in *Poems and Letters* edited by H. M. Margoliouth (1927; 2nd edition, 1952).

[1] J. Morley, *Cromwell* (1900) pp. 429–30.

[2] Thomas Burton, M.P., *Diary. 1652–1658*, edited by John Towell Rutt (1828), Vol. 1, Introduction, xv, footnote.

[3] ibid., Vol. 2, Appendix, p. 531.

already seen that by about 1640 polyphony was becoming intellec-
tualised and in danger of losing its original purposiveness. The
chief anger of the Puritans must have been directed against such
ornamental polyphony as was practised in the Church service.

Not that this aspect of Puritan ideology could be condemned as
deliberately destructive. Puritanism in every sphere combated
obscurantism and absolutism, it struggled for the independent
relation to God, against the revived mysticism of the Anglican
Church. No longer does the responsibility for God and man lie
with priest and king. In the case of the Puritans this positive side of
man's increased sense of power is, however, doomed by its
character to be unfriendly to profound music.

They accelerated a process which the public at large had felt long
ago. It has already been pointed out that only a few polyphonic
fantasias found their way to the printing-press. This points to the
fact that they were in demand by a somewhat limited number of
people. Towards 1640 it was, indeed, only a small circle in London
and Oxford who practised them, and these people were usually
associated with the hated Anglican outlook.

As we noticed earlier, the polyphony that was used by the composers of Court and Church was of a kind that placed all parts of
the score on an equal footing. There was no 'chief melody' which
the ear of the listener could catch easily. The complex polyphonic
results of the combination of a multitude of parts demanded a far
more attentive, intellectually alert and emotionally subtle attitude
on the side of the listener than the new era would allow.

Puritanism fought Anglican polyphony, especially when it
became excessive and hyper-complex, just as the Anglican Reform
100 years before had fought Catholic polyphony. Not only out-
spoken Puritans did so, for as early as 1601 the opinion is
expressed in 'To the Reader' in Philip Rosseter's *A Booke of Ayres*:

> . . . so in Musicke we yeeld the chiefe place to the grave, and well
> invented Motet, but not to every harsh and dull confused Fan-
> tasie, where in a multitude of points the Harmonie is quite
> drowned.

Instead the melodic ideal of the 'charming air' was advanced, as
William Strode expressed it in one of his most beautiful poems,
one which reflects the beginning of this change from the old to the
new attitude towards music:

The Commendation of Music

Oh lull me, lull me, charming air,
 My senses rock with wonder sweet;
Like snow on wool thy fallings are,
 Soft as a spirit's are thy feet:
  Grief who need fear
  That hath an ear?
  Down let him lie
  And slumbering die,
And change his soul for harmony.

(William Strode, 1602–1645).

The end of the development is shown in a statement by
Christopher Simpson:

> . . . this kind of music (fantasias of the polyphonic kind) is now
> much neglected, by reason of the scarcity of auditors that
> understand it; their ears being better acquainted and more
> delighted with *light and airy music*.[1]

Light and airy music. This was indeed what was asked of the
composers; moreover the demand was for light and airy
instrumental music rather than vocal. In 1659 Anthony à Wood
testified that 'Puritans used to love and encourage instrumental
musick; but did not care for vocall . . .'[2] 'Man may play a Lesson
on a Lute or other Instrument to refresh his Spirits.'[3]

The earlier stages of the development of such light instrumental
compositions have already been studied in reviewing consort
dances and suites. A large corpus of such music was produced even
in the critical period before the Civil War. Apart from the works of
the already mentioned John Adson[4] many tunes and suites were
composed by men like Thomas Mudd[5] (dates unknown), Davis
Mell (1604–1662)[6] and Maurice Webster (d. 1635),[7] to mention
only some of the better-known among this group of musicians.

---

[1] *Compendium*, 1667, p. 15.
[2] *Life and Times of Anthony à Wood*, ed. Llewellyn Powys, London, 1932, p. 70.
[3] T. F. Minister of Exon., 1653, quoted by Davey, p. 252.
[4] There are 54 dances in *Courtly Masquing Ayres* (1652); at least 5 in Brit. Mus. Add. 15118
and a few more in Bodleian Mus. Sch. E. 451.
[5] Pieces in Add. 1840–4 and other MSS.
[6] 12 suites in Christ Church, Oxford (treble part only).
[7] Various music by him in Thomas Simpson, *Taffel-Consort* (Hamburg, 1621), Lbm Add.
MS. 18940–4, and Bodleian Mus. Sch. E 451.

Their compositions may be characterised as pleasant but unimportant.

A whole school of composers tried to adjust the polyphonic fantasia – with which they had been educated and had grown up – to the new ideal. No doubt a strange compromise; but the composers who chose such a course are no more to blame than their ancestors of 100 years before who, having been brought up in the tradition of the Catholic polyphonic motet, turned to the In Nomine in order to reconcile the opposing demands of the Anglican Reform with the polyphony that was their proper sphere.

The result of this compromise which was arrived at during the era of rising Puritanism might be named the 'pseudo-polyphonic fantasia'. The influence of the more popular and homophonic dance consorts was very obvious in this kind of music, of which the already mentioned fantasias a 5 by Michael East of 1610 were the first examples.[1] A later publication of fantasias by East (1638) includes items for 2 bass viols, and for 3 and 4 viols. While the interesting pieces for 2 bass viols are more deeply rooted in the old polyphonic traditions of the Morley type,[2] the 3 and 4 part fantasias are definitely of the new 'compromise' type. All these pieces have characteristic titles, some of them religious, others madrigalesque and sometimes slightly perfumed ('Love cannot dissemble' – 'Name right your notes' – 'Desperavi', 'Peccavi', 'Vidi', etc.; the 9 fantasias a 3 bear the names of the nine Muses).

These 'literary' titles indicate a desire on the part of the composer to appeal to a wider public than, for instance, Gibbons' more abstract and complex art aspired to reach. In East's fantasias we find no genuine polyphony built on the simultaneous sounding of several independent parts. There is always one chief part which attracts the attention of the listener, while the other parts form a semi-homophonic accompaniment. This 'melodic thread' travels from part to part, yet most of the time it stays in the descant.

A fancy for four parts, 1638 ('Name right your notes'), by Michael East, appears in the Appendix (No. V).

The whole character of such pieces is homophonic and 'airy' (East himself calls his four-part fantasias in particular 'ayerie fancies'). There is no pretence of any great degree of intellectual

---

[1] East published 37 fantasias in these collections. Brit. Mus. and Royal College of Music. Fantasias a 3 have been edited by Freda Burford (Viola da Gamba Society 1970, 1973)

[2] See also above, pp. 104 ff.

vigour. One seeks in vain in them for anything which recalls the art of Lawes.

John Okeover (d. about 1664),[1] Martin Peerson (d. 1651),[2] Henry Loosemore (d. 1670),[3] Richard Mico (d. about 1650),[4] Thomas Brewer (1611–?),[5] and other composers, most of whom were not Court musicians but in private service or independent, contributed simplified fantasias of the Michael East type. John Hilton (1599–1657)[6] provided a more personal note by the use of interesting and lively forms and by the introduction of popular and striking themes, such as:

Example 70: from fantasia a 3, by John Hilton:

This is agreeable and easy-going art, but less inspired than the production of the Gibbons-Ferrabosco-Tomkins era. Only one master had enough vitality to contrive within the lighter fantasia style, a chamber music of a more profound character and of deeper and more radiant colours: Simon Ives (1600–1660). Ives is too personal a musician to be called an eclectic or revivalist, although he did not contribute any vitally new elements of style to the period. Among his numerous fantasias and In Nomines[7] are to be found real gems that sparkled once more with the old melodic optimism and originality of the golden age. Ives worked for the Court as well as for the wider public. He displayed in his works a certain nobleness of spirit combined with simplicity of means. His

[1] Fantasias and pavanas in Add. 17786–91, 17792–6 and Bodleian, Oxford, Mus. Sch. D. 245–7.

[2] Fantasias, almains, etc., in Add. 17786–91, Christ Church, Oxford, Mus. MS. 423–8 and 716–⁴.

[3] Add. 34800.

[4] 30 fantasias and some dances in Christ Church, Oxford, Mus. MS. 2, 353–6, 403–8, 436, 473–8 and others.

[5] 6 fantasias a 4 and dance movements in Bodleian, Oxford, C. 100, F. 568–9 and others.

[6] Fantasias and præludium a 3 on Christ Church, Oxford, Mus. MS. 744–6.

[7] Fantasias a 2–6, one In Nomine a 5 and innumerable dance movements in Add. 31424, Bodleian, Oxford, Mus. Sch. C. 64–9, Christ Church, Oxford, 716–20 and others.

finest instrumental composition is a fantasia a 4, a gay piece in D-major.[1]

But while some composers were thus trying to reconcile Court style with popular demands, the real popular art was going through a crisis of its own. It is true that by no means the least important or the least valuable part of the output of the period, is the 'home-made' aids and tunes of the people themselves: 17th-century folksongs and dance tunes some of which are today still just as familiar as they were at the time of their origin. A considerable number of popular instrumental dance tunes appeared in John Playford's collections, such as *The English Dancing Master* (1650, 1652, 1657, etc.), *Musick's Hand-maide* (1663), *Musick's Delight on the cithren* (1666), *Courtly masquing ayres* (1662), *The pleasant Companion* (Thomas Greeting, (1682), and others). Here are a few of them:

Example 71: Tunes from 'The English Dancing Master'.

(*a*) Parson's Farewell:

(*b*) Scotch Cap:

---

[1] Add. 17792–6.

(*c*) Pell Mell:

(*d*) The Fit's Come on Me now:

(*e*) The Merry Merry Milk Maids:

The rapid development of capitalism and wealth meant also the rapid development of class differentiation and division both among townspeople and peasantry, and all the genuine, unrestrained production of the English people, amusing and colourful though it was, could not come to the rescue in this hour of crisis of English music as a powerful rejuvenating factor. And whatever productive energy remained in this kind of unsophisticated music-making, it certainly was not made use of or developed into a great new musical life by the cultural initiators of the upper classes who disputed the key positions, ideological and material. The rival authoritarians – the reactionary Court and High Church on the one hand, and the sober Puritan leaders on the other – aimed alike at the rigid control of the individual.

Once the Commonwealth was installed Cromwell turned against the party of the 'Levellers', the most determined promoters of popular revolutionary advance. After this great rebel movement had been destroyed much of the creative initiative of the people was discouraged: it dried up in those regions of art which had started to blossom during the turbulent years of the Civil War. The Commonwealth government was concerned to strengthen state power and to spread Puritan theories and doctrines but not concerned about an intense cultural life for the people. The now ruling strata of the bourgeoisie, itself a class power, could not afford to concede too much cultural freedom of movement in any sphere of life.

This, then, was the situation: English chamber music, that was universally acknowledged and magnificently homogeneous during the golden age, was split into halves. Here, appeared an inbreeding of hyper-delicate and non-popular chamber art at Court and in related circles, there, a simple tune-playing, or at best a compromise style of pseudo-polyphonic dances and fantasias. And when in 1649 the last remnants of Court and High Church were suppressed, only the simplified art of the new middle classes was left. A fresh impetus that might have brought new life by developing the vital productive powers of the people themselves disappeared among the social changes that took place during the following periods.

Once again, we do not want to give the impression that the Puritans were, as they are sometimes said to have been, wilful destroyers of English music. They were not against all music, but only against Church music, and even in this question there were exceptions. Cromwell and Milton both cared for Church music, as also did other prominent Puritans. The general trend of Puritan musical policy was fairly clear, but the movement as a whole was not always completely sure of itself. Light and pleasing music, for instance, was recommended very warmly by many Puritans, though others, such as Prynne, in *Histrio-Mastix* or a Scourge for *Stage Players* (1633), came down heavily upon music as well as on most of the popular amusements of the day.

An atmosphere of indecision lay heavy over many regions of

English thinking in the first half of the seventeenth century. The age of Newton and John Locke had not yet arrived; among the various religious and political thinkers there was difference of opinion about music as about many other important questions. The strongest opposition came from the Quakers, led by George Fox. There were even such extreme cases as that of the composer Solomon Eccles (1618–1683) who became a Quaker and, in 1660, after showing himself to be an excellent musician,

> publicly burned his instruments and music on Tower Hill and took to shoemaking. To show his contempt for 'steeple-houses' he for two Sundays running insisted on making shoes in the pulpit of a London church during service, and had to be removed by the constable.[1]

Milton, whose father was a composer, spoke enthusiastically as a poet about music, even though he gave purely utilitarian views when appearing as a politician or philosopher. In his early *At a solemn Music* he even proclaimed himself a great admirer of religious music:

> Oh may we soon again renew that song
> And keep in tune with Heaven, till God ere long
> To his celestial consort us unite,
> To live with him, and sing in endless morn of light!

In his *Areopagitica. A speech against the licensing of books* (1644), he says:

> If we think to regulate printing, thereby to rectify manners, we must regulate all recreations and pastimes, all that is delightful to man.

Then he gives a list of the dire results which he feels will follow in the field of music were such a censorship to be imposed:

> No music must be heard, no song be set or sung, but what is grave and Doric . . . It will ask more than the work of twenty licensers to examine all lutes, the violins and the guitars in every house; they must not be allowed to prattle as they do, but must be licensed what they may say. And who shall license all airs and madrigals that whisper softness in chambers?[2]

---

[1] Scholes, *Oxford Companion*, 1939. Later Eccles contributed to *The Division Violin*.
[2] John Milton, *Areopagitica, A Speech for the Liberty of Unlicensed Printing* (1644, edited with a commentary by Sir Richard Jebb, 1918) p. 26, l. 27–p. 27, l. 7.

Furthermore there is no doubt that there really was much publication of music during the Commonwealth, if of 'light and airy' character and of no outstanding value. The Puritans may have done harm to the development of music by refusing to admit the art to the serious thoughts of a serious age. But it cannot be said that they suppressed the art or even tried to. The time between 1648 and 1660 was a musically active time. The only question is what kind of music was played, written and encouraged. That is all that matters.

In view of all this evidence it is surely an over-simplification of the case to assert that English music was destroyed by the Puritans. Such indeed is the power of a title (especially a political nickname such as this one), that one is apt to forget that Puritans were no more and no less than ordinary men in peculiar circumstances. It is these circumstances which made them Puritans, and it is these circumstances which destroyed English music. Chief of the dominating conditions of the time was the way in which economic expansion, in permeating the inner life of the country, produced increasing class divisions and developed, among the decisive sections of society, the general attitude of mind which was discussed and illustrated in the earlier part of this chapter. It was this spirit which degraded music to the level of a toy, a plaything, a restorative to be applied to men to make them fit for labour. At the same time it glorified all arts and all qualities in art which make for steady application to duty, whereby riches may be made.

The worldly rewards of this cultural policy were immense. The second great forward surge in the history of the economic and political advance of England took place in the Commonwealth.

But in the same period, and by the same process, the fate of English music was sealed.

CHAPTER VII

Last Rise – Eclipse

And yet, once again before the great ebb the creative power of English music was to show itself in full force.

It was the unusually happy combination of several peculiar circumstances that restored to English chamber music once more, if only for a short time, its lost greatness.

The immediate external reason for this remarkable recovery was the Restoration of 1660 itself by which Charles II became king – so it seemed at first.

The restoration of the Court was by no means altogether a restoration of the pre-Commonwealth order. On the contrary, on the basis laid by the revolution of 1640–60, industry and trade could expand rapidly. The independent power of the crown as an executive authority had gone. The king was a 'king by the grace of merchants and squires'.[1]

But, at the same time, reactionary forces *were* strengthened, and they were conspicuously represented at Charles II's court. On the one hand the most democratic elements of the Commonwealth period (Levellers) had been defeated (the Dissenters, for instance, were forthwith excluded from municipal government and the universities). Yet the compromise of the Restoration had brought back to power, on the other hand, a clique of courtiers and landowners with a semi-feudal mentality, an essentially static and conservative outlook. While the bourgeoisie was developing strongly and economic prosperity progressed considerably, the restored Court, with the advancing years, pursued a new and cleverly camouflaged policy of action.

Charles II's policy in matters of art reflects quite clearly the narrow selfishness of his ambitions.

He was only concerned with the cultivation of art at the Court. He did not care one iota about what happened to musicians outside the Court. There was no question of improving their lot; many musicians of earlier fame were forgotten. In general cultural life at the Court did not strike impartial observers as particularly sympathetic. There were many silly fashions and much empty showing-off. Typical of the time were the dress fashions – costumes

[1] Hill.

'burst into a wild efflorescence after the "close time" of the Commonwealth'; 'men's gloves were fringed, scented with jasmine or orange', and 'both men and women used muffs'.[1] The people at the Court are described by the famous Anthony à Wood as 'rude, rough, whoremongers; vaine, empty, carelesse'.[2] Roger North (1650–1733) speaks similarly of their musical incompetence, if more politely: 'Nothing advanced musick more in this age than the patronage of nobility, and of men of fortunes,' but '. . . the Lords and the rest that subscribed (as the good King Charles II) had ears, but not artificial ones, and those were necessary to warrant the authority of such a court of justice'.[3]

However, as Court life differed so much from the busy capitalist working day of commercial and early industrial England, there was at least plenty of time to spend in the pleasures of the mind.

Charles himself was not disinclined to play the musical Mæcenas. It was his ambition to surround himself with the splendours of a great chapel. In addition, the patronage of a few of the more cultured men of 'nobility and fortune' around the court advanced and intensified musical activity on a wider scale.

The masters who were patronised included most of the great musical talents in the country. Some of the former coryphæi of Charles I's chapel had managed to survive the upheaval of the Commonwealth. Luckiest among them, from the point of view of maintaining their tradition, were those who had found temporary refuge in and around Oxford, the asylum of Anglicanism during the critical years.[4] They were recalled and once more given an opportunity to employ their great skill and learning with official recognition.

At the beginning of the Restoration the most important among these men were Jenkins, Coleman, Christopher Gibbons, Christopher Simpson, Banister, Cooke, Humfrey, Jeffreys, Locke, Brewer and Rogers: later, only two more great names appeared, Blow and Purcell. Of all these men only Humfrey, Blow and Purcell were born after 1630: the other men belonged to the old school. Their musical education was deeply-rooted in the tradition of polyphonic music in which England had excelled during the first

[1] A. C. A. Brett, *Charles II and his Court*, 1910, pp. 198 ff.
[2] *Life and Times of Anthony à Wood*, ed. Llewellyn Powys, London, 1932.
[3] Roger North, *Memoirs*, 1728; ed. E. F. Rimbault, 1846.
[4] Anthony à Wood wrote in 1656: 'The Musick masters who were now in Oxon and frequented the said (weekly musical) meetings were William Ellis, Proctor, Wilson and others' (ed. L. Powys, p. 51).

decades of the century. But Humphreys, Blow and Purcell also belonged indirectly to the older school, since their teachers were formerly active members of the musical establishment attached to the pre-Commonwealth Church and Court.

So the restored Court commended the services of men schooled in the technique of their craft. Composers were neither forced to continue in their polyphonic tradition nor prevented from so doing; though Charles personally tried to divert the attention of the musicians from the particular form of the old-style fantasia and especially from the use of viols, which he considered old-fashioned, to less intimate and more showy forms of art (and to the use of instruments that better suited his Court ambitions). Wood testified that 'Charles did not like the viols; preferring the violins as being more airie and brisk than viols'.[1] Roger North reported that 'Charles II had an utter detestation of fancys'.[2]

At the same time, the Court composers themselves, although they had been brought up in the tradition of the past, were not by any means untouched by the progress of social life outside the Court, fortunately for their work. The lewdness of Court etiquette (which brought the Court increasing unpopularity) would not have been any inspiration, once the first intoxications of royalist enthusiasm had passed away. The Court was, after all, an island of old-time aristocratic mentality in a wide and fast-flowing current of commercial realism. But the combination of Court patronage with certain modern forms of practice arising from life outside the Court offered new scope for the composers and proved a healthy influence. And is it not a fact that the very nastiness and soullessness of his surroundings sometimes causes the artist to create the more soulful and passionate works of art? just as Charles's xenophilism helped to strengthen the new nationalism among great composers as the examples of Matthew Locke and John Blow show.

The first years of Charles II's absolutism were based on a compromise, as neither the commercial-capitalist nor the aristocratic forces could do entirely without one another.[3] There was a state of dispute in cultural life, too. A lively interest in topical

[1] Ed. L. Powys, p. 212.
[2] Ed. Rimbault, p. 103.
[3] See Arthur Bryant, *Charles II* (London, 1949, rev. 1955) and K. H. D. Haley, *Charles II* (London, 1956).

problems and ideas was taking place, which is always a healthy sign in cultural life.

Despite the 'Restoration' of the old state form and the persecution of Puritans, the English Enlightenment grew from the roots of the bourgeois revolution with its forward-reaching ideas and its passionate impetus. Indeed the Restoration age was not only characterised by the 'noble' rogues of Charles II's court, but to a much higher degree by Newton and the Royal Society which was founded in 1662 in order to support science in the spirit and interests of early capitalism which was expanding rapidly. Locke and Hobbes introduced new conceptions of materialist thought and of government and social structure. The genius of Milton continued to inspire English literature from Bunyan and Aphra Behn to Defoe and Swift. Art and writing of the time were permeated by ideas of the freedom of the citizen, of the dignity of man and of humanism. Just because of its prophetic greatness the English Enlightenment exercised an immense influence on progressive thought throughout Europe.

How actively musicians of the period in particular were searching for a way out of the spiritual crisis can be judged from the flood of theoretical treatises that appeared between 1660 and 1680. Locke, Mace, Pepys, Wood, Simpson, John Philips, Th. Salmon, J. Playford and others all discussed burning problems of musical practice and theory, tending to consider music in its philosophical aspects and often displaying a vivacity and fighting spirit that reminds one of France as it was during the second half of the eighteenth century.

So Restoration musicians proved to be (to use a hackneyed phrase) as much children of their time as any before them.

Of all the new forms of practice that were developing outside the Court the evolution of the *public concert* was the most momentous.

We have seen that even in early sixteenth-century chamber music performances there existed a much more subjective attitude on the part of the player or listener towards the art than had been the case in any previous musical practice. The public concert represented a further penetration of the individualist spirit into musical life. It became one of the most important cultural manifestations of the advance of capitalism. The consequences of the arrival of this new way of performing music and listening to it were enormous.

Public concerts which first arose in the 1670s on the initiative of John Banister, musician, and Thomas Britton, coal-merchant, were an important part of the reorganisation of public life altogether. The gates to musical pleasure were opened wide to new strata of citizens. Concerts were an essential contribution to countering the cultural privileges of the aristocracy.

The new character of concerts was already manifest in their outer appearance. They were conducted, as Roger North describes them, in 'alehouse fashion', with the public sitting at small tables in a hired hall in Whitefriars near the famous George's Tavern. While the concert was going on listeners could smoke and have drinks (this was changed in 1680 when a larger hall was required). Whoever paid a shilling was allowed in, and these concerts were announced in the *London Gazette*. From 1683 onwards highlights of these performances were the celebrations of St Cecilia's Day, for which the first 'Musical Society' was founded – composed of musicians and amateurs with different social background.

By 1700 such Concerts had already become functions of considerable cultural weight. Thus through these concerts an important extension of the music-loving public was made possible.

It was no more a closed society,[1] but an anonymous and practically limitless public that heard the performances. This concert public had few forerunners in English history. The aristocratic visitors who attended the performances of plays and masques during the earlier years of the seventeenth century may have helped to pave the way for gatherings of the new kind. The Music Acts in Cambridge and Oxford during the Commonwealth (musical celebrations of examinations and other prominent occasions) attracted a large public though the audiences were mainly academic. Cromwell introduced 'state concerts' in Whitehall.

With these 'concerts for everybody' England was well in advance of musical life in Germany. With the exception of Hamburg, the Hansa trade metropolis, where some years later a popular type of opera with the active participation of the people came into being, the dominant position of feudal-absolutist courts as centres of

---

[1] Private chamber music circles and other closed musical societies continued to exist throughout the century. Only one example of many: Roger North mentions that after 1660 'shopkeepers and foremen came weekly to sing in consort' in London taverns (*Memoirs of Musick*).

music-making persisted in Germany up to the end of the eighteenth century, and concert enterprises similar to those in England grew from the bourgeois-popular *Collegia Musica* and *Stadtpfeifereien*, but gradually, and despite much ridicule and opposition.

A new attitude on the part of the listener resulted from the birth of the concert, the significance of which increased from year to year. Not only did new circles of music-lovers who had been kept out of musical life by aristocratic privileges in matters of culture enter the public scene; not only did this new concert-going public visit these recitals with lively expectation, but their whole relationship to music changed.

The concert-going public proper evolved as the logical result of the increase in the habit of passive listening. The public went to music-meetings in the hope of finding 'much pleasure, consolation and recreation', as Charles Butler had expressed it thirty years before. Each member of the audience would sit in his chair, imbibing harmony and happiness, and relate all the happenings in the music to the memory of his own emotional experiences, or his current state of mind. And he would pay for this hour of pleasure in coin of the realm.

Here is the second important novelty. *Music became a commodity.* As such it was sold in the market and obeyed all those laws of supply and demand to which every product of capitalism was subjected. It became available to whoever cared and could pay – and dating from the economic revival about the middle of the Restoration period quite a number of citizens could afford to attend concerts. Musical life became, to an increasing degree, dependent on the commercial initiative of those who ran concert and operatic enterprises, and who often had only the commercial interest in mind.

The bigger the demand for music in concert halls grew, the larger became the halls. After d'Avenant's still modest attempts in 1656, the first concerts of John Banister and Thomas Britton, dating from 1672, drew more and more numerous audiences.[1]

[1] It is interesting to note how Banister's concert meetings came about. Banister repeatedly had trouble at the Court; in Anthony à Wood's MS. notes in the Bodleian Library it is said that he was eventually dismissed from the service of Charles II for saying 'he had better have the English' after the king had called for the Italian violins. On the other hand, among the state papers is a 'Remonstrance' (29 March 1667) against his fraudulent conduct in keeping for himself most of the £600 a year which should have been paid for 'extraordinary services of the violins'. Then he started his weekly musical meetings. He turned to commercial and

The new attitude of the public led to the development of styles and forms in music acquiring more and more the unified character of complete emotional entities. Some form of dramatic consistency was now absolutely essential in the new work of art. In it there was indeed variety, but, to an increasing degree, variety of musical characters acting in the same drama. It was already Milton's opinion that 'variety (as both music and rhetoric teacheth us) erects and rouses an auditory like the masterful running over many chords and divisions . . .'. At the same time the polyphony of the old age changed. Old English chamber music had been, after all, music for the players rather than music for the listeners. In the 'golden age' each performer (and each achieved an equally high standard of musical proficiency) took equal delight in playing his independent melodic line inside the contrapuntal whole. In the new concert the work of art had to adjust itself to the wishes of a non-playing public. The new patterns of musical form, for the most part, consisted of a subjective and emotional melody, accompanied by subservient parts, easy to understand, easy to 'put over'.

Thus the *'gestic'* (i.e. emotionally-rhetorical) ideal of music was gaining ground. All that has been said about Italian music at the beginning of the century as opposed to English chamber art now began to apply to this country. No wonder the instruments of modern subjective expression replaced the viols. After a period of opposition on the part of the representatives of the old chamber music, the violin family finally rose in triumph. In 1631 Owen Feltham had shown his disgust with the instrument:

> It is a kind of disparagement to be a cunning fiddler. It argues his neglect of better employment, and that he hath spent much time on a thing unnecessarie.[1]

In 1657 Anthony à Wood of Oxford wrote in his diary that gentlemen in private musical meetings

> esteemed a violin to be an instrument only belonging to a common fiddler, for feare of making these meetings to be vaine and fiddling.

But soon things changed, and the special ability of the violin to

public music, the very antithesis of that at the Court. His concerts took place at first at his home, from 1678 in that of Thomas Britton. Soon an annual fee of 10 shillings was charged.

[1] *Resolves*, 1631.

respond to subjective and expressive interpretation of music was found to be completely in accordance with the *new* attitude of the listener. And so, very shortly afterwards, the same Anthony à Wood reported excitedly:

> I saw Thomas Baltzar (the German violinist) run up his fingers to the end of the finger-board of the violin, and run them back insensibly, and all with great alacrity and very good time, which I nor any in England saw the like before.[1]

The king's preference for violins had a somewhat different origin: it was not so much the emotional quality of the violin as its greater fitness for pomp and display that caused him to recommend it so strongly. However, the patronage of the king very much helped to popularise the instrument. Roger North also alludes to the violoncello (bass violin) which began to be used at that time:

> There was a set of gentlemen at that time in towne who frequently mett for pure private diversion. And their musick was, of ye Babtist (Lully) way, very Good. They were most violinists, and often hired base-violinns (which instrument as then used was very hard & harsh sounded Base & nothing so soft & sweet as now) to attend them.[2]

How quickly and completely the violin finally conquered is shown in a passage of Thomas Mace who deplores bitterly the disappearance of the true spirit of old English chamber music:

> Very little of *This so Eminent Musick* [for viols] do we hear of in *These Times*, (the *Less* the *Greater Pity*.)
>
> Then again, we had all *Those Choice Consorts*, to *Equally-Sciz'd Instruments*, (*Rare Chests of Viols*) and as *Equally Perform'd*: For we would never allow *Any Performer to Over-top, or Out-cry* another by *Loud Play*; but our Great Care was, to have *All the Parts Equally Heard*; by which means, though sometimes we had but in-different, or mean *Hands to Perform* with; yet *This Caution* made the *Musick Lovely*, and very *Contentive*.
>
> But now the *Modes* and *Fashions* have cry'd *These Things* down, and set up a *Great Idol* in their Room; observe with what a *Wonderful Swiftness* They now run over their *Brave New Ayres*; and with what *High-Priz'd Noise*, viz. 10, or 20 *Violins*, &c. as I said before, to a *Some-Single-Soul'd Ayre*; it may be of 2 or 3 *Parts*, or

---

[1] *Diary*, 1657 and 1659.
[2] *Musicall Grammarian*, ed. H. Andrews, 1925, p. 31.

some *Coranto*, *Seraband*, or *Brawle*, (as the *New-Fashion'd-Word* is)
and such like *Stuff*, seldom any other; which is rather fit to make
a Mans *Ears Glow*, and fill his *Brains full of Frisks*, &c. than to
Season, and Sober his Mind, or Elevate his Affections to *Goodness*.[1]

Thomas Mace alludes to another innovation which is
foreshadowed in this short and yet portentous period, the *orchestra*.
Together, the large public and the new 'gestic' function of
instrumental music greatly accelerated the evolution of orchestral
music as opposed to private chamber music. It is true that there are
examples of almost orchestral performances before this time;
again, especially in the masques. In Ben Jonson's *Love Freed from
Ignorance and Folly* (1611) payment was given to the following
musicians:[2]

To the 12 Musitions that were preestes that songe
   and played   24[li]
It'm to the 12 other Lutes that suplied, and wth fluits   12[li]
It'm to the 10 violens that contynualy practized
   to the Queen   20[li]
It'm to 15 Musitions that played to the Pages and Fooles   20[li]
It'm to the 13 hoboyes and sackbutts   10[li]

and there are plenty of instances of the contrivance, at almost every
Tudor and Stuart court, of instrumental mass effects which played
no small part in the founding of the modern orchestra. But such
performances were based on the demand of kings for splendid
display rather than on the demand of subjects for entertainment.
Only with the evolution of the general public did the orchestra
secure widely-based economic support and become an established
institution. Roger North insisted strongly on the establishment of
the orchestral ideals which indeed had been anticipated in the
masques of James I: 'Magnitude and force of sound is among the
chief excellencys of music.'[3]

These developments were not without effect on the performers'
attitude. The concert artist was in a position entirely different from
that of the organist in the church or the minstrel in the dancing-
hall. In him the individualistic ambitions of every member of the
public were personified. He became so much the centre of interest

---

[1] *Musick's Monument*, 1676.
[2] Duncan and Crowest, *Minstrelsy*, 1907, p. 198.
[3] *Memoirs*, p. 83. The reader may be referred to Lafontaine's book, *The King's Musick*, for
more facts on orchestras at Stuart courts.

that a certain exaltation of his personality was the natural consequence. It is in Wood's description that first mention is made of the *virtuoso*.[1] An artist who finds himself in the position of an idol soon tends to increase idolatry by startling the public with double-stoppings, passages and ornaments played at lightning speed. Though sober standards of true musicianship were still upheld by many of the numerous English and foreign virtuosos who entered the musical life of the country during the last decades of the century, the showing-off spirit of the concert virtuoso had appeared. The public, responding, soon began to show such curious predilections as an enthusiasm for male sopranists and contraltists.

The establishment of public concerts in London during the 1680s coincided with, and may partly have caused a sudden interest in, chamber music of a type virtually unknown in England before this time. Purcell turned, in his 1683 set of sonatas, to the 'fam'd Italian masters', thought by some to have been Colista, Vitali, Bassani and Corelli.[2]

Curiously, Purcell's English contemporaries seem to have turned not to these contemporary Italian composers, but to an earlier type of sonata, still Italian in origin, but received from Austrian and German composers of the mid-century. Several English manuscripts of the post-restoration period[3] contain copies of sonatas by Vienna composers such as Bertali, Schmelzer and others, as well as German sonatas by Rosenmüller, Nicolai, Schnittelbach and others. These are found side by side with sonatas in the same style, by the English composers William Young (whose sonatas were published at Innsbruck) and Henry Butler. A number of these sonatas use the bass viol in virtuoso style, most typically in sonatas for violin, bass viol obbligato and continuo. One of the chief popularisers of this German-Austrian style in England contemporary with Purcell was the Moravian 'Capellmeister'

[1] Apart from Baltzar, Nicola Matteis is an important figure. He lived in England for many years as a virtuoso and composer of violin music, and his influence in the direction of a more brilliant style was great. North also mentions 'Scheiffare' (Scheiffler), Voglesang, 'and other names to fright one' (*Grammarian*, p. 30), to whom we may add Godfrey Keller, Godfrey Finger, and Gerhard Diessener (Disineer), all three German or Bohemian by birth. Wood further reports that the violinist Mell 'was not so admired, yet he played sweeter, was a well-bred gentleman, and not given to excessive drinking, as Baltzar was'.

[2] For instance see Michael Tilmouth: 'The Technique and Forms of Purcell's Sonatas', in *Music and Letters*, April 1959, pp. 109–21.

[3] For instance, Dolmetsch Library II. c. 25; Durham Cathedral Library D 2, D 4, D 5; British Library Add. 31423, Add. 31500; Bodleian Library, Mus. Sch. o. 80, Mus. Sch. d 249.

Godfrey Finger, who arrived in London in about 1686, and after a brief spell in royal employment, did much to develop public concert life.[1] His six sonatas of 1690, three for violin, and three for recorder with continuo are virtually the earliest solo sonatas to be written in England. They seem to have impressed his contemporaries, since many sonatas of the 1690s, particularly those of Daniel Purcell and William Croft,[2] clearly show their influence. Finger's other printed collections include 6 sonatas for two unaccompanied recorders (Op. 3, c. 1700), which are part of a sudden fashion for this scoring started by Raphael Courteville in 1686;[3] 10 impressive sonatas for recorder and continuo (Op. 10, c. 1700), 10 trio sonatas for two violins and continuo (Op. 5, c. 1705), 12 trio sonatas for two recorders and continuo (Op. 4 & 6, c. 1705), and four recently discovered sonatas for the unusual combination of two recorders, two oboes and continuo.[4]

Many other sonatas also exist in manuscript, including some for bass viol.[5]

Other enthusiasts for the German sonata style include Godfrey Keller, who contributed two sonatas for 2 recorders, 2 oboes and continuo to Finger's collection mentioned above, and who wrote a number of others, mainly for wind instruments, in Finger's style;

[1] See: Arthur Marshall: 'The Chamber Music of Godfrey Finger', in *The Consort*, 1970, pp. 423–432.

[2] Daniel Purcell, *Six sonatas or solos, three for a violin, and three for the flute. . . . I Walsh . . . & I. Hare: London* (1698); *Six sonatas or solos, three for a violin and three for the flute . . . Compos'd by Mr. Wm. Crofts & an Italian Mr. . . . John Walsh . . . & John Hare . . . London* (1700).

[3] *Sonatas of two parts, compos'd and purposely contrived for two flutes . . . I Walsh . . . London* (1686).

[4] *Six Sonates a 2 Flustes et 2 Hautbois . . . et 1 Basse Continue . . .* Amsterdam, E. Roger (undated); unique copy in the possession of Baron Carl de Geer, Lefusta Bruk, Sweden. In *William Lawes* by Murray Lefkowitz (London, 1960) on pp. 106–125 the opinion is expressed that the stylised fantasia-alman-galliard setts written in England early in the seventeenth century by Coperario, William Lawes and others sufficiently resembled Sonatas to be known by that name. He offers no evidence that they were known as such in England at the time of their composition, and, in my opinion, to refer to them as sonatas, or so to label them in modern editions, is quite incorrect. Neither do all numerous German dance 'suites' of the same time bear that name. The first Italian sonatas in the meaning of sets of dance movements, airs, canzoni, etc., do not appear until 1637 when Tarquinio Merula published his *Sonate da Chiesa and Sonate da Camera*. On the other hand non-dance sonatas of the late sixteenth- and early seventeenth-century Italian type (Gabrieli, Marini, Uccellini, etc.) were not written by English composers until Young (1653, in Innsbruck!) and Jenkins, nor do any solo sonatas appear in England until much later in the century.

Lawes gave no collective name to the violin setts in his autograph MSS.; however, a non-autograph source from the same period (Ob MSS. Mus. Sch. C. 89 a–d) is entitled 'Mr. William Lawes' Fantazias and Ayres for two trebles and a base to the organ'. There is accordingly some authority for labelling these setts 'Fantazias and Ayres'.

[5] See Arthur Marshall, *The Viola da Gamba Music of Godfrey Finger*', Chelys, 1970, pp. 16–26.

James Paisible, Robert King and Benjamin Hely. The end of this style in England was marked by the sudden departure of Finger from England in about 1701, and the increasing popularity of Corelli's music through imported publications at about the same time, a development succinctly described by Roger North:

> Then came over Corelly's first consort that cleared the ground of all other sorts of musick whatsoever. By degrees the rest of his consorts, and at last the conciertos came, all which are to the musicians like the bread of life . . .[1]

The influence of *foreign music* began to be of decisive importance during this time. At first it seemed as though its influence would be productive of a permanent reconstruction of English music. So, alas, it was. But not as one might have hoped.

We have repeatedly drawn attention to certain Italian elements of style. Such influences developed up to about 1635 only on very general lines. Wherever details of Italian music were taken over they were kept within the limits of experiment. On the whole English chamber music (as distinct from vocal music) had kept remarkably independent of continental influence for a long time, compared for instance with German music which was deeply affected by Italian art. English composers were very conscious of their originality and of the purity of their style, and whenever Italian influence threatened to grow they raised, like Morley, their warning voices.[2] Yet the powerful subversive element of Italian music – so full of that 'fire and fury' which Roger North admired[3] – could not be checked for ever. More and more features of Italian music were utilised. Italian instrumental music itself became popular.[4]

During the Commonwealth the infiltration of continental elements into English chamber music made rapid progress. In 1656 Matthew Locke had protested: 'I never saw any foreign instrumental music (a few French Corantos excepted) worthy an Englishman's transcribing.' But during this time, the harmonic basso continuo, a definitely foreign element in British art, was gaining ground. In 1639 William Child issued a psalm work for voices 'with a continuall base either for the organ or Theorbo

---

[1] John Wilson: *Roger North on Music* (London, 1959), pp. 310–11.
[2] See above, p. 188 (footnote).
[3] *Musicall Grammarian*, p. 24.
[4] In 1622 Peacham made a list of great composers of his time (*Compleat Gentleman*, p. 100) which includes sixteen continental masters of whom twelve were Italians.

newly composed after the Italian way'. This, it is true, was vocal music; and some years before Deering composed madrigals with basso continuo. But in the instrumental field William Lawes was already compromising with the continuo, and about 1655 several composers of instrumental music used it. Even if the basso continuo in some works written during the Commonwealth by composers like Jenkins, Locke and Jeffreys was no more than a kind of short score of the polyphonic parts, the 'vertical' harmonic attitude slowly won through – entirely in accordance with the new spirit that began to dominate cultural and social life in general.[1]

The influence of Italian emotionalism is felt in the more and more frequent appearance of *dynamic* and *tempo* indications. In a MS. by George Jeffreys both kinds of direction are found.[2] In a fantasia a 3 by John Hilton we are told to play 'softly' (piano), 'away' (faster) and 'long tyme' (slower).[3] Effects based on the change from piano to forte are exploited in 'echoes' such as were written by Thomas Mudd, William Lawes, Maurice Webster and others.[4]

French and German influences had been operative before the Restoration – chiefly expressed in the appearance in this country of certain forms of French dances and German sonatas.[5] Yet such elements played an insignificant part in the development of English chamber music before the Restoration.

But with the restoration of Charles II to the throne, the whole 'foreign policy' in matters of musical practice and production entered an entirely new phase. Just as Charles's political aims were more and more closely linked with those of other powers, so he

[1] Although Jacobean consort music was generally accompanied by written out parts some composers were already abandoning accompaniments in lute tablature in favour of unfigured bass.

[2] Add. 10338.

[3] See above, p. 226.

[4] MSS. in the British Museum and in Christ Church, Oxford.

[5] French 'fantasies' written during the first half of the seventeenth century were themselves derived from the fancies of this country, as we can see by studying the works of Claude Lejeune, Eustache Du Caurroy, and Nicolaus Metru. Certain types of dances from France became familiar over here, but the forms were used as a mere mould for the English idiom. The introduction of the sonata form into this country from Italy *via* Germany dates from the middle of the century. Sonatas imitating the typically German, rather than the expressive and emotional Italian style were composed by William Young (printed collection, 1653; also single sonatas in Durham Cathedral Library), Henry Butler (ibid.), and also John Jenkins (ibid.). Young's edition of sonatas a 2–5 with basso continuo appeared in Innsbruck and cannot be discussed here, being really part of the German production. The rest of his sonatas, also most of those by Butler and Jenkins, are virtuoso compositions for 1–3 bass viols, and will be treated later on in this book.

pursued to an increasing degree a musical policy which favoured foreign elements of style. Italian, German and now especially French musicians, were invited to take positions at the Court at high salaries. For a period of great splendour had started in French music. Opera, under the patronage of the Roi Soleil, received an impetus hitherto unknown. It became a centre round which French music developed into an imposing art radiating the whole grandeur of Louis's absolutism. It was Charles's ambition to appear in a similar halo of artistic glorification. He could not be behind his colleague on the other side of the Channel. Opera in England, which was of only small significance about the middle of the century entered a phase of considerable success, largely owing to French influence. At his Court Charles established a band of 24 violins on the lines of the model at Paris where Charles had spent his years of exile. Louis Grabu, French violinist (d. about 1694) replaced the English Nicholas Laniere (1588–1666) as master of the Chapel Royal in 1665. The number of French composers and performers employed henceforth at the Court was high.

Ballet, dances and other instrumental forms of the French Court, such as the Overture Suite, were adopted. The works of master Lully were soon hailed almost as enthusiastically here as in Paris. Scores of arrangements of his works for all kinds of instrumental combinations are in the British Museum.[1] French influence had come to stay in English musical life. This conquest was, however, at first confined to the Court, where it amounted to a 'veni-vidi-vici'. Amateurs, teachers and the general public were slower in submitting to the startling new French style.

> The French manner of Instrumentall musick did not gather so fast as to make a revolution all at once, but during the greatest part of that king's [Charles II] reigne, the old musick was used in the countrys, and in many meetings and societys in London,

says Roger North who adds, however: 'But the treble-violl was disregarded and the violin took its place.'[2]

The fusion of the old English tradition of polyphonic mastery and the new continental achievements proved exceedingly healthy for English music for a time, as we shall see.

It was indeed a happy combination of circumstances which made possible the brief renaissance of English chamber music.

[1] MSS. Add. 29283–5, 31429, 33236, 10445 and others.
[2] *Memoirs*, p. 105.

For, at a time when its absolutist ambitions kept the Court in constant conflict with the great and growing commercial classes outside it, chamber music was able to derive benefit from both sets of antagonists: the Court granted lavish patronage, gave composers places and pensions, work to do and bread to eat; while the greater world provided the audiences for public concerts, a development that greatly enhanced our composers' financial chances. There was another lucky coincidence in the fact that foreign music, which for a time did English music so much good, happened to be favoured both in the small world of privilege and in the great world of enterprise, the Court cultivating it for the sake of its elegance and its association with a more successful despotism abroad, the city liking it for its eloquent, showy, emotional qualities. But these propitious circumstances, even in their fortunate combination, would have availed English chamber music nothing, if there had not been a vigorous remnant of high musical culture surviving the Civil War and the Commonwealth – a body of men skilled in its practice, to whom chamber music still meant all that is best in the art. And again it must be emphasised that the chief centre of musical activity was the Court – whatever was its moral and political outlook.

*

The main stylistic developments of chamber music from Jenkins to Purcell are the slow evolution from polyphony to homophony, and the final victory of dramatic and lyrical, of subjectively emotional elements.

Let us now turn to John Jenkins (1592–1678), one of the most important and most amiable musical figures of the whole century. His career is a study in itself. Jenkins is essentially a polyphonist, but at the same time his immense output includes pieces in all styles current during his long life, from the most backward to the most advanced. Much of his life was spent in the households of East Anglian nobility, though when the King's Musick was restored he was called with other great musicians, although he was then already sixty-eight years old.[1] He was an excellent virtuoso on various instruments as Roger North tells us in his biographical

---

[1] He was honoured by an unusual act of generosity on the part of his colleagues; he was allowed to draw his fees without actually performing, in recognition of his great reputation as the doyen of English music.

notes on the composer.[1] Only a few slight items from his enormous output are definitely known to have been published in contemporary collections;[2] the cost of printing the more elaborate compositions was apparently prohibitive.[3]

But Jenkins' music was very well known in its time. Wood writes in 1676, two years before the composer's death: 'John Jenkyns . . . most famous; for his compositions enter into the hands of all men.'[4] Roger North, who was an amateur pupil of Jenkins (his actual profession was the law – he was Attorney General), refers both to the number and to the quality of the composer's works which were 'more voluminous, and in the time more esteemed

---

[1] John Wilson (ed.), *Roger North on Music*, London, 1959, pp. 21–23, 295–299, 343–348. More detailed biographies of Jenkins can be found in the following: Robert A. Warner, *The Fantasia in the Works of John Jenkins*, unpublished Ph.D. dissertation, University of Michigan, 1951; Andrew Ashbee, *The Four-Part Instrumental Compositions of John Jenkins*, unpublished Ph.D. dissertation, University of London, 1966; Carolyn Coxon, *John Jenkins: A Critical Study (with editorial transcription) of His Instrumental Music*, unpublished Ph.D. dissertation, University of Edinburgh, 1969. See also A. Ashbee, 'Genealogy and John Jenkins', *Music and Letters*, 46 (1965), pp. 225–230.

[2] Mostly by Playford. All are listed in *RISM: Recueils Imprimés: XVIᵉ–XVIIᵉ Siècles*, Munich, 1960. Both Burney, *A General History of Music*, London, 1789 (reprint New York, 1957), ii, p. 322, and Hawkins, *A General History of the Science and Practice of Music*, London, 1776 (reprint New York, 1963), ii, p. 584, mention 'twelve Sonatas for two violins and a bass, with a thorough-bass for the organ, printed at London about the year 1660, and at Amsterdam in 1664'. Although no copy of either edition is known to exist, Rudi A. Rasch, 'Seventeenth-Century Dutch Editions of English Instrumental Music', *Music and Letters*, 53 (1972), pp. 270–273, suggests that a collection entitled *J. Jenkins, Engels Speel-Thresoor van CC. de nieuwste Allemanden, Couranten, Sarabaden, Ayres, etc. gesteld door elf de konstighste Violisten deser tydt in Engeland voor Bass en Viool, en ander Speel-gereetschap, mede LXVII Speelstucken als Allemanden, Couranten, etc. voor twee Violen en Bass, als mede een Bassus continuus ad placidum. Amsterdam, 1664* (mentioned by C. F. Becker, *Die Tonwerke des XVI. und XVII. Jahrhunderts*, Leipzig, 1855, p. 282, and by A. Goovaerts, *Histoire et Bibliographie de la Typographie Musicale dans les pays-bas*, Antwerp, 1880, pp. 406–407) was derived from Playford's *Courtly Masquing Ayres* (1662) with a second part comprising 67 pieces by Jenkins, perhaps 'the same as the 1664 Amsterdam edition of Jenkins's "Twelve Sonatas for two violins and a base, with thorough-bass"'. Clearly these 'Sonatas' were really suites of dances like those in, e.g., Christ Church, Oxford, MS. 1005. A catalogue of musical publications offered at the Frankfurt fair in 1667 mentions 'Joan. Jenickens 5-stimmige Balletten und Sarabanden mit 2 Violinen, 2 Viola da Braccio und 1 Violon mit Basso Continuo; Magdeburg, 1667' (see K. A. Goehler, *Verzeichnis der in dem Leipziger und Frankfurter Messkatalogen angezeigten Musikalien*, 1901–2). This rather looks like a German edition of some of his sarabands and ballets with basso continuo, possibly arranged for 5 parts by a German in accordance with the German practice which at that time preferred five- and six-part music to the Italian solos and trios. There is, however, no further proof that 'Joan. Jenickens'' work is really by our composer; no copy of this publication is known to be available.

[3] Christopher Simpson, *The Division-Viol*, 1665, facsimile ed., Curwen, 1955, p. 61, writes: 'The Charge of Printing *Divisions* (as I have experienced in the *Cuts* of the *Examples* in this present Book) doth make that kind of Musick less communicable.'

[4] II, 335.

than all the rest, and now lye in the utmost contempt'.[1] Wood also calls him 'the mirrour and wonder of his age for music'.[2] Jenkins' works were passed from hand to hand by copying and indeed many manuscript copies of his music still exist in various libraries throughout the world. Of several pieces, e.g. certain four-part fantasias, we can still count seven or eight handwritten copies.

The number of Jenkins' instrumental compositions is exceptionally large. Like Lawes, he wrote, almost exclusively chamber music. Among his works are 16 pieces a 6 (12 fantasias, 2 In Nomines and 2 pavans – including the 'Bell Pavin'); 17 fantasias and 3 pavans a 5; 17 fantasias and c. 52 airs a 4; 32 'Ayres' and 8 fantasia-suites for two trebles, two basses and organ; 27 fantasias, a pavan and nine fantasia-suites for treble, two basses and organ; 21 fantasias, 10 fantasia-suites, 22 fancy-air sets and c. 210 airs for two trebles and a bass; 19 fantasia-suites and c. 165 airs for treble and bass; more than 50 works for 1–3 bass viols (some including continuo) and c. 220 pieces for lyra viol(s). Special mention must be made of his several sets of airs for 'one treble, one base, one lyra and harpsichord' which continue the tradition of the 'broken consort of the 'golden age'.[3]

Apart from its abundance the most surprising feature of Jenkins' work is its variety. Almost every style of the whole seventeenth century is represented. Studying this vast production one seems to be regarding a complete panorama of the development of chamber music from Elizabethan times to the 'Glorious Revolution'. There are fantasias of the Ferrabosco type and melodies that seem to anticipate Handel.

It is difficult, if not impossible, to consider all of Jenkins' musical works in chronological order. Most MSS. are undated, though as our knowledge of their copyists and provenance grows, chronology of the music they contain becomes clearer. Some groups of works definitely belong to certain periods of Jenkins' life. No examples of his music are known in MSS. dating from before the 1620s – such as British Library, Egerton MS. 3665, the great score-book copied by Francis Tregian (d. 1619) – and it

---

[1] *Roger North on Music*, p. 343.

[2] I, 208–209.

[3] The most complete list of Jenkins' output yet published is Carolyn Coxon, 'A Handlist of the Sources of John Jenkins' Vocal and Instrumental Music', *R.M.A. Research Chronicle*, IX, pp. 73–89. See also *Chelys*, I, pp. 45–53, III, pp. 35–38 and V, pp. 86–95 for lists of Jenkins' music in the Viola da Gamba Society of Great Britain Provisional Index (in progress, ed. Gordon Dodd).

seems reasonable to conclude that he achieved maturity and recognition as a composer from the 1620s on. Most, if not all, of his supreme fantasias and associated works for four, five and six viols were undoubtedly composed prior to the Commonwealth.[1]

Seen as a whole, these fantasias of Jenkins appear among the last islands of genuine polyphony at a time when all over Europe composers were rapidly moving away from it. In spite of many progressive details they mark the conclusion of a style. However, if it does not contain any vitally new elements, nevertheless, in Jenkins' hands, the fantasia reached new heights of perfection through his unsurpassed lyric gifts and his grasp of large-scale form allied to an adventurous exploitation of key-relationships – a feature not hitherto explored to the same extent by other consort composers. The flexible nature of the fantasia as a form gave Jenkins a free rein for his imagination and enabled him to produce works of inexhaustible richness both in invention and in emotional warmth.

In Chapter VI stress was laid upon the dualism in the production of chamber music during the years before the republican period. There was the hyper-complex Court art, as represented by Lawes, and there was, on the other hand, the simplified and popularised fantasia of the East-Okeover-Brewer era. Now Jenkins wrote music in both styles. Some of his pieces breathe the same spirit as many of William Lawes' works. These lively and highly elaborate pieces are based on polyphony in an extreme form.[2] Their counterpoints are just as intricate and just as difficult as Lawes' fantasias. This polyphony is even harder to disentangle because the melodic lines in all parts are even longer. If the intervals and figures in Jenkins' pieces are not quite as wild and jumpy as those of the other master, their structure is even more personal. There are hardly any 'full stops'. Whenever a cadence seems to prepare to settle down, one may be sure that it will turn back at the last moment and run into some new contrapuntal development.

---

[1] Jenkins' fantasias are discussed in the dissertations by Warner, Ashbee and Coxon cited above. Modern editions are: *John Jenkins: Consort Music in Six Parts*, ed. R. Nicholson and A. Ashbee, London, 1976; *John Jenkins: Consort Music in Five Parts*, ed. R. Nicholson, London, 1971; Four-part fantasias: No. 3, ed. A. Mangeot, London, 1936; Nos. 5 and 6, ed. S. Beck in *Nine Fantasias in Four Parts by Byrd, Bull, Ferrabosco, Jenkins and Ives*, New York, 1947; Nos. 7, 9, 12, 15 and 16, ed. A. Ashbee in *John Jenkins: Consort Music of Four Parts*, Musica Britannica, XXVI, 1969 (2nd ed. 1975). See also R. A. Warner, 'John Jenkins' Four-Part Fancy (Meyer, No. 14) in C minor: An Enharmonic Modulation around the Key Circle', *The Music Review*, 28 (i), February, 1967, pp. 1–20.

[2] E.g.: Nos. 2, 9 and 12 a 6; Nos. 1, 4 and 5 a 5; Nos. 1, 3 and 4 a 4.

Rhythmically these pieces are incredibly complex. Syncopes veil
the changeover from bar to bar; accents are more often against the
beats than on them. The main difference between Jenkins' noble
and distinguished art and Lawes' music lies not in its intricacy and
elaborateness but in the fact that his music is usually less 'showy'
than that of Lawes. Jenkins is the more typical chamber-music
composer. His art is not based on stormy, extravagant or even
particularly expressive thematic ideas. It is as intimate, objective
and detached as chamber music can possibly be. In fact, it is the
ideal chamber music, as exemplified in a fantasia a 4;[1] see
Appendix VI.

Most composers since the days of Morley differentiated between
two-, three- and four-part fantasias on the one hand and five- and
six-part ones on the other. The former were much livelier and
more richly figured than the latter. Certainly this is generally true
of Jenkins' fantasias, but one finds the same diversity of style and
form in the four-, five- and six-part groups. Alongside the intricate
polyphony of some fantasias – for instance a number of the
monothematic ones – can be set others which bear many traces of
the more popular dance idiom. The historical dualism in English
chamber music during its period of crisis is now illustrated in the
production of one and the same man. A striking example of a
ballad-melody type of theme in Jenkins' fantasias is that from his
fantasia No. 6 a 4, perhaps a recollection, conscious or unconscious, of 'All in a Garden Green' or 'Gathering Peascods':

Example 72: theme from fantasia No. 6 a 4 and the opening of
'All in a Garden Green'.

Some of his four-part fantasias in particular contain wonderful
long melodies, while many works include centrally placed
homophonic passages, or a series of shorter and more-easily
comprehensible phrases, which act as a foil to the extensive
contrapuntal working found elsewhere.[2] The detailed planning of

[1] No. 1.
[2] E.g.: Nos. 1, 5 and 6 a 6; Nos. 7, 8 and 10 a 5; Nos. 5 and 6 a 4.

these fantasias is infinitely variable, but due consideration is always given to the overall form. The two In Nomines are, as North remarked, 'most elaborate' and the pavans are very fine. 'Bell' pieces like the 'Bell Pavin' may sometimes have originated as memorial tributes to patrons or friends of the composer. A number of Jenkins' works in the genre enjoyed great fame in their time, as Roger North, among others, confirms.[1]

The trio fantasias for two violins and bass viol[2] are in a more modern style, though at least four or five of them apparently date from the same period as the four-, five- and six-part works. The whole collection would appear to have been completed by 1650 or so, since it seems likely that the beautiful score of them in Jenkins' hand (British Library, Add. MS. 31428) was written for Sir Nicholas Le Strange (1604–1655). These concise fantasias are much livelier, more optimistic, playful and understandable than the intricate earlier works, with contrasts between sections clearly defined. Some pieces contain episodes which must have appeared very daring to Jenkins' contemporaries. A well-known example occurs in fantasia No. 1 of the series:[3]

Example 73: from fantasia No. 1 a 3 by John Jenkins (c. 1645).

[1] *Roger North on Music*, pp. 272, 296 and 346.
[2] Nos. 3, 4, 9, 10 and 20 ed. Helen J. Sleeper, *John Jenkins: Fancies & Ayres*, Wellesley Edition No. 1 (Wellesley College, 1950). Nos. 3, 5, 8, 11, 13, 16 and 19 ed. Nathalie Dolmetsch, *John Jenkins: Seven Fancies in Three Parts*, Hortus Musicus No. 149 (Bärenreiter, 1957).
[3] Thematic index in *Chelys*, I, 1969, pp. 47–48.

Among other works from Jenkins' middle years are the marvellous series of 27 fantasias and a pavan for treble, two basses and organ[1] and of 32 'ayres' for two trebles, two basses and organ.[2] Of great interest here is the use of an obbligato organ part, sometimes in a solo role and at other times adding independent counterpoints to the strings. Undoubtedly this innovation was copied from similar parts in the emerging fantasia-suite – a form which was to replace the single fantasia as the 'chiefest kind of [instrumental] musick' from the middle years of the century. Stylistically both sets of pieces maintain earlier traits rather than break new ground, with reliance still upon polyphonic techniques. The 'ayres' are no light-weight works. Their serious, poetic nature is given rich colouring through the employment of two basses, resulting in a mellow and sometimes even sombre mood. The flash of battle in 'Newark Siege' hints that they were written during the years of civil strife. Jenkins lived in Norfolk with two defiantly Royalist families – the Le Stranges and the Derhams – and here, perhaps, is his own musical reflection of 'these distracted times'.

There is yet another side of Jenkins' music: his work as the composer of fashionable dance suites. There are an amazing number of his pieces in this genre and many of the earlier ones imitate the masque music enjoyed by the aristocracy in James' and Charles I's reigns.[3] By the 1640s we find him grouping dances into suites of two or three pieces: the 84 airs he scored in Christ Church, Oxford, MS. 1005, are for two trebles and a bass and are compatible in style with the three-part fantasias for the same instruments. They were completed in 1644–5 and include the only works by Jenkins which can be dated precisely.[4] Other airs by him are sometimes found grouped in sets of six or seven pieces, all in one key, from which performers perhaps made up their own suites.[5]

It would be impossible here to go into a detailed account of his

---

[1] Thematic index in *Chelys*, I, 1969, p. 53. Nos. 1–10 ed. W. Davies, Viola da Gamba Society (Great Britain) Supplementary Publications, Nos. 26–28, 43, 79, 104, 108, 116–118. No. 25 ed. C. Arnold, *Consort Transcriptions Keel*, 1963.

[2] Transcribed complete, ed. A. Ashbee, in *Musica Britannica*, XXVI, pp. 1–77. See also his dissertation (cited above) and his paper 'The Four-Part Consort Music of John Jenkins', *Proceedings of the Royal Musical Association*, 96, pp. 29–42.

[3] See especially the four-part dances in, e.g., Christ Church, Oxford, MSS. 367–70. A thematic index and list of modern editions of these is in *Chelys*, V, 1973–4, pp. 92–95.

[4] See A. Ashbee, 'Towards the Chronology and Grouping of Some Airs by John Jenkins', *Music and Letters*, 55, 1974, pp. 30–44. A thematic index is in *Chelys*, V, 1973–4, pp. 86–91.

[5] E.g. the lyra consorts in Bodleian Library, Mus. Sch. MSS. C. 84, C. 85 and C. 88.

astonishingly varied and colourful dance music, just as it remains a mammoth task to try to count or put in order his hundreds of melodies, shapely and flowing, skilfully invented, always pleasant and interesting. It is a proud, a great period of creative work, and it is high time that all this lovely music was revived.

North wrote of Jenkins that

> his lute and lyra violl wrought so much upon his fancy . . . that he diverted to a more lively ayre, and was not onely an innovator, but became a reformer of musick. His Fancys were full of ayery points, grave's, triple's, and other varietys, and his lesser pieces imitated the dulcor of Lute Lessons, of which he composed multitudes; and all that he did, untill his declining age, was lively, active, decided, and, (if I may be credited) *cappriccioso* . . . And they were coveted because his style was new, and (for the time) difficult, for he could hardly forbear devisions, and some of his consorts was too full of them. . . . But this is further to be sayd of him, that being an accomplisht master of the viol, all his movements lay fair for the hand, and were not so hard as seemed.[1]

There is, for instance, a large group of pieces for from one to three bass viols, with or without thorough bass,[2] virtuoso compositions in which demi-semiquavers are a normal feature in all parts of the score.

Jenkins is not the originator of this curious 'concertante' and ornamental style. A direct line runs from the early divisions by Norcombe, Hume and others through the viola da gamba duets or trios of composers such as Coperario and Ward to Jenkins and his fellows.[3] But Jenkins' employment of the style is especially interesting, illustrating the versatility of the master. His own virtuosity once caused him to be 'brought to play upon the lyra viol afore

---

[1] *Roger North on Music*, pp. 344–345.

[2] Thematic index in *Chelys*, III, 1971, pp. 35–38. See also Janet M. Richards, *A Study of Music for the Bass Viol written in England in the Seventeenth Century*, unpublished B.Litt. dissertation, Somerville College, Oxford, 1960–1.

[3] East and Ives and the above-named composers as well as some more masters of slightly later date (including also Christopher Simpson, Matthew Locke, William Young, John Hingston and Benjamin Hely) wrote a number of pieces for 2 and 3 bass viols of equal pitch. The use of this combination represented yet another form of compromise between the old and the new attitudes. It was an attempt to reconcile the tradition of the contrapuntal fantasia with the growing popularity of the bass viol virtuoso-solo. Here again the predominance of one instrument over the others is the chief feature. The honours go round from viol to viol. Typical sources for such pieces are Brit. Mus. Add. MSS. 31424 and

King Charles I, as one that performed somewhat extraordinary'[1] and the techniques of division playing traditionally employed in 'divisions on a ground' – and so brilliantly described in Simpson's *Division-Violist* – dominate many of Jenkins' fantasias and dances for bass viols.

Example 74: from Sonata for two viole da gamba (conclusion),[2] by John Jenkins.

31430 and Bodleian, Mus. Sch. MSS. C. 59–60. East remarks in his *Seventh Set of Books* which contain the duos for bass viol: 'Wherein are Duos for two Base Viols, so composed, though there be but two parts in the eye, yet there is often three or four in the eare'; meaning that he endeavoured to achieve a full polyphonic and also harmonic effect although only two parts are employed.

[1] *Roger North on Music*, pp. 343–344.
[2] Durham Cathedral, Mus. MS. D. 5, No. 10.

A 'Sonata'[1] and an aria with variations by Jenkins, composed for violin, viola da gamba and basso continuo, composed in the same highly ornamental style, are especially attractive. The melody of the latter might have been written in the early eighteenth century:[2]

Example 75: Aria for violin, bass viol and continuo by John Jenkins (c. 1660).

Incidentally in this piece, violin as well as bass viol already displays a considerable range; we note that the violin climbs up to f-sharp.

The infiltration and acceptance of the violin into seventeenth-century chamber music undoubtedly spearheaded radical changes in the character and scoring of fantasias. Jenkins' later music is strongly influenced by the new style and his main preoccupation turns from the composition of single fantasias to suites in which the fantasia is grouped with two airs in common-time and triple-time respectively; sometimes the last of these is omitted.[3] Fantasia-

---

[1] Durham Cathedral, Mus. MS. D. 5, No. 6. Modern editions: (a) ed. P. Evans, *John Jenkins: Fantasia in D Minor*, London, 1958; (b) ed. C. Arnold, *John Jenkins: Sonata a 2 in D Minor*, London, 1958.

[2] Durham Cathedral, Mus. MS. D. 5, No. 7. Modern edition, ed. C. Arnold, *John Jenkins: Aria in A major*, London, 1958.

[3] The generally accepted term 'Fantasia-Suite' for this genre seems to have been coined first by Helen Joy Sleeper, as in 'John Jenkins and the English Fantasia-Suite', *Bulletin of the American Musicological Society*, 4, 1940, pp. 34–36. For a full study of the form see Christopher D. S. Field, *The English Consort Suite of the Seventeenth Century*, unpublished Ph.D dissertation, New College, Oxford, 1971.

suites of this kind seem to have been pioneered by Coperario and what may be Jenkins' earliest examples of the form[1] are closely modelled on the older man's pattern; indeed there are partial copies of Coperario's suites extant in Jenkins' own hand.[2] Typical features are a galliard-type third movement (with a common-time coda), passages for solo organ, and more extrovert thematic material suited to the violin (though in Jenkins' case still playable on the viol for the benefit of those country houses lacking violin virtuosi such as were present at Court).

However, these suites pale into relative insignificance beside the large-scale virtuoso works which apparently succeeded them. Division writing of the utmost complexity and brilliance dominates the nine fantasia-suites for treble, two basses and organ,[3] two others for treble, bass and organ[4] and the seven Fantasia-Ayre ('Divisions') sets for two trebles, bass and organ,[5] the effect of which is heightened in the fantasias by its being placed between the opening fugato section and a relatively simple homophonic passage (often in triple time). There are numerous double-stops in the bass parts and few works of the period demand so consummate a technique from all the players. The second movements maintain the brisk vitality typical of the dances from which they originated, with divisions introduced for the repeat playing of each strain. However, in the Fantasia-Ayre ('Divisions') sets in particular, these airs grow in stature and significance: a worthy foil to the preceding fantasias. A modern corant replaces the outmoded galliard as the third movement and the common-time coda is now dispensed with. The introduction of elaborate divisions was Jenkins' particular contribution to the development

[1] 17 suites for treble, bass and organ in Bodleian, Mus. Sch. MS. C. 81 and 10 suites for two trebles, bass and organ in Bodleian, Mus. Sch. MS. C. 82. Modern editions of the C. 81 pieces are: (a) No. 4 in G: ed. C. Arnold and Marshall Johnson, London, 1957; (b) No. 5 in A minor: ed. C. D. S. Field, London, 1976; (c) Nos. 12 and 17: ed. H. J. Sleeper in *Fancies & Ayres: John Jenkins*, Wellesley, 1950. No. 5 in C major from C. 82 is ed. C. Arnold and M. Johnson, London, 1957.

[2] In British Library, Add. MS. 23779, originally from the library of Sir Nicholas Le Strange. See: (a) P. J. Willetts, 'Sir Nicholas Le Strange and John Jenkins', *Music and Letters*, 42, 1961, pp. 30–43; (b) C. D. S. Field, 'Musical Observations from Barbados', *Musical Times*, July, 1974, pp. 565–567; (c) A. Ashbee, 'A Further Look at Some of the Le Strange Manuscripts', *Chelys*, V, 1973–4, pp. 24–41.

[3] Bodleian, Mus. Sch. MSS. D, 241–4 and D. 261. See A. Ashbee, 'John Jenkins's Fantasia-Suites for Treble, two Basses and Organ', *Chelys*, I, 1969, pp. 3–15 and II, 1970, pp. 6–17.

[4] Five incomplete sources. Damaged treble parts in Jenkins' hand are in Royal College of Music, MS. 921.

[5] Bodleian, Mus. Sch. MSS. D. 241–4 and D. 261. Modern edition, ed. R. A. Warner, *John Jenkins: Three-Part Fancy and Ayre Divisions*, Wellesley, 1966.

of the fantasia-suite and Christopher Simpson was undoubtedly right to single out these works as a model for all to follow:

> In these several sorts of *Division* of *two* and *three Parts*, my self, amongst others more eminent have made divers Compositions, which perhaps might be useful to young Musicians, either for their Imitation or Practice: . . . Howbeit, if you desire written Copies of that sort, . . . none has done so much in that kind, as the ever Famous and most Excellent Composer, in all sorts of Modern Musick, *Mr. John Jenkins.*[1]

Perhaps the latest of Jenkins' fantasia-suites, and probably the most significant compositions of his later years, are the eight four-part works[2] and the fifteen remaining Fancy-Ayres set for two trebles, bass and organ.[3] These continue the trends towards more concise movements, more clearly defined and contrasted sections, varied textures and firm tonality. Divisions become both less stereotyped and less demanding technically.

Much of this music leads directly to Purcell and even to Handel. Jenkins' work need fear no comparison with Purcell's in respect of musicianship and technical resourcefulness. No one can deny Purcell's right to be widely celebrated, but surely Jenkins' importance ought to be recognised. For he gathers to himself and displays to the best advantage all that was of practical value in the whole of his period. His vitality is boundless, his variety unfailing, his productivity immense. He may be called the great all-rounder of English chamber music.

The Jenkins of these fantasia-suites[4] should really be given a seat of honour alongside the progressives of the day. Yet a good proportion of his earlier work belongs to the more conservative

---

[1] Simpson, *The Division-Viol* (1665), p. 61.

[2] Ed. A. Ashbee, *Musica Britannica*, XXVI, pp. 78–132. See also his dissertation and paper read to the Royal Musical Association, cited above.

[3] British Library, MSS. 27550–4 and Bodleian, Mus. Sch. MSS. F. 564–7. These works are discussed in Warner's dissertation, cited above.

[4] Much attention has recently been given to John Jenkins by musicologists. In 1950 Helen Joy Sleeper issued an edition of 4 Fancies for 5 viols and organ, 5 Fancies for 2 trebles and bass, 2 sets of Fancy-Almaine-Ayre for violin, bass and organ, 3 sets of Fancy and Ayre for 2 trebles and bass, 5 Ayres for 4 viols. An excellent introduction is included in this edition, *John Jenkins (1592–1678) Fancies and Ayres*, published by Wellesley College, Mass. In 1969 a *Provisional Index of Works by John Jenkins* appeared in *Chelys* I (Gordon Dodd). Further editions have been published by the Viola da Gamba Society. Other studies are: R. A. Warner, *The Fantasia in the Works of John Jenkins* (cf. G. Dodd in *Chelys* I), A. Ashbee, *John Jenkins, Consort Music of 4 Parts*, 1969 (*Musica Britannica*, XXVI).

category which properly concerns us now. Some further attention is due to these conservatives.

George Jeffreys (d. 1685) wrote creditable fantasias for descant, tenor and bass.[1] There is no question here of concert ambitions. They are examples of old-style polyphony. The same can be said of a rather more primitive fantasia a 3 by Henry Loosemore (d. 1670).[2]

John Hingeston was Cromwell's house musician. We can recommend his compositions for careful study: there are numerous fantasias and suites a 2–6, mostly contained in two old Oxford MSS.[3] all of them original and distinguished in their thematic material.

Example 76: from fantasia (a) No. 8 a 2 (introduction to suite), by John Hingeston.

(b) fantasia-suite No. 1 a 5:

and very competently worked out. He wrote two fantasy suites, one for cornet, trombone and organ, and one for two cornets, trombone and organ.

Christopher Simpson is the chief representative of a rather large group of musicians who stand between the conservatives and the 'modernists' of Restoration chamber music, with a natural inclination to the more traditional. Simpson and his fellows composed much solo music with and without accompaniment – that kind of instrumental solo which we found in the works of the beginning of the century and which managed to keep fairly independent of foreign influences for a comparatively long time.

Simpson's series of fantasias, *Monthes and Seasons*, with virtuoso violin and bass viol parts, must be mentioned as particularly

[1] Add. 10338.
[2] Add. 34800.
[3] Bodleian, Oxford, Mus. Sch. D. 205–11 and E. 382.

valuable.[1] Each piece bears the name of a month or a season (we
can discover no relation, however, between the programmatic
titles and the music). There are passages of great technical
difficulty. When all the three parts of the score perform their own
'ornamental concertos' at the same time, the result must have
appeared neck-breaking to the composer's contemporaries:

Example 77: from fantasia 'Spring' for violin, two bass viols and
basso continuo by Christopher Simpson.

---

[1] Bodleian, Oxford, Mus. Sch., C. 54–8. A large number of copies of this work has
survived. Among his fantasy suites in the Bodleian MSS. are two for cornet, trombone and
organ and 2 cornets, trombone and organ respectively. Published by Musica Rara.

Simpson, however, is the undisputed master of the 'Divisions on a Ground', i.e. the set of variations on a given bass which is repeated again and again. Here he employed a fine art of figuration which is on the whole originally English. It is melodically simple and mostly based on passages and broken chords; there is nothing speculative or intricately polyphonic in this music.

The viola da gamba was Simpson's instrument. His *Division Violist* (1659) constitutes an important landmark in the history of the instrument as well as of the 'tema con variazioni'.[1] This technique can be traced back in English viol music at least to Tobias Hume, and in the lute repertoire to the middle of the sixteenth century. In Italy there is evidence of it in use at the beginning of the sixteenth century. For a century, the English were supreme at this art, latterly at a time when it was falling into disuse elsewhere.

Apart from Simpson, Captain Cooke (1616–1672), Henry Butler (dates unknown),[2] Daniel Norcombe (1576–1647), and many others wrote viol divisions of this kind, many of which are contained in Playford's *Musick's Recreation on the Violl* (1652). Such divisions were, however, not confined to the viola da gamba. Divisions appeared for the violin in the *Division Violin* (1685, 1688 and 1693) which includes pieces by Simpson, Mell, Beckets, Tollet, Solomon Eccles and others; for trios of strings in Lenton's and Tollett's Consorts (published 1695); later also for recorder in the *Division Flute* (1706) which contains works by Banister sen. and others.

Simpson was, however, not entirely preoccupied with the viola da gamba. He wrote suites and other pieces for 2 and 3 viols, 2 trebles and bass and other combinations, rather in the average style of the period.[3]

A considerable number of composers like Simpson worked chiefly outside the Court. Thomas Farmer (d. about 1693) was one of the 'Waits of London', which is to say he was in the service of the municipality. His *Consort of Musick in four Parts* (1687) and *A Second Consort of Musick in four Parts* (1690) containing lessons, grounds and overtures in the French style, are pleasantly invented though oc-

---

[1] Copies in Brit. Mus. and Durham Cathedral; there were many editions up to 1712.
[2] See above, p. 244 (footnote 5).
[3] Add. 18940–4, Christ Church, Oxford, 1021, 1027, 1083; Tenbury 296–9.

casionally amateurishly arranged.[1] The activities of John Banister, sen. (1630–79), as composer, covered works for 1–4 strings, chiefly suites and grounds of the familiar type.[2] His melodic gift was recognised by his contemporaries, and much of his work was included in collections of the time.[3] The already mentioned 'Captain' Henry Cooke (1616–1672) was a well-known figure in the musical life of the Commonwealth and Restoration, as a composer as well as in his capacity as a teacher (in which he was very successful). The contributions of a namesake, Richard Cooke, to instrumental music include pieces for two viols in Jenkins' average dance-music style, and also for trio combinations.[4] The name of Sylvanus (Silas) Taylor occurs in MSS. and collections of the time. He is essentially an amateur and is represented by single airs and suites.[5] William Ellis, a friend of Anthony à Wood and organiser of weekly concert meetings in Oxford from the time of the Commonwealth onwards,[6] appears also as composer of suites a 1–4.[7]

A substantial amount of light chamber music had been composed during the years of the Commonwealth, and the publication of such music continued unabated after the Restoration. Most of these were in the easy-going style of Jenkins' and Simpson's melodious suites, though they were not always as well invented and worked out. The influence of the popular tunes of the day is easily recognisable in many pieces.

Invigorated by the work of the great composers of the time, popular instrumental music of the Restoration in general was a spate of happy, cheerful compositions. Even though it was not very profound art, it profited from the active participation of the leading masters, just as much as in turn these composers derived from the response of the popular masses a degree of inspiration which the Court and its bloodless, sottish nobility was never able to give.

Not only the concert halls and playhouses but also many homes

---

[1] Further compositions for 1–5 parts in Brit. Mus. Add. 17853, 24889, 29283–5, 31429 and 31466.

[2] See Brit. Mus. Add 151184, 18940–4, Harleian, 3187–8; Christ Church, 361–2, 1125, 1183; Bodleian, c. 54–8, e. 410–4. A suite with trumpets includes 7 part books.

[3] *Division Violin* (1685), *Musick's Recreation on the Viol* (1652), *New Ayres & Dialogues* (1678), etc.

[4] Suites in Bodleian, Oxford, D. 220, E. 405–9 and 110–4.

[5] Bodleian, Oxford, E. 429 a–e.

[6] See above, p. 233.

[7] Christ Church MSS. 1022 and 1236. Some notes on S. Taylor in Westrup's *Domestic Music under the Stuarts*, *Mus. Ass. Proc.* 1941–2, p. 43 f.

of upper and lower-middle-class citizens were the centres of such light instrumental music. Most of this music is for one or two violins, with or without basso continuo. At the end of the period the editor of *Apollo's Banquet* (1690) goes so far as to say (preface):

> The Treble-Violin is at present the only instrument in fashion, and the delight of most Young Practitioners in musick for its chearful and sprightly sound.

*

It is not possible to deal in detail with all the composers of light chamber music who thrived between 1660 and 1688. Only a few names and titles of works can be given for the benefit of students who may wish to pursue this line of research.

Among the more important collections of such music not so far mentioned (much was edited by the house of Playford), were *Courtly Masquing Ayres* (1665), which contains suites by many noted composers; *Choice Ayres and Dialogues* (1676–85); *New Ayres and Dialogues* (1678), which contains many violin solos and duos; *Ayres and Dialogues* (1669 and 1685); *Ayres and Symphonys for ye Bass Viol* (1682);[1] *The Pleasant Companion* (1682), an instruction book for the flageolet by Thomas Greeting, with many tunes by Banister, Locke, Humphreys, Robert Smith and others; also the *Genteel Companion* and the *Delightful Companion*, both instruction books for recorder by Humphrey Salter and Carr, with a large number of tunes; the slightly later *Sprightly Companion* (1695)[2] for the oboe, with pieces a 1–4 instruments; *Youth's Delight on the Flageolet* and *A Vade Mecum for Recorder* (about the same time). Further, there are publications of works by individual composers, such as James Sherard, 12 *Sonatas for 2 Violins and Bass* (1701),[3] published by Roger in Amsterdam; and John Banister jun.'s *The compleat Tutor to the Violin, with the Newest Tunes now in Use* (1688). In addition there are countless MS. dances, suites, tunes and other pieces by John Birchenshaw (d. about 1681),[4] John Dowdon,[5] Richard Girdler,[6] George Hudson,

---

[1] All works in the British Museum, except the last one which is in Durham Cathedral Library.

[2] Available only in Brit. Mus. K. 4. b. 22, 3.

[3] Copy in Oxford, Bodleian and Amsterdam, University Library.

[4] 12 tunes for violin & bass (Christ Church, Oxford, 1016–7), suites a 3 (Bodleian E. 410–4).

[5] Many pieces a 1–3 (Christ Church, 90–1, 361–2).

[6] 6 pieces a 2 violins & bass (about 1685) (Add. 29283–5).

the violinist (d. 1678),[1] Robert Smith (d. 1675),[2] Thomas Tollett (d. after 1696),[3] and many others, including Anthony à Wood himself.[4]

The names of Christopher Gibbons, Locke, Blow and Purcell, the 'progressives' among Restoration composers, occur again and again in the huge repertoire of general-purpose dances, fantasies and divisions. The importance of these few modernists lies, nevertheless, not in the number of pieces which they added to this corpus, however large their share of instrumental airs may have been, but in the fact that they developed some elements of style which were revolutionary in English music.

Christopher Gibbons (1615–1676),[5] son of the great Orlando, is the oldest composer of the group and decidedly one of the most fascinating musicians of this interesting period. He introduced a new personal and almost ecstatic note into instrumental music. This originality is best seen in his three- and four-part fantasias, most of which are introductions to suites of dances.[6] These are pieces of a grimly passionate nature, abounding in sudden dissonances and queer passages. Some of his scores are alive with 'false relations'. Suspensions are not resolved but just left 'in the air', however dissonant they may be. Oddest is the behaviour of the melodic line which shows none of the traditional decorum of the earlier English fantasias. The bass in particular jumps up and down in ninths, twelfths and other unusual intervals.

The reader is referred to Christopher Gibbons's fantasia a 3 (Appendix VIII of this book).[7]

Even Lawes' music did not go to such lengths of eccentricity as this angular effort. This is radically expressionistic emotionalism, or as North calls Christopher Gibbons' music 'bold solid and strong but Desultory & not without a little of ye Barbaresms'.[8]

The life-work of the great 'futurist' Matthew Locke (1630–1677) recalls Christopher's nervous, unstable and often violent art, combined, however, with greater emotional depth.

---

[1] Suites a 3 (Christ Church, 1006–9).

[2] Many Brawls and other dances as well as chaconnes a 3–4 & basso continuo (Christ Church 90–1, 361–2, 1003, 1025–7).

[3] Tunes for strings a 3 (Add. 39565–7) and a 4 (Christ Church 1183).

[4] 3 pieces for 2 trebles and bass (Brit. Mus. Add. 31429 and possibly 29283–85).

[5] See Sheila Finch Rayner and Clare G. Rayner, 'Christopher Gibbons: "That Rare Musitian"', *Musica Disciplina*, Vol. 24 (1970), p. 151.

[6] Chief MSS.: Bodleian, Oxford, C. 102, D. 231 a–g, Christ Church MSS. 8 and 21; Brit. Mus. Add. 30487 and Add 31431.

[7] Add. 30487.   [8] *Musicall Grammarian*, p. 27.

Locke was one of the few great composers of the Republican period who were very active in the operatic field as well as in that of instrumental music. By 1660 he had established himself as one of the leading musicians of the time. He was made 'composer in ordinary' to the king, the first to hold this post under the restored monarchy.

Locke's earlier works show clearly enough the generally progressive tendency of the master. Among them are the three- and four-part fantasias, some of which have found their way to the modern printing press. They include also such original and enjoyable musical pictures as this two-part ayre of 1654:

Example 78: from fantasia-ayr a 2[1] by Matthew Locke.

---

[1] Add. 17801. A complete list of sources appears in Matthew Locke, 'Chamber Music', edited by Michael Tilmouth. *Musica Britannica*, Vols XXXI and XXXII (1971 and 1972).

He wrote numerous suites, such as the famous *Little Consort of three parts*, composed 'at the request of Mr. William Wake for his schollars in 1651' and printed by Playford in 1656; the *Broken Consort* of six suites for three instruments, all consisting of fancy, corant, aire (or almand or echo) and saraband; the *F flat Consort for my Cousin Kemble* of 1656 (obviously so called because most of the pieces are in D-minor, C-minor, E-flat-major, etc., which have many 'flats'); and many more suites and single movements of all kinds. Locke wrote movements for 'His Majestie's Sagbutts and Cornets' which were actually performed at King Charles II's Coronation during his procession through the town. They are dated April 22, 1661.

In most of these works Locke is an experimentalist and innovator. True, some of his music is sophisticated, and several of his combinations are really far-fetched, as has been pointed out by earlier historians. But on the other hand Locke could invent striking popular melodies such as this:

Example 79: Hornpype by Matthew Locke.

which can only be called the work of a genuine musician.

Locke's music is in several respects the counterpart of Lawes'. It

is still essentially polyphonic, but polyphonic in a style which so far
we have only found in Lawes' works, where we first met a curious
transmutation of polyphony. We noticed a certain contradiction
between Lawes' traditional polyphonic language and his readiness
to accept certain elements of foreign modernism, while at the same
time developing a very personal expression within the polyphonic
idiom. Locke goes far beyond either William Lawes or Christopher
Gibbons, as far as extravagant polyphony is concerned. The
extravagance of his melodic line is sometimes extraordinary. The
polyphonic combination of several of these lines often results in
open friction. Typical of his procedure is his modification of the
techniques of imitation on which the whole of the polyphony of the
previous period was based. He loosens the strict rules of literal
imitation by imitating only the direction of a motif, not its
intervals:

Example 80: from fantasia a 4 by Matthew Locke.

(*a*) Initial subject

(*b*) Imitation (direction kept but intervals reduced); bar 13

(*c*) Imitation (intervals augmented); bar 16

Moreover, into the polyphonic system, especially of the fantasia,
he eagerly introduces every modern element which he can get hold
of from anywhere in Europe, and everything is elaborated with
such passionate personal conviction that in the end the polyphony
of the old fantasia changes from top to bottom. There is often a
great eloquence in Locke's polyphonic melodies, such as is only
found elsewhere in contemporary Italian sonatas:

Example 81a: from fantasia a 4 by Locke.[1]

[1] Same piece, second section.

and similarly:

Example 81b: from fantasia a 3 by Locke.[1]

Locke's harmonies are surprising, and quick modulations are familiar in his works.

Example 82: from fantasia a 3.

Daring though he was before, the 'new era' after 1660 seems to have given a new impulse to Locke's modernism, and his most interesting works were written during the years immediately preceding his death, though not exclusively for the Court. By far the greatest of his later works, and one of the most extraordinary documents of old music of all countries, is Locke's incidental music for Shadwell's *Tempest* of 1672, written for strings.

I owe my acquaintance with these eleven instrumental masterpieces to Professor Dent who revived the work in a public performance in Cambridge in 1933. Nobody will fail to recognise

<hr>

[1] Fantasia a 3; ibid.

the dramatic strength and originality of every one of these musical microcosms. The portentous gravity of the Introduction (strongly influenced by the new French Ouverture); the excited dialogue of first violin and tutti in the Galliard, the resolute directness of the Gavot; the strange, tender beauty of the Saraband and its otherworldly dissonances; the rhythmical finesse of the Lilk (lilt), are obvious even to those who are not used to listening to old music. The 'Curtain Tune' is the culmination of the whole work. It depicts the storm, its slow and sinister approach, its violent raging, interrupted by sudden lulls, and its final settling-down to calmness and serenity. A miniature *Pastoral Symphony*.

Example 83: Matthew Locke, Curtain Tune from *The Tempest*:[1]

[1] Copies in Brit. Mus., in Prof. Dent's Library, etc., new edition by G. Whittaker, Oxford University Press, 1935. See also E. M. Harding, *A Thematic Catalogue of the Works of Matthew Locke*, Oxford, 1971. *Musica Britannica*, XXXI–XXXII, contain Matthew Locke's 'Chamber Music', transcribed and edited by M. Tilmouth, London, 1972. This includes the music discussed in this chapter and its sources.

This piece not only contains an early orchestral tremolo, expressing the threatening force of the storm, and several musical 'stage directions' such as 'soft', 'lowd', 'violent', but it definitely has the first crescendo, diminuendo and ritardando in the history of music ('lowder by degrees', 'soft and slow by degrees'), specially marked by the composer in the score.

Much could be said about the remaining items of the suite, the gay Rustick Air, the graceful Minoit (surely one of the first minuets in English music), the Corant, Martial Jigge and concluding canon; space forbids me to go into details.

A number of manuscripts contain similar music probably dating from the end of Locke's career.[1] Their four-part texture and style of writing suggest that they were designed for orchestral use; possibly they were written for various theatrical productions for which Locke is known to have written music.[2]

Most interesting of all are the suites found in *Tripla Concordia* (London, 1677), which includes 26 pieces in three suites a 3 for 'treble and basse-violins'. In this collection Locke is seen as the leader of a group of composers: Robert Smith, John Banister, Francis Forcer, William Hall and Robert King, who popularised

---

[1] New York Public Library, Drexel MS. 3849: 'Thomas Britton his book, 1680'; Drexel MS. 5061; Drexel MS. 3976; 'The Rare Theatrical', a score collected by William Hayes in the mid-eighteenth century from sources now lost. A selection from the last two is available in *Four Suites made from Consort Music by Matthew Locke*, edited by Sydney Beck (New York, 1947).

[2] For instance: *The Step-Mother* (Lincoln's Inn Fields, November 1663); *The Empress of Morocco* by Elkanah Settle (Duke's Theatre, 1673); *The Siege of Rhodes* by Sir William Davenant (Rutland House, 1656); *The History of Sir Francis Drake* by Sir William Davenant (Drury Lane, 1633); *The Cruelty of the Spaniards in Peru* by Sir William Davenant (Drury Lane, 1658).

the French orchestral style of Lully in England, and who are equivalent to the German group, *Les Lullistes*.[1]

It was this kind of music that called forth the bitter and eloquent protests of Thomas Mace. The representatives of the old gentle polyphonic age could not follow Locke's stormy advance.

Locke is an ingenious, courageous and highly intelligent musician. To us he is particularly interesting as his personality reflects very clearly the difficult and complicated social situation of his time, a time of hopes, disappointments, inhibitions, possibilities and new opportunities. He is the real revolutionary in English music. It was in great part owing to his efforts that English music was extricated (at least temporarily) from its conservative position. The great strength of Locke's work lies in the fact that it belongs to two neighbouring ages, and that it benefits from both. The later productions of the early-deceased master belong essentially to the new age which was to culminate so brilliantly in Purcell.

Locke admitted fairly freely elements of foreign style. Especially French features appear in increasing frequency in his music, notwithstanding the fact that Locke himself was a very determined champion of English musical independence, as against Charles's dependence on continental countries.

For some reason, Locke and his contemporaries dropped the characteristic five-part scoring (violin, 3 violas, bass violin) of the French court orchestra, which was also used by the English court band before the civil war. Instead they adopted the more modern Italianate scoring with two violins, with or without a single viola part. At the same time they infused the forms of French dance music with a very individual attitude to dissonance and angular counterpoint, creating a style which was taken up by Blow (1649–1708)[2] and Purcell in their early works. This modified enthusiasm for the forms of French music lasted from the Restoration up to the middle of the 1680s, and takes in the suites of

---

[1] For discussion of this group, see Arthur Hutchings, *The Baroque Concerto* (London, 1961), pp. 114–132.

[2] John Blow's importance lies, of course, in his songs, anthems and organ compositions. Instrumental pieces known to be by Blow are a sonata and ground for two violins and bass, a symphony for 2 flutes and bass and some shorter items (see Brit. Mus. Add. 29283–5 and Add. 33256). His ballet music, such as the famous *Venus and Adonis* masque, is less orchestral than Locke's *Tempest* music.

William Gregory[1] and the printed collections of John Lenton and Thomas Tollett, *A Consort of Musick in Three Parts* (London, 1692) and Thomas Farmer, *A Consort of Musick in Four Parts containing 33 Lessons beginning with an Overture* (London, 1686). A second collection by Farmer, apparently published two years after his death in 1689, appears to have survived only in manuscript.[2]

London taste in the middle 1680s, strongly influenced by the new public concerts, began to show a preference for abstract music and the sonata, following either the German or Italian model. Nevertheless, the French style continued to be used in the theatres as act music which prefaced the overture and the play proper. The fashion for publishing such suites for the benefit of amateurs was started by Frances Purcell in 1697, with the posthumous publication of her husband's theatre music entitled *A Collection of Ayres, compos'd for the Theatre*. This was followed by a large number of similar publications of theatrical music issued in series by Walsh, of theatrical music by Paisible, Eccles, Simons, Croft, Finger, Lenton, Daniel Purcell, Barrett and others. This French style can still be felt in the stage works of Pepusch, Handel and other composers of the middle eighteenth century.

The problems which English music had to face towards the end of the seventeenth century are most clearly seen in the work of Henry Purcell (1658–1695), the man who succeeded in overcoming them all.

Purcell, born in the year of Cromwell's death, won a position for English music never equalled before.

His output of chamber music includes 4 fantasies a 3, 9 a 4, 1 a 5, 1 In Nomine a 6, 1 a 7, 23 trio-sonatas, of which one is a reconstruction by Thurston Dart, and a number of smaller pieces.[3] Some of the fantasias were written when Purcell was only twenty-two. They were the last chamber-music fantasias ever written – they say farewell to the form in which English chamber music had celebrated its greatest triumphs. The purpose of these pieces is, however, not quite clear: were they just studies, undertaken to keep Purcell familiar with the old tradition of polyphonic fantasias; or were they written in order to put new life into an outdated form? For though Purcell's forms have much in common

---

[1] See James Riley, 'The Identity of William Gregory', *Music and Letters*, July, 1967, pp. 236–246. James Riley's article ignores an important set of 16 suites a 3, in Brit. Mus. Add. 31430.

[2] For instance Lbm Add. 29283–5, nos. 225–57, with the date 1691.

[3] *Sonatas of III parts*, edited by Roger Fiske, 2 vols (London, 1975–6).

with those of his great predecessors, the language of these pieces is very new indeed.

If we are really to understand these works we shall have to consider Purcell's position in English music.

It is not unlike that of Mozart in German music. Indeed these two personalities have so much in common that we cannot help remarking the similarity of their cultural role. Revolutionary and individualist ideals, inhibited by the influence of a social reaction, yet proclaimed with the greater insistence and intensity, inspired both composers. Mozart's surroundings are known to have been dark and narrow. Purcell similarly grew up in an atmosphere of Court brutality, tyranny and intrigue that could not but repel every decent human being, and most of all a great artist. Ideas of reform, professed by the more radical supporters of the 'glorious revolution', must have filtered through to the musician at the Court, just as the equalitarian theories of Rousseau, Voltaire and Diderot were later to work in the prisoner of the See of Salzburg. These ideas incited Mozart to side with the progressive and democratic freemasons' movement, to rebel against his tyrannous employer and to expose the whole rottenness and corruption of the nobility, a desire which is so strikingly expressed in *Figaro*. Purcell, too, must have been familiar with ideas which were at least strongly critical of the ruling society and the governing authorities. In 1681 the play *The Sicilian Usurper* (an adaptation by Nahum Tate of *Richard II*, with music by Henry Purcell) was banned after the first performance on political grounds.[1] So Purcell took the risk of setting to music texts of a bitingly satirical character.[2] Yet quite apart from such occasional direct documentation of politically progressive tendencies (Purcell was, of course, not primarily a 'political' composer), ease and freedom of living, thinking and inventing, coupled with profound personal passion, and a struggle

[1] See Vol. XX of Purcell's *Collected Works*, Introduction by Dr Alan Gray.

[2] The text of a song contained in *The Marriage Hater Matched* (Comedy by Durfey; Purcell edition, Vol. XX) ends with these words:

> Be moral in thought,
> To be merry's no fault,
> Though an Elder the contrary preaches;
> For never, my friends,
> Was an age of more vice,
> Than when knaves would seem pious,
> And fools would seem wise.

thus recalling the words of Gibbons' famous *Silver Swan* (see above, p. 174).

for free, individual expression are common to both masters. This atmosphere of freedom and progress, and the healthy influence of advanced foreign styles in combination with a tremendous technical mastery based on a glorious tradition, produced similar results in both composers: an almost volcanic eruption of production ever intensifying and ever deepening, until each died, exhausted, at an early age.

It has been said that there is a 'heroic atmosphere' in Purcell's sonatas.[1] This quality is very similar to the noble and courageous eloquence of Mozart's G-minor symphony or C-minor fantasy.

A new breath of fresh air enlivens every one of Purcell's works. There is a new 'human touch' in his dramatic compositions. The stiff and official-minded libretti dealing with subjects of classical antiquity (some of which Purcell in his official capacity had to set to music) are outnumbered by stories from the everyday life of the common citizen such as *The Rival Sisters* (Gould), *Rule a Wife and Have a Wife* (Fletcher), *The Old Bachelor* (Congreve), *The Double Dealer* (Congreve), and many others. The heroes of his plays are characterised by their human qualities, their weaknesses, passions, and sufferings. These people really *live* through Purcell's music. Even in *Dido and Æneas* Dido is no more the marble figure from some ancient Greek frieze, but *the* suffering, tragic woman.

Purcell's instrumental works, even his earliest, breathe the new spirit, too. There is nothing left of the awkwardness and violence that sometimes occurred in Locke's works, or of the hyper-contrapuntal intellectualism which we noticed in Thomas Ford's fantasias and in at least some of William Lawes' works. Purcell took over from his predecessors all that was bright, colourful, tuneful, and passionate. There is an intensity of sentiment, a sense of dramatic power, and at the same time a sensual tenderness such as we have never met before. We feel that something new has happened to English music.

The last traces of medieval scholasticism, still apparent in many of the compositions of his immediate forerunners, have vanished. An astonishing freedom of expression prevails. Startling suspensions, insistent accents, chromatic passages with audacious harmonisation abound in Purcell's fantasias and sonatas.

French, German and Italian influences are too obvious to be explained away by those who would like to proclaim Henry Purcell as the 'exclusively English' composer. Although Purcell is in many

---

[1] A. Einstein, *Greatness in Music*, trans. Cesar Saerchinger, New York, 1941.

respects the natural heir of Jenkins, Locke and Blow; although there is much in Purcell's melodies and harmonies (especially their brightness and popular qualities) that is unthinkable without the whole history of both English folk music and art music; he must be called an international as well as a national artist. Purcell himself was quite open about his fondness for foreign styles. He called his son John Baptista (after Lully), and says in the foreword of his Sonatas a 3 of 1683 that they 'imitated the Italian way'.

The ardour of Purcell's emotions is most convincingly evident, in spite of the archaic *fantasia* form, in his fantasia for 5 viols 'upon one note'.[1] If we listen to the change from C-major to a plaintive F-minor, and the sudden and dramatic trumpet-like entry of a new C-major, we feel that a new age is approaching, the age of the Vienna classics.

There are good studies of Purcell. I shall not repeat what has already been pointed out by his biographers,[2] and I shall not expatiate on all the exciting features of the other pieces, the harmonic ventures of the four-part fantasias, the ingenuity of the three-part pieces, the heroic calmness of the six- and seven-part In Nomines, the radiance of the trio-sonatas. I must leave it to individual study to delve into these masterpieces.

Purcell has had at least as much influence on the development of the mind and character of the British people as had many a general, statesman, or philosopher. He belongs to the people. Much of the liveliness in Purcell's rhythms can be traced to the 'English Dancing Master', that great collection of popular tunes and dances which is a source of inspiration even to composers today. He used melodies of a type known and understood by common men. In his passionate harmonies, which were so new in his time, he expressed their hopes, struggles and desires. Thus in his works he gave back to the people an even greater wealth and beauty than he had drawn from them. Therefore the public today should know of his work, not only that part which is generally performed.

Our love and admiration for Purcell will not lose but gain, his

[1] The note C is kept in the third viol part throughout the piece. It is reprinted in full in the Appendix (No. IX).

[2] J. A. Westrup in his comprehensive study deals particularly with the master's instrumental works. In 1963 F. B. Zimmerman issued *An Analytical Catalogue* of works by H. Purcell (London, Macmillan). Purcell is discussed fully by S. Demarquez (Paris, 1931), and R. Sietz (Leipzig, 1955). Purcell's Sonatas are analysed in M. Tilmouth, *The Technique and Form of Purcell's Sonatas (Music and Letters,* XL, 1959).

greatness will increase if we view his work in the context of the social forces surrounding and inspiring him. Life, wonderful, stimulating, radiant life prevails in the creations of this great artist. Like Antæus who was strong so long as his feet touched earth, Purcell was great, because throughout his life he was always able to gather fresh strength from the life of the people.

*

The question of the position of the composer in society, suggested by our discussion of Henry Purcell, has been raised more than once in these pages, where we have already indicated disagreement with the theory that the individual genius alone, by virtue of his own personal endowments, 'makes', advances or moulds the history of art.

The directions in which an artist develops his function, style and talent is largely conditioned by the social factors of his time, its fashions and conventions (with which the artist may or may not feel himself in harmony) the ascendancy of one set of ideals, the suppression of another, as this or that social group predominates, all play their part in influencing his development. The general state of a society is thus reflected in the art it produces.

However, the example of Purcell shows once again clearly that a creative artist is no mere photographer of conditions, but a living human being in his own right, reacting to *all* important tendencies of his time; a great work of art often contains elements which are mere undercurrents in contemporary society. The problems which the great artist sets out to solve will be recognised by his fellow-men as their own, and they will be individually enriched by his profounder insight. The composer, in particular, can make people think and feel with a depth and illumination hitherto unknown to them. Listening to great music, such as a Purcell Sonata or Aria, they perceive 'what oft was felt, but n'er so well express'd'. At that time man's emotional and intellectual experience was enormously widened, his individual initiative and joy of living powerfully stimulated by such a great artist as Henry Purcell.

The vital creative role which the composer fulfils places a heavy responsibility on him. The more truthfully he faces the realities of life – in all its aspects – the more will be the enduring inspiration he gives to his fellow-men, turning many of them towards *progressive* undercurrents which the dominant interests of the day may studiously ignore or positively suppress. There is in every classical work of art an element of protest, more, there is in each great artist something of a revolutionary. The relationship between the artist and his society is a reciprocal one; he is neither a passive tool nor yet a dictator but a man of his time, open to its influences, a vehicle through which they flow, expressing in an art form the impression his social consciousness has received; his knowledge of the role played by social forces – together with his creative genius as an artist – will be the measure of his greatness through which his creative power may influence and mould society afresh.

To represent all composers as consciously 'political' artists, and their best work as what is often called 'propaganda' art would be a gross mistake, equivalent to ignoring the fact that each of the arts has its own distinct medium of imaginative expression.

During the lifetime of many a composer there are occasions when he makes use of his art for an immediately political purpose (although such occasions have been comparatively rare in the careers of most recent composers). Mozart, the composer of the freemason cantatas, is a political composer, but the Mozart of the C-major symphony is not. Chopin's Polish national dances, the mazurkas and polonaises, were written to inspire Polish independence; but not so his piano preludes. Tallis's harmonisation of the plain-song responses of the Anglican service were composed with an ecclesiastico-political aim; his string and keyboard music was not. However, they all contributed to the shaping of minds of listeners and players alike, helping to form their consciousness; in this wider aspect they served a philosophical, social, political purpose. Byrd kept himself aloof from the political and religious changes of his time but his music did much to free the mentality of his age from stiffness and medieval prejudice and helped to humanise those who heard it, to thaw, with its warmth of feeling, their emotional frigidity. Social influences often act in an indirect, roundabout, delayed and even contradictory way, but no great work of art has ever been conceived by the complete negation of social forces. Therefore great art will only be fully understood when viewed within the context of these social forces. This should be kept in mind in particular by art critics and art historians. To try to explain the artist's work in isolation from the social life around him would be like first strangling a man in order to demonstrate on his dead body the working of the breathing organism.

CHAPTER VIII

Aftermath

At the end of the seventeenth century English chamber music collapsed.

It is true that for some years a fair average level of achievement was maintained. Several musicians worked on into the new century: Henry Purcell's brother Daniel (1663–1717), John Eccles (1650–1733), John Banister junr. (d. 1735), Raphael Courtevil (d. after 1700), Robert King (d. after 1711), Richard Goodson (1655–1728), Benjamin Hely (d. after 1700), James Paisible (d. after 1700) and others. But they sacrificed the English idiom, and their art became subservient to Corelli, Vitali and the Scarlattis, Lullys and L'Oeillets, the Fingers, Kellers, Fuxes and Keisers. To an even greater extent this is true of the music of the eighteenth century. I say this with all the respect due to such composers as Arne, and the able and wellmeaning Croft, Boyce and Wesley.

What were the causes of this sudden eclipse?

It was brought about by a change in the 'cultural climate' of England. The Revolution of 1689 was the final triumph of those elements in English society whose struggle, during 150 years of history, had been accompanied in the sphere of art by activities fitting to times of struggle and forward drive. Success, however, brought an end to the struggle, and subsequently there came a profound change in the attitude of the successful class.

Instrumental chamber music was the music of the rising merchants and the progressive sections of the aristocracy as they were fighting their way through progress and set-backs, to final victory. The new forces in the days of Elizabeth were advancing vigorously in the economic and political field, always engaged in a struggle against those at home and abroad who wished to re-establish the old order of life. This condition of conflict filled the leaders, as well as the mass of citizens, with a fighting spirit, with hope, vigour and emotional profundity. In its forward march, this new society again and again encountered obstacles which had to be overcome. The Elizabethan was preoccupied with problems of the mind and soul – as the Athenian was during the era of Pericles. In such societies and at such times men are not only inclined towards music and poetry, they *need* them. Hence the profoundly personal spirit in Elizabethan music, poetry and drama; and hence the stupendous progress especially of chamber music.

The patronage of bourgeois aristocracy under these conditions had led to a state where chamber music was the art of the time. It had become a favourite way of expressing personal emotion. The musical artist had expressed for society what everybody was feeling: from the political to the personal, from black despair to rosiest hope, from all-embracing metaphysical visions and problems to the intimate human considerations of friendship and love.

The age of Elizabeth was followed by a period of sharpening conflict between burgherdom and a feudal absolutism culminating in the great English revolution which constitutes the climax of the history of Britain up to that time; its ardour and drive live on in the great scientific, philosophical and literary achievements of the English Enlightenment.

Through the victory of the merchant-adventurer or producer-classes a new mental attitude gained ascendancy, the attitude of the busy businessman. The new leaders in their temporary security turned towards external, commercial conquest. Their philosophy was concerned with work and religion. They set themselves to instil the spirit of Puritan zeal and sobriety into all parts of society. The Republican leaders were unable – though perhaps willing – to give musical life new depth and a new impetus. By nature they faced the other way.

After 1660, when Puritanism and Republic were beaten a last wave of creative musical activity arose. Not that the monarchy then restored was a particularly inspiring factor in itself; but certain circumstances combined to give some English composers another great chance to develop – in an activity which was chiefly centred round the Court.

This was the time when Locke, Blow, Humfrey and Jeremiah Clark flourished, and this was also the time when many an old music lover seemed to be able to breathe again. It was in 1668 that Samuel Pepys wrote:

[I went] with my wife and Deb. to the King's House, to see 'The Virgin Martyr'.

. . . That which did please me beyond anything in the whole world was the wind-musique when the angel comes down, which is so sweet that it ravished me, and indeed, in a word, did wrap up my soul so that it made me really sick, just as I have formerly been when in love with my wife; that neither then, nor all the evening going home, and at home, I was able to think of anything but remained all night transported, so as I could not believe that ever any musicke hath that real command over the soul of a man as this did upon me.[1]

But a new change was on the way.

Charles II's court was soon as isolated as that of his predecessor. The final downfall of the backward and narrow old aristocracy which had been temporarily swept to the surface by the Restoration was only a question of time. The 'Glorious Revolution' followed; and forthwith ensued the final establishment of a bourgeois nobility whose ancestors in the middle ages had been rebels; and in its final hour of triumph this class itself became the main bulwark of conservatism.

The bourgeois nobility which was then finally enthroned controlled the destiny of Britain for many decades, and for many decades it tended to impress its cultural ideals on the people of this country. In the eighteenth century these ideals were, above all, those of 'practical' culture, outward-looking, taking account of purposes and effects rather than of origin and cause. The triumphant practical achievements of these decades of English history bear witness to the qualities of the men who built up an empire, and with it a colossal agricultural, industrial and commercial machine; powerful men, calm and confident, thoroughly sure of themselves and their mission, enterprising, highly intelligent and, above all, practical in all things – practical in their philosophy, practical in their sensible outlook on this world and the next, practical especially in their encouragement of applied science, practical in their very humanitarianism, practical even in their liberal patronage of fine arts. For they spent handsomely on those arts which a practical man can understand – upon paintings of their wives and daughters, and later upon landscapes showing the richness of their land, upon architectural magnificence, upon finely wrought furniture and fabrics.

And what of music?

The attitude of the English gentleman towards music underwent a radical change. We may recall the good old days as they are illustrated in an incident mentioned in Thomas Morley's treatise (1597). Somebody had confessed that he was unable to take part in

---

[1] *Diary*, 27.ii.1668. The play is by Massinger.

a homely performance of music, 'as is the custom', 'and everyone began to wonder', says Morley, 'yea some whispered to others demanding how he was brought up'. The new outlook, so far as participation in musical performances is concerned, is clearly defined 100 years later by John Locke, the philosopher, who wrote in 1693:

> A good hand upon some instruments is by many people mightily valued; but it wastes so much of a young man's time, to gain but a moderate skill in it, and engages him often in such odd company.[1]

Here is Romain Rolland's description of the sovereign aristocrat at his musical best –

> the distinguished English gentleman, statesman and artist, thoroughly sane and well-balanced, with the quiet activity, the serenity of mind, the good humour and the rather childlike optimism which one often meets with north of the Channel, pleasantly gifted as a musician, but superficial and seeking in music a wholesome pleasure, as Milton advised, rather than a passion beyond his control.[2]

The music he favoured was the music proper to an age of realism and empiricism: first of all patriotic songs which were produced in great abundance all through the eighteenth and nineteenth centuries; then for diversion, pleasant airs for the voice, made and sung as pastorals and glees in the eighteenth, as drawing-room songs and ballads in the nineteenth century; and finally, if instrumental music must 'invade' the home, piano solos by the women folk.

As for opera, he would patronise it, to be sure, as a foreign affair, which indeed, alas, it was, and his patronage and riches in the end brought into being one of the most remarkable musical phenomena of our time – the Covent Garden Opera Season, a great national festival of foreign music. This institution was born of the spirit to which Dr Burney, the father of musicology, confessed when talking about Italian Opera in England, that it

> . . . is a Manufacture in Italy, that feeds and enriches a large portion of the people; and it is no more disgraceful to a

---

[1] Quoted by P. A. Scholes, *Oxford Companion*, p. 282.
[2] *A Musical Tour through the Land of the Past*, trans. B. Miall, 1922, p. 43.

mercantile country to import it, than wine, tea, or any other production of remote parts of the world. . . .

Music, once a 'ladder to the intelligence of higher things'[1] became, in the words of Dr Charles Burney, in the eighteenth century 'an innocent luxury, unnecessary, indeed, to our existence, but a great improvement and gratification of the sense of hearing'.[2]

As such, it may properly be bought and paid for, and bought with money rather than with application and study. The public concert, at which music was purveyed as a commodity, developed enormously in the eighteenth century.

Passive listening to music (at least as far as instrumental music was concerned) became the part that the public had to play in English musical life, and the creative as well as the performing part was left to visitors from other countries.

And for listening to music, this country, rich and yearly growing richer, could pay well. There was a spirit of cosmopolitan toleration and broadmindedness among the comfortable upper-class musical amateurs in the eighteenth century. Foreign musicians were engaged by the hundred, and these continental masters were attracted by English concert life as by nothing else. Among them were some of the greatest of all, from Corelli via Handel, and the sons of Bach to Haydn, Mozart, Mendelssohn. England could afford to invite them; she enabled many a great musician from the Continent to live and thrive. Though this patronage is a contribution of England to European musical life which should not be overlooked, the creative supremacy of continental music was absolute for many, many years, again particularly in the field of instrumental chamber music. Throughout the eighteenth century English chamber music, so far as it existed, was quite unable to withstand the competition of more vital foreign influences.

The healthy influx of foreign styles into English music became an invasion. Symbolic of the fate of English music was the enormous vogue of Handel, by whose internationalism English music and all that was great in it was completely absorbed – English, German, French and Italian elements are about equally matched in his works.

So far as education was concerned, the subject of music 'largely

[1] Morley.
[2] *A General History of Music*, 1776, Vol. I, Preface, p. xiii.

dropped out of the British curriculum'; amateur cultivation, which is of such vital importance as an 'echo' to professional art, tended to be 'left to the female portion of the "comfortable classes", and even so to be regarded as a mere "accomplishment"'.[1]

It is true that the finest folksongs were still sung in the seclusion of the eighteenth-century countryside. All the emotional depth and liveliness of British music is reflected in many immortal folk melodies. Altogether, singing – and in particular folksong – continued with surprising vigour, in view of the collapse of the more elaborate types of music.

But all this music of the villages was then chiefly of local significance; it became less and less important for national culture as a whole[2] and after 1800 the centre of gravity, the main force of production, the main source of the country's prosperity, finally shifted from the land to the towns.

It was a new cultural climate in which, as Matthew Arnold said in speaking of the poet Gray, 'there was a spiritual east wind blowing'. The result was that the creation of speculative, imaginative, inward sorts of music ceased for a long time, and this climate was far more severe upon music than upon any other art. In the case of chamber music especially, it killed education and thus destroyed the means whereby musical appreciation and ability might have been preserved against the time when the climate should change.

For change the climate did, in the course of this century and the next, when a great impulse of humanitarianism and liberal thought energised the culture of this country. In fact, throughout the eighteenth century something like a spiritual revolt was going on, a revolt against the 'official' trend in cultural life. From the time of Pope and Hogarth this revolt was a wonderful stimulus to creative thought and impulse in literature, painting and architecture, and in poetry it culminated in the romantic revival about the turn of the century. Throughout this time great artists, carried forward by successive waves of popular movements, expressed in all the arts except in music, the people's desire for life, independence and freedom, and their irrepressible creative genius.

But in the elaborate art of instrumental music, that art in which

---

[1] P. A. Scholes, *Oxford Companion*, p. 282.

[2] See A. L. Lloyd, *The Singing Englishman*, Keynote Series Book No. 4, London, 1944, pp. 41 ff.

the greatest triumphs were being celebrated on the Continent, alas, there was no Byron, no Wordsworth, no Shelley; there was no new Purcell, no English Beethoven. Instrumental music could not rise above the reserved romanticism of a John Field.

The time came, but the art was forgotten. The tradition had too long been broken.

It does not take very long for a break in continuity to take effect upon an art like chamber music, as indeed upon any music that makes demands on the technical accomplishment of listeners and participants. In all the more highly evolved instrumental music, and thus particularly in chamber music, these demands are high.

We have already seen how near the Commonwealth hiatus came to taking the life out of instrumental music, and how the renaissance of the Restoration was made possible only by the survival from earlier days of a small number of masters who worked round the Court. Moreover the general standard of musical education was quickly debased. We saw for instance that the Chapel Royal was unable to find boys who could read music, and all this after a break of some twenty years; half a generation. What chance had instrumental music of a revival, however improved the prospects, after a century had elapsed?

In a similar way, around 1600 the chamber music of the Netherlands (a beautiful, elaborate art) gradually withered after the victory of Calvinism; church schools which had provided its educational background were closed. In the interests of historical progress these measures were necessary, since the old music schools were tied to the Catholic Church. But Netherlands merchants on whose behalf the cultural policy of Calvinism was carried out, cared even less than the Puritans about creating conditions in which music could blossom anew. The breach was fatal, and the colourful instrumental music imported from Germany into Holland half a century later could not bring back the musical supremacy of that country, even though there were one or two individually great composers such as Carolus Hacquart.

In music a breach of tradition is a particularly serious matter because the *active* participation of a musically educated public is absolutely indispensable to a flourishing and intensive musical life. The great tradition of English chamber music was interrupted by the change in the 'cultural climate' about the middle of the seventeenth century. And neither Thomas Mace's raging nor John

Hingeston's warnings were able to restore the lost paradise of English music.

Two centuries elapsed before musicians and music-lovers started to become aware of the immense riches to be discovered in early English musical achievement. Today it forms an integral part of British musical life – this is largely due to the research work of a whole generation of enthusiastic young musicologists carried out during the past thirty-five years.

Select Bibliography

Ashbee, A., *The Four-part Instrumental Compositions of John Jenkins*. Unpublished diss., London (external) Ph.D., 1966

Baines, Anthony (ed.), *Musical Instruments through the ages*, Harmondsworth, 1961

Baines, Anthony, 'James Talbot MS. Wind Instruments', *Galpin Society Journal*, Vol. I, 1948, pp. 9–26

Bowles, Edmund A., 'Musical Instruments in the Liturgical Service in the Middle Ages', *Galpin Society Journal*, 1957, Vol. X, pp. 40–56 and subsequent correspondence from Robert Donington, 1958, Vol. XI, pp. 85–87, and Edmund A. Bowles, 1959, Vol. XII, pp. 89–92

Boyan, P. A., and Lamb, G. R., *Francis Tregian, Cornish Recusant*, London, Sheed and Ward, 1955

Brett, Philip (ed.), *Musica Britannica*, Vol. 22 – *Consort Songs*, London, Stainer and Bell, for the RMA

Brown, David, *Thomas Weelkes*, London, Faber and Faber, 1969

Brown, Howard Mayer, *Instrumental Music Printed Before 1600. A Bibliography*, Cambridge, Mass., 1967

Bukofzer, Manfred F., *Music in the Baroque Era*, London, 1948

Cocks, William A., 'James Talbot MS. Bagpipes', *Galpin Society Journal*, Vol. V, 1952, pp. 44–47

Cole, Elizabeth, 'In Search of Francis Tregian', *Music and Letters*, Vol. 33 (1952), pp. 28–32, London, Oxford University Press

Cole, Elizabeth, 'Seven Problems of the Fitzwilliam Virginal Book', *RMA Proceedings*, 79, (1952–3), pp. 51–64

Cooke, Deryck, *The Language of Music*, London, Oxford University Press, 1959

Dart, Thurston, 'Robert ap Huw's Manuscript of Welsh Harp Music, (c. 1613)', *Galpin Society Journal*, Vol. XXI, 1968, pp. 52–65

Dart, Thurston, 'The Printed Fantasias of Orlando Gibbons', *Music and Letters*, Vol. XXXVII, 1956, pp. 342–349.

Dodd, Gordon, *Viola da Gamba Society Thematic Index of Music for Viols*, London, 1980

Donington, Robert, 'James Talbot MS. Bowed Strings', *Galpin Society Journal*, Vol. III, 1950, pp. 27–45

Dowland, John, *Lachrimæ or Seaven Teares* (1604), with a commentary by Warwick Edwards. (Boethius Facsimile, 1974)

East, Michael, *The Fifth Set of Bookes*, 1618

Edwards, W. A., *The Performance of Ensemble Music in Elizabethan England*, in *RMA Proceedings*, 97, 1970–1

Edwards, W. A., *The Sources of Elizabethan Consort Music*. Unpublished Ph.D. diss., Camb. Univ. 1974

Ferrabosco, Alfonso II, *Lessons for 1, 2 and 3 Viols*, London, 1609
— Facsimile, Da Capo Press, 1973

Gill, Donald, 'The Orpharion and Bandora', *Galpin Society Journal*, 1960, Vol. XIII, pp. 14–25

Gill, Donald, 'James Talbot MS. Plucked Strings. The Wire-strung Fretted Instruments and the Guitar', *Galpin Society Journal*, Vol. XV, 1962, pp. 60–69

Gill, Donald, *Gut-strung Plucked Instruments Contemporary with the Lute*, Lute Society Booklets No. 2, London, 1976

Gill, Donald, *Wire-strung Plucked Instruments Contemporary with the Lute*, Lute Society Booklets No. 3, London, 1977

Goldstein, David (ed.), *20 Light Fantasias* from the Fifth Set of Books, Provincetown, Mass., Provincetown Bookshop Editions, 1969

Harding, Rosamond E. M., *A Thematic Catalogue of the Works of Matthew Locke*, Oxford, Blackwell, 1971

Harwood, Ian, *A Brief History of the Lute*, Lute Society Booklets No. 1, London, 1975

Jeffery, Brian, 'Instrumentation in the Music of Anthony Holborne', *Galpin Society Journal*, 1966, Vol. XIX, pp. 20–26

Mould, Charles, 'James Talbot MS. Harpsichord', *Galpin Society Journal*, Vol. XXI, 1968, pp. 40–51

Munrow, David, *Instruments of the Middle Ages and Renaissance*, London, 1976

Neighbour, Oliver, *The Consort and Keyboard Music of William Byrd*, London, 1979

Nicholson, Richard, 'A Note on Gibbons and the Anonymous Six Part Fantasies in Christ Church Library', in *VdGSB* 27, July 1967

Nordstrom, Lyle, 'The Cambridge Consort Books', *Journal of the Lute Society of America*, Vol. V, 1972, pp. 70–103

Poulton, Diana, *John Dowland*, London, 1972

Prynne, Michael, 'James Talbot MS. Plucked Strings. The Lute Family', *Galpin Society Journal*, Vol. XIV, 1961, pp. 52–68

Rayner, Clare Gill, *Christopher Gibbons 1615–1676*. Unpublished Ph.D. diss., Indiana University, 1963

Reese, Gustave, *Music in the Middle Ages*, London, 1941

Rimmer, Joan, 'James Talbot MS. Harps'. *Galpin Society Journal*, Vol. XVI, 1963, pp. 63–72

Schofield, Bertram, and Dart, Thurston, 'Tregian's Anthology', *Music and Letters*, Vol. 32, (1951), pp. 205–16, London, Oxford University Press

Stevens, John, *Music and Poetry in the Early Tudor Court*, London, 1961

Stokes, E., 'Lists of the King's Musicians', *Musical Antiquary*, Vols I–IV, 1909–12

Traficante, Frank, 'Music for the Lyra Viol: The Printed Sources', *Lute Society Journal*, Vol. VIII, 1966, pp. 7–24

Traficante, Frank, 'Lyra Viol Tunings: All Ways have been Tryed to do It', *Acta Musicologia*, Vol. XLII, fasc. III–IV, Basel, Bärenreiter-Verlag

Traficante, Frank, 'Music for Lyra Viol: Manuscript Sources', *Chelys*, Vol. 8, 1978–9

Tyler, James, 'A Checklist for the Cittern', *Early Music*, January 1974, Vol. 2, No. 1

Vaught, Raymond, *The Fancies of Alfonso Ferrabosco II*. Unpublished Ph.D. diss., Stanford University, 1959

Warner, R. A., *Jenkins: Four-part Fancy Meyer 14 – an Enharmonic Modulation round the Key-circle*, London, *Music Review*, February, 1967

Warner, R. A., *The Fantasia in the Works of John Jenkins*. Unpublished Ph.D. diss., University of Michigan, 1951

Weidner, Robert (ed.) *Tye, Christopher, the Instrumental Music*, New Haven, Conn. A–R Editions Inc., 1967

Willetts, Pamela J., 'Sir Nicholas L'Estrange and John Jenkins', *Music and Letters*, Vol. 42, No. 3, April, 1961, London, Oxford University Press

Willetts, Pamela J., 'Sir Nicholas de Strange's Collection of Masque Music', *The British Museum Quarterly*, Vol. XXIX, (1965) pp. 79–81

Willetts, Pamela J., 'John Lilly, Musician and Music Copyist', *The Bodleian Library Record*, Vol. 7, No. 6, February, 1967, Oxford, Bodleian Library

Willetts, Pamela J., 'Musical Connections of Thomas Myriell', *Music and Letters*, Vol. 49, No. 1, January, 1968, pp. 36–42, London, Oxford University Press

Willetts, Pamela J., 'The Identity of Thomas Myriell', *Music and Letters*, Vol. 53, No. 4, October, 1972, pp. 431–3, London, Oxford University Press

Woodfill, Walter L., *Musicians in English Society*, Princeton University Press, 1953

Early Music. This journal was initiated by the Oxford University Press in 1973 with J. M. Thomson as editor. Four numbers appear each year. It includes articles on all aspects of medieval, renaissance and baroque music; among the contributors are to be found the names of some of the most distinguished workers in these particular fields.

Appendix

I. Alfonso Ferrabosco, jun., fantasia for four stringed instruments

II. John Bull, fantasia for four stringed instruments[1]

[1] This fantasia is now accepted as being by John Bull. See Gordon Dodd, 'Coperario or Bull?' *Chelys* I (1969), p. 41.

III. William Lawes, fantasia for six stringed instruments

IV. *William Lawes, fantasia for two violins, bass viol (cello) and harp (or any keyboard instrument)*

V. Michael East, fancy for four stringed instruments

VI. John Jenkins, fantasia for four stringed instruments

* Style of bowing non-legato: between legato and portamento

VII. *John Jenkins, fantasia for two violins and bass viol (cello)*

(poco rit.)

(Andante)
(60)

VIII. *Christopher Gibbons, fantasia for two trebles (violins) and bass viol (cello)*

*IX. Henry Purcell, fantasia 'upon one note' for five
stringed instruments*

(Moderato, ma con moto)

(poco allargando)

(ritard.)

Index*

* compiled by Maxine Smith